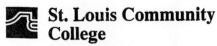

Through the Storm,
Through the Night

The African American History Series

Series Editors:
Jacqueline M. Moore, Austin College
Nina Mjagkij, Ball State University

Traditionally, history books tend to fall into two categories: books academics write for each other, and books written for popular audiences. Historians often claim that many of the popular authors do not have the proper training to interpret and evaluate the historical evidence. Yet, popular audiences complain that most historical monographs are inaccessible because they are too narrow in scope or lack an engaging style. This series, which will take both chronological and thematic approaches to topics and individuals crucial to an understanding of the African American experience, is an attempt to address that problem. The books in this series, written in lively prose by established scholars, are aimed primarily at nonspecialists. They focus on topics in African American history that have broad significance and place them in their historical context. While presenting sophisticated interpretations based on primary sources and the latest scholarship, the authors tell their stories in a succinct manner, avoiding jargon and obscure language. They include selected documents that allow readers to judge the evidence for themselves and to evaluate the authors' conclusions. Bridging the gap between popular and academic history, these books bring the African American story to life.

Volumes Published

Booker T. Washington, W. E. B. Du Bois, and the Struggle for Racial Uplift
    Jacqueline M. Moore
Slavery in Colonial America, 1619–1776
    Betty Wood
African Americans in the Jazz Age: A Decade of Struggle and Promise
    Mark Robert Schneider
A. Philip Randolph: A Life in the Vanguard
    Andrew E. Kersten
The African American Experience in Vietnam: Brothers in Arms
    James Westheider
Bayard Rustin: American Dreamer
    Jerald Podair
African Americans Confront Lynching: Strategies of Resistance
    Christopher Waldrep
Lift Every Voice: The History of African-American Music
    Burton W. Peretti
To Ask for an Equal Chance: African Americans in the Great Depression
    Cheryl Lynn Greenberg
The African American Experience during World War II
    Neil A. Wynn
Through the Storm, Through the Night: A History of African American Christianity
    Paul Harvey

Through the Storm, Through the Night

A History of African American Christianity

Paul Harvey

ROWMAN & LITTLEFIELD PUBLISHERS, INC.
Lanham • Boulder • New York • Toronto • Plymouth, UK

Published by Rowman & Littlefield Publishers, Inc.
A wholly owned subsidiary of The Rowman & Littlefield Publishing Group, Inc.
4501 Forbes Boulevard, Suite 200, Lanham, Maryland 20706
http://www.rowmanlittlefield.com

Estover Road, Plymouth PL6 7PY, United Kingdom

British Library Cataloguing in Publication Information Available

Library of Congress Cataloging-in-Publication Data

Harvey, Paul, 1961-
  Through the storm, through the night : a history of African American Christianity /
by Paul Harvey.
    p. cm.
  Includes bibliographical references (p. 195–201).
  ISBN 978-0-7425-6473-2 (cloth : alk. paper) — ISBN 978-0-7425-6475-6 (electronic)
  1. African Americans—Religion. 2. United States—Church history. I. Title.
  BR563.N4H3783 2011
  277.3'0808996073—dc22

                                                            2011006486

∞™ The paper used in this publication meets the minimum requirements of
American National Standard for Information Sciences—Permanence of Paper
for Printed Library Materials, ANSI/NISO Z39.48-1992.

Printed in the United States of America

For Suzi

Contents

Acknowledgments

Thanks first must go to Nina Mjagkij and Jacqueline Moore, who solicited me to write this volume, encouraged me throughout, and then worked over every detail of this book ("sort of like a Waring blender," as Warren Zevon once wrote) with unflagging energy.

Leon Litwack first sparked my interest in African American history, and participation in a 1998 National Endowment for the Humanities seminar at the Du Bois Institute of Harvard on Teaching the History of the Civil Rights Movement, led by Waldo Martin and Pat Sullivan, furthered some of the ideas presented in this book. So did conversations with too many historians and religious studies scholars to mention here, but a special shout out to Anthea Butler, Jonathan Walton, Sylvester Johnson, Tracy Fessenden, Curtis Evans, Albert Raboteau, Patrick Rael, Joanna Brooks, Kelly J. Baker, Randal Jelks, and Yvonne Chireau, whose work has been particularly influential for me.

From 2007 to 2009 I was fortunate to lead (together with Amanda Porterfield) a class of Young Scholars in American Religion through a series of seminars that were personally and professionally transformative. For that, I thank my scholarly co-conspirator Philip Goff of Indiana University-Purdue University Indianapolis, who so skillfully directs the Center for the Study of Religion and American Culture, and the peerless group in that "class" who enriched my life in every way: Edward J. Blum, Randall Stephens, Becky Goetz, Kate Carte Engel, Kathryn Lofton, J. Spencer Fluhman, Charles Irons, Tisa Wenger, Darren Dochuk, and (last but not least) Matthew Avery

Sutton. Also, from 2007 I have created and run the blog Religion in American History, at http://usreligion.blogspot.com, and the ever-growing list of contributors and commentators there have given me a scholarly community of which I could only have dreamed in years past.

Finally: this one goes out to the one I love.

INTRODUCTION

∼

Themes in African American Religious History

"Among our people generally the church is the Alpha and Omega of all things," the black intellectual, abolitionist, and nationalist Martin Delany wrote in 1849. "It is their only source of information—their only acknowledged public body—their state legislature—their only acknowledged advisor."[1] As a founder, along with Frederick Douglass, of the seminal antebellum black newspaper the *North Star*, Delany was a keen observer of the role of the black church in providing a public forum for a people generally enslaved, ignored, or scorned by white Americans. If hyperbolic, his description of the role of the church is a common one in many assessments of African American religious life. "The Negro church of to-day is the social centre of Negro life in the United States, and the most characteristic expression of African character," the great black intellectual W. E. B. Du Bois wrote in his 1903 classic *Souls of Black Folk*.[2] Delany and Du Bois both described how a history of African American Christianity would show that religious institutions and practices had brought black Americans through centuries of turmoil and struggle. They both produced works that could have gone by the title of this book: *Through the Storm, Through the Night: A History of African American Christianity*.

Were Delany and Du Bois alive today, they surely would have been shocked to read that "the Black Church, as we've known it or imagined it, is dead," as the African American religious scholar Eddie Glaude recently wrote in an online polemic. African Americans still go to church in large

1

numbers, he admitted, and identify with religious institutions in higher proportions than virtually any other group in American society. Nonetheless, Glaude concluded, "The idea of this venerable institution as central to black life and as a repository for the social and moral conscience of the nation has all but disappeared." Glaude called for a renewal of the historic prophetic energies of the black church: "The death of *the* black church as we have known it occasions an opportunity to breathe new life into what it means to be black and Christian. Black churches and preachers must find their prophetic voices in this momentous present."[3]

Glaude's posting provoked a firestorm of response from both scholars and contemporary black church activists. From the scholarly perspective, the idea that there is such a singularized thing as "the black church" was always a fiction created by black scholars such as Carter G. Woodson and Du Bois. Once they invented the term, they invested it with portentous meaning. Through all periods of American history, black churches were expected to answer to all social needs—to really be the "Alpha and the Omega of all things"—ignoring the socially repressive conditions in which African Americans have lived their lives and practiced their faiths. The "burden of black religion" is that it has been weighed down with too heavy a load.[4]

Regardless of the more esoteric pronouncements of scholars, black churches are alive and well. Nothing made this more evident than the brouhaha created during the 2008 presidential election by the Reverend Jeremiah Wright, former pastor to Barack Obama during his years in Chicago. "God bless America? No! God damn America," Wright thundered from the pulpit, shocking whites who watched the same clip endlessly replayed on cable television and the Internet. But Wright's sermons, in fact, arose from a prophetic tradition dating back over two centuries, including many of the texts to be discussed in this book. They were jeremiads, sermons that called out and condemned the sins of a people and a nation.

Beyond this kind of publicity, black religious institutions continue to thrive in less spectacular ways, and black ministers and churchpeople still exercise a significant influence in their communities. For all these reasons, historian Edward J. Blum, in response to Glaude, noted that throughout the twentieth century, scholars continually had pronounced the black church dead, only to have to reverse their pronouncement when it sprang back to life. He concluded that "in the hearts and minds of many African Americans, 'the church' still moves and inspires their lives."[5]

But Glaude was not really saying that the black church was dead. Instead, he was following in a long line of pastors, scholars, activists, and churchpeople who called for a renewal of the prophetic mission of black religious thought and practice. Their calls came with a deep sense of the history of the role of African American religious institutions. Indeed, no study of African American history could suffice without a close accounting for black American religious thought and practice. Yet, despite the occasional prominence of black churches and churchpeople in significant American historical events—most recently, the civil rights movement—most Americans have little sense of their rich and complex history.

Black religious traditions provided theological, institutional, and personal strategies for cultural survival during bondage and the era of Jim Crow laws, which was characterized by at best partial freedom. Likewise, black religious institutions have contained *within* them the tensions and complexities of African American communal life. Black churchpeople, for example, have fought an ongoing tug-of-war between a drive toward "respectability" in the eyes of the larger white society and valorizing practices derived from African religious influences. From the eighteenth century to the present, black Americans adopted Christianity amid a critique about the acceptance of the "white man's religion." Beyond the varied responses to Christianity itself, black churches have attracted congregations of widely disparate educational levels, incomes, and worship styles. In short, the history of African American Christianity captures the complexity, strength, and fragility of African American communal institutions set within a country and culture that for centuries denied the humanity of black people.

This book aims to be a short, lively, introductory narrative history of African American Christianity and an invitation to press further the specific issues, controversies, and theoretical discussions covered here. While this book discusses the rise of particular black religious institutions and organizations, it also stresses the cultural products originating or emerging from the African American religious experience. Of those, the most important is music, which historically has been a primary form by which African Americans have expressed their deepest longings, hopes, and concerns. The field hollers, from which blues music originated, the spirituals of slaves, the rise of black gospel music in the early twentieth century, the "freedom songs" of the civil rights movement, and the bitter skepticism of some contemporary rap all speak to the deepest issues of African American religious culture. In African American history, music and religion cannot be separated, for religion fundamentally has been *defined* through musical expression. Even more important, it is vital to understand the origins of African American religious culture, for it has been the basis for much of broader American culture, particularly popular music.

A few caveats are in order. First, while much recent literature has focused on the history of the African diaspora (the dispersal of African peoples during and after the slave trade) throughout the Americas, this volume retains a focus on North America, and more specifically on the lands that became the United States. Where appropriate, this work draws comparisons with African American religions elsewhere in the Western Hemisphere—as, for example, in contrasting African American conjure and magic with Afro-Caribbean Vodun, the African-based religious tradition rooted in Haiti that in America became "voodoo."

A second caveat is that this volume will focus especially, although not exclusively, on African American *Christianity*. In recent years, scholars have devoted much attention to excavating the non-Christian African and African American traditions, including the sizable proportion of slaves who practiced Islam in Africa and America, the varieties of African religious expressions that survived in North American slave societies, and the explosion of African American "ethnic" religions in twentieth-century urban settings, such as the Black Muslims known best through the transcendent figure of Malcolm X. Moreover, the final chapters briefly consider the pluralization of African American religions since the 1960s, focusing especially on the impact of recent immigrants from Africa, the Caribbean, and South America. Thus, in many urban areas, Dominican Catholicism, Afro-Brazilian religious expressions, Ethiopian Eastern Orthodoxy and Judaism, and Nigerian spirit-filled worship have assumed an important place in African American religious life. Despite recent pluralization trends, African American Christianity has remained the dominant form of religious expression among black Americans since the late eighteenth century. It thus demands extensive attention in any volume on African American religion.

A few introductory concepts may help sort through the contentious relationship between the contested terms *race* and *religion*. What does "race" mean? What does "religion" mean? A short introduction here cannot answer these difficult questions but can suggest some ways to think about them.

Complex historical factors influenced the construction of modern racial categories. One was the gigantic global enterprise of colonizing the New World and then populating it with Europeans and African slaves. Beyond these economic factors were the religious practices and beliefs that each group brought to North America, including stories from the Old Testament and diverse indigenous American and African traditions. Euro-American Christianity was hardly the sole or even primary force in this process. Yet, religious myth, originating from interpretations of biblical stories as well as speculations about God's Providence, played an important role in the formation, revision, and reconstruction of racial categories in the modern world. In short, *religion* played a significant part in creating *race*. More specifically,

Christianity was central to the process of *racializing* peoples—that is, to imposing categories of racial hierarchies upon groups of humanity or other societies.

Yet if Christianity fostered racialization, it also undermined it. Biblical passages were powerful but ambiguous, and arguments about God's Providence in colonization, the slave trade, and Christian missions to slaves were contentious. Christian myths and stories were central to the project of creating racial categories in the modern world. But the central text of Christianity, the Bible, was also amenable to more universalist visions. In that sense, it could never be a fully reliable ally for theorists of racial hierarchy.

For much of the eighteenth and nineteenth centuries, race and religion defined "civilization." Christianizing others involved civilizing them. Sometimes this meant brutally stripping African Americans of the garments of their own civilizations. At other times, the correlation of Christianization and civilization supported idealistic crusades of bringing formerly enslaved peoples into U.S. citizenship, as in the abolitionist movement and in the creation of black schools and colleges during Reconstruction. In other instances, the intertwining of Christianity, civilization, and whiteness justified the complete exclusion of African people from the American republic. The first U.S. citizenship law of 1790, for example, defined membership in the republic as a privilege of white men, just as early black church leaders were petitioning Congress for their rights. Likewise, the 1857 *Dred Scott* Supreme Court decision insisted that black men had no rights that white men were bound to respect, even as black churchpeople organized conventions to pressure for respect of those rights. In short, the connections between religion and race have been complicated. Idealism and brutality often went hand in hand, as did notions of inclusion together with the instruments of exclusion. Idealism and imperialism often joined in projects both inspiring and ignoble. For example, the enslavement of African American people and the explosion of Protestant evangelicalism occurred virtually simultaneously.

In the twentieth century, Christian thought helped to undermine the racial system it had been instrumental in creating. In the 1950s and 1960s, black civil rights activists emerged from black churches and finally penetrated the walls of segregation, still guarded by conservative white churchmen and opportunistic politicians. The civil rights revolution in American history was, to a considerable degree, a religious revolution, one whose social and spiritual impact inspired numerous other movements around the world.

Well past the civil rights movement and the end of officially sanctioned segregation in America, religious institutions have remained largely, and voluntarily, separated by race. Even while scholars dispute the singular notion of the "black church," the term remains widely used in public discussions. In short, if religion is no longer racialized in the ways it was in previous centuries, religious congregations nevertheless tend to be racially separated, a simple reality of how Americans of diverse ethnic backgrounds have ordered their lives. Religion still has a color, even while the public rhetoric of American religion is ostensibly raceless and colorless. Thus, in a society sometimes said to be moving into a "postracial" era, ethnic and racial constructions remain a central ordering fact of religious life. That is why, even though the black church is not the Alpha and Omega of all things, it remains a significant and identifiable presence on the American cultural landscape.

Historically, African American Christianity has faced a number of paradoxes that have arisen from the ambiguous status of black people as Africans and Americans. The first fundamental paradox is this: white Americans spread Christianity among black Americans intending not only to evangelize people of color but also to make them more content in their enslavement. The end result was precisely the opposite: ultimately, African American Christianity provided the language and the spirit of African American survival under slavery, and of African American freedom efforts to destroy legal segregation. Black Christian parishioners, for example, empowered the civil rights movement, the most important social movement of twentieth-century American history. During the civil rights era, they seemed to be the most powerful body of Christians in America, capable of moving a nation socially and politically. The United States once was called the nation with the soul of a church; riffing on that, one scholar has referred to the black church as the "church with the soul of a nation."

Yet, black churches often have not been able to realize their potential as central institutions that speak for African Americans. They have been internally divided by slave versus free churches, by cultural practices, by skin tone and levels of education, by theological traditions, and by region. And that is the second paradox this book explores. On the one hand, the very popularity and singularity of the term "black church" suggests a unified force that emerged from the Christianization of black Americans during the Great Awakenings. The black church encompasses, for example, the creation of black denominations and other religious structures, and the effective political movements that arose in part out of those institutions during the civil rights era. Historically, black Christians in America have been identified with Protestant denominations, a legacy of the simultaneous rise of slavery and Protestant evangelicalism in the Deep South; more specifically, black Protestants historically have been mainly Baptist and Methodist. Indeed, African Americans have been one of the most Protestant ethnic groups in the country per capita. That factor alone helps to explain the continued power of the concept of a black church.

On the other hand, the black church and its leaders have been the target of relentless criticism. Critics have challenged the worship behavior of African Americans, including shouting and other emotionally enthusiastic practices. Black music, literature, and film have parodied "jackleg," or fraudulent, ministers. Academic critics have blasted "otherworldly" ministers and church organizations for their failure to provide practical programs of social reform. Facing such an array of criticisms, black Protestantism has been as beleaguered as it has been powerful. Its most eloquent defenders and its fiercest critics have come from within the black community, as in Glaude's polemic "The Black Church Is Dead." In short, the church with the soul of a nation has been, for much of its history, a symbol of frustrated longings.

There is a final paradox. Black Christians provided many of the shock troops for the social revolution of the civil rights movement. Moreover, African Americans since the New Deal of the 1930s have become associated with a powerful and solid voting bloc for the Democratic Party, even though the theology of many black churches historically has been conservative and devoutly evangelical. In short, a conservative Christian theology has fueled a history of social activism associated with liberal causes. In the civil rights years, black churches empowered a movement that cleansed the soul of a nation, in part by rejecting the fundamental premises of mid-twentieth-century optimism and returning instead to the prophetic tradition of biblical texts.

The black church that became largely identified with the struggle for civil rights faces both opportunities and dilemmas in a post–civil rights era. Black churches have been one of the relatively few black institutions to survive and thrive in the post–civil rights era. This is because African Americans since the late eighteenth century nurtured their churches as their own institutions. In recent years, the historic contrast between the often conservative theology and the liberal politics of black churches has been narrowing and even closing to some degree. White activists on the religious-political right have developed ideological alliances, especially in the areas of abortion and gay rights, to forge interracial political blocs that focus on issues of gender and sexuality. Nonetheless, black churches also remained aligned with the civil rights agenda, and black voters still turn out for Democratic and liberal candidates. Thus, the political impact of black Christianity is mixed.

In recent years, black parishioners increasingly have responded to the "megachurch" (huge nondenominational congregations) phenomenon, and to the charismatic call of white and black televangelists and prosperity gospel proponents. The term "prosperity gospel" refers to a contemporary theological movement stressing that Christian obedience ensures material prosperity. Assuming this continues, one may ask whether mainstream denominations such as Baptists and Methodists will come to be seen as irrelevant. In African American Christianity, this is most evident in the rise of Thomas Dexter (T. D.) Jakes. Born to a working-class family in West Virginia and now a preacher in Dallas, Jakes pushes "prosperity theology" to an integrated crowd of enthusiastic listeners.

The black church is a figment of academic imagination. As such, it could never be the "Alpha and Omega of all things" for black Americans. That was, and remains, too heavy a burden to put on black churches. In recent years, the rise of interracial megachurches has challenged the historic role of black churches as central institutions in the African American community. But since black religious institutions remain alive and well, and black churches have been at the center of the most important struggles for justice in American history, it is critical to understand their history. This book provides a brief interpretive introduction to that history.

CHAPTER ONE

~

Middle Passage for the Gods

African and African American Religions from the Middle Passage to the Great Awakening

A wide variety of peoples and cultures came to the New World from disparate parts of West and Central Africa during the years of the international slave trade. These men and women brought with them a remarkable array of religious beliefs and practices. Some came from societies that already had been Christianized or Islamicized prior to or during the slave trade. Others brought their local religious traditions with them.

African slaves employed a variety of strategies and developed new forms of religious expressions in acculturating to their lives on the new continent. Many underwent the process of "creolization," a term referring to the assimilation and acculturation of Africans into African Americans from the first generation to the second. By the eighteenth century, enslaved people showed that their religious beliefs could not only survive the tortuous passage but also empower resistance. Both the Stono Rebellion in South Carolina in 1739 and the "Great Negro Slave Plot" in New York in 1741 evidenced the religious roots of slave resistance, a theme of many American slave revolts. By that time, evangelical Christian missionaries were just beginning to make their first successful forays into preaching a message of gospel equality to small, scattered, but receptive African American audiences.

The religious beliefs and practices of enslaved African peoples clearly influenced the development of African American history. But the transmission of African religious traditions and their transformation in the New World have been the subject of a long and vigorous debate among scholars of African American history. Students of the subject have disagreed with each other on whether African religious traditions could have survived the horrifying slave voyages of the Middle Passage and the brutal conditions on New World plantations. But they did.

According to the most recent estimates, from 1501 to 1866 around 12.5 million people were transported from various regions of Africa to Europe and the Americas during the slave trade (see table 1.1). Other estimates have placed the total anywhere from about eleven million to upwards of fifteen million. Of this total number, relatively few individuals as a percentage of the total, perhaps about half a million, came directly or indirectly (usually via the Caribbean) to the North American colonies, and almost all of those from the late seventeenth century to the ending of the legal slave trade in 1808. By the Civil War, that number had grown to four million African Americans: about 3,600,000 slaves and 400,000 free people of color.

The accompanying map of the African slave trading regions shows the depth and geographic extent of the slave trade. The Middle Passage from Africa to the Americas involved well over twelve million humans, who brought to the New World their beliefs and religions. The slave trade wrecked millions of lives and permanently altered the religions of everyone involved. Conquest, violence, dispossession, and subjugation characterized the capture of and trade in humans, while despair, struggle, and creativity marked the religious responses of African peoples to their enslavement.

West and Central Africa supplied the human labor for the plantations of the New World. During the era of the slave trade, from the late fifteenth century through the mid-nineteenth, people captured from those regions and sold in the Americas followed a variety of African religions, as well as Islam and Christianity. Traditional African religions were largely *Orisha* religions, from the Nigerian Yoruba term for spirit manifestations of the high God Olorun. Orisha religions predominated in most of the supplying areas of the slave trade until the ninth century, when Islam started to spread throughout North Africa and into the northernmost districts of the slave-trading regions, namely, Senegambia and the Kingdom of Ghana. Far to the south and east, Christianity exercised its greatest influence in the kingdoms of Kongo and Ndongo, north of present-day Angola.

Slaves taken from these diverse regions of Africa filled the ships of the Middle Passage. Scholars once thought that slave traders deliberately mixed imported slave populations to lessen the chances for revolt among Africans of differing languages and ethnicities. In fact, while this sometimes happened, slave traders more often bought and sold humans from particular cultural regions in Africa. Thus, slaves routinely ended up being resettled forcibly with people from their home regions.

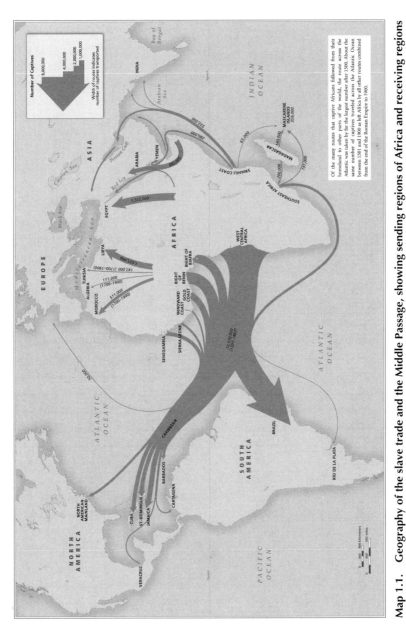

Map 1.1.   Geography of the slave trade and the Middle Passage, showing sending regions of Africa and receiving regions of the Americas. Reprinted by permission from David Eltis and David Richardson, *Atlas of the Transatlantic Slave Trade* (New Haven, CT: Yale University Press, 2010).

Table 1.1. Africans Transported during the Slave Trade

	Spain & Uruguay	Portugal & Brazil	Great Britain	Netherlands	U.S.A.	France	Denmark & Baltic	Totals
1501–1525	6,363	7,000	0	0	0	0	0	13,363
1526–1550	25,375	25,387	0	0	0	0	0	50,763
1551–1575	28,167	31,089	1,685	0	0	66	0	61,007
1576–1600	60,056	90,715	237	1,365	0	0	0	152,373
1601–1625	83,496	267,519	0	1,829	0	0	0	352,843
1626–1650	44,313	201,609	33,695	31,729	824	1,827	1,053	315,050
1651–1675	12,601	244,793	122,367	100,526	0	7,125	653	488,064
1676–1700	5,860	297,272	272,200	85,847	3,327	29,484	25,685	719,674
1701–1725	0	474,447	410,597	73,816	3,277	120,939	5,833	1,088,909
1726–1750	0	536,696	554,042	83,095	34,004	259,095	4,793	1,471,725
1751–1775	4,239	528,693	832,047	132,330	84,580	325,918	17,508	1,925,314
1776–1800	6,415	673,167	748,612	40,773	67,443	433,061	39,199	2,008,670
1801–1825	168,087	1,160,601	283,959	2,669	109,545	135,815	16,316	1,876,992
1826–1850	400,728	1,299,969	0	357	1,850	68,074	0	1,770,979
1851–1866	215,824	9,309	0	0	476	0	0	225,609
Totals	1,061,524	5,848,265	3,259,440	554,336	305,326	1,381,404	111,041	12,521,336

Source: Compiled from data in the Trans-Atlantic Database, available online at www.slavevoyages.org.

Slave traders not only focused on certain regions of Africa to purchase human cargo but also targeted particular areas in the Caribbean and North America to sell their merchandise. Those who purchased slaves in the New World often expressed decided preferences for Africans from specific regions, believing that one group was somehow more suited for labor or less prone to revolt than another. For example, the Central African regions of the Kongo kingdom became the largest source of humans forcibly imported into South Carolina during the early eighteenth century. These Africans shaped the emerging slave culture that developed in the rice-growing regions near Charleston. In contrast, French Louisianans imported Senegambians in large numbers, largely due to the trading patterns of slave supply ships and the demands of French colonists. Meanwhile, Virginians received people stolen from the Gold and Windward Coasts and the bights of Biafra and Benin, again largely due to the sea routes of the ships that supplied the Chesapeake colonies. In all these cases, slaves from individual African regions frequently ended up in the New World with other Africans of similar ethnicities, languages, and religions.

Despite the differences separating African peoples taken from the multitude of different cultures, particular religious beliefs and ritual patterns were relatively common throughout the slaving regions. Africans generally held a profound belief in an overarching but relatively distant Spirit, who oversaw a huge variety of deities. These lesser gods, in turn, inhabited objects in the world. Africans venerated and provided sacrifices to ancestors, invoking their spirits through ritual music, dancing, and chanting. Their practices involved beseeching and appeasing the lesser deities who were responsible for the world of matter and spirit. These were, in the Yoruba tongue of present-day Nigeria, the orishas, spirits who commanded a variety of religious practices. Their power was not by definition good or evil. Religious or ritual specialists (priests) divined messages from the orishas, who communicated to humans via natural objects and whose power might be manipulated through material "fetishes." Among the most common material fetishes were *gris-gris*. These were pouches of natural materials, including roots, fingernails, animal parts, soil, and other natural objects, and sometimes scraps of sacred scriptures such as verses from the Qur'an. Africans carried gris-gris to ward off evil or invoke success.

African practices also emphasized forms of healing that combined medical and social conceptions of illnesses. Africans believed that diseases were caused by breakdowns of not only the biological body but also the social life of a community. They employed particular medicines and rituals that sought to mend the social conflicts causing communal strife and bodily disease. For this purpose, religious specialists prepared healing potions or foods, which they gave as sacrifices to spirits and ancestors.

These lesser gods, who had various names in different parts of West and Central Africa, including *vodun*, *loas*, *orisha*, and others, governed the world and affected the course of human life both for good and for ill. Like many other human civilizations, Africans over generations handed down stories of the personalities and propensities of individual gods. These mythical tales explained the workings of the divine hierarchy. The orishas were both benevolent and malevolent. Because of the willful personalities and volatile potentials of the spirits, it was incumbent on people to offer them the right combination of ritual praise, veneration, and obedience. Africans wore colors preferred by the spirits, avoided taboo foods, and performed ritual ceremonies in prescribed ways that honored the ancestors.

In the African religious worldview, when people died they became spirits, and as spirits they continued to interact with living human societies and to influence human life. Africans regarded these spirit beings as personalities who possessed their own distinct preferences, propensities, and strengths. Because human life and social harmony involved balancing dangerous and unpredictable spiritual forces, devotees sought professional help from religious specialists who could perform the proper rituals of appeasement, make up the right herbal medicines for ailments, and divine the future of individuals, family, and kinship groups.

To ensure the continued appeasement of the deities/gods, West and Central Africans organized societies that introduced converts to secret and sacred ways. These secret societies put initiates through ceremonies in which they figuratively died and were resurrected as new people. Individual societies prepared sacrifices to particular orishas, and devotees became mediums of those gods. In trances and other ritual acts, Africans acted out in song and dance the character of individual spirits. As mediums, they became that god's "horse." Spirits "mounted" and rode individuals, who then responded to the demands of the spirit-rider with bodily movement, singing, shouting, and chanting. African song and dance styles arose from these religious ceremonies and deeply imprinted black American religious cultural expression.

Besides these rituals of song and dance, rituals of medicine also shaped religious life in West and Central Africa. In the Kongo kingdom, religious life focused on *minkisi*, spirits who could harm or cure. The Kongolese held widely shared beliefs in a transcendent, benevolent God, who was the creator and ultimate source of providence. They also understood the world to be inhabited by a number of gods who were present in everyday life. In religious rituals devoted to these gods, Africans from the Kongo made sacrifices to powerful spirits that they believed inhabited and animated material and natural objects. Engaging in these acts, they hoped, would honor the gods and ensure the proper balance of forces on earth. They consulted priests and others with practical knowledge of the workings of the gods and saw the actions of the spirits in human bodies during times of spirit possession. In ritual possessions, humans served as mouthpieces for the spirits, communicating messages about present-day affairs and granting to living humans fertility and health.

As part of the religious belief patterns of these societies, men and women carried on the customs and traditions of the family, kinship groups, and societies. The Kongolese, as well as many other African societies, believed that the ancestors were reborn in their descendants. An important part of those sacred customs involved burial rituals. Done properly, burial ensured the entrance of the deceased spirit into the next world, where, as an ancestral spirit, he or she could intervene in the affairs of men and women on earth. Funeral rituals involved elaborate mourning ceremonies, and burials included broken pottery and other vessels that allowed for the release of the spirit into the next world and the continuation of the cycle of life. In this way, life on earth and life in the spirit realm always maintained a close connection. Disruptions of social harmony predicted similar ruptures in the realm of the gods. By contrast, social harmony on earth could be assured by the proper acts of homage to the beings who populated the spirit world.

During the early years of the slave trade, the religious world of Africans encountered competitors from religions that had originated in other parts of the world. Christian and Islamic missionaries from Europe and the Middle East often perceived a vast gulf between their religious practices and those of Africans. From the standpoint of comparative religions, however, there were many parallels between African, Islamic, and Christian religious rituals. In the ninth century, when Islam started to expand into northern Africa, Africans incorporated Muslim practices and objects into their religious patterns. In many cases, African elites in the kingdoms and courts adopted Islam, while ordinary Africans continued their long-held religious customs. In some cases, the two could be combined. Thus, Africans put verses from the Qur'an in their gris-gris, prayed to Allah in addition to beseeching the orishas, and invoked the protection of the ancestors for the trading networks they had developed with Islamic kingdoms in the north.

Likewise, when the Kongo monarch Nzinga a Nkuwu adopted Christianity as the official state religion of his kingdom in 1491, ordinary Kongolese accepted Catholic rites because they paralleled their own, easing the entrance of Christianity into this region. Catholics prayed and gave ritual offerings to a diverse array of divine beings such as saints, angels, Mary, and other figures who stood between men and God. The Kongolese, similarly, prayed to familial ancestors and ritually manipulated natural objects to unleash the extraordinary spiritual power within them. Thus, Kongolese Christians combined religious traditions, engaging in ritual sacrifice to and invoking the obligatory favors of orishas, ancestors, and beings from the Christian world. All of them might provide succor and protection to humans who lived in a world precariously balanced on competing spiritual forces. Further, Portuguese missionaries starting in the fifteenth century borrowed the names of African gods when outlining the Christian spiritual universe to attract potential African converts. This religious *syncretism*, the melding of religious traditions, which was common in Africa in such places as the Kongo, continued in North America.

The initial encounters of Europeans and Africans in the New World started during an age of great religious ferment and expansion following the Protestant Reformation and Catholic Counter-Reformation. While the trade was economically motivated, the European participants sought some religious sanction for their coercive and brutal trade in human souls. Europeans sought justification in the Bible, but Judeo-Christian stories were not inherently amenable to providing a religious basis for modern racial slavery. Biblical characters lived in an ancient Semitic, Mediterranean, and North African world, one in which modern understandings of "white" and "black" people would have been meaningless.

Once slavery took root in the Americas, it was inevitable that religious authorities would decree that, if slavery existed, God must have a reason for it—and that reason must be in the Bible. But slavery in the Americas was specifically a *racial* form of bondage. This was in contrast to traditional forms of slavery found worldwide, which were not racially based. Thus, any religious defense of slavery in America would have to clarify God's providence in having one race of people enslave another. In this way, Euro-Americans developed some of the meanings of "race" in the modern sense. They began to define what constituted whiteness and blackness, categories that would long outlive slavery itself. And those categories were, at least initially, fundamentally religious ones.

White supremacist racial thought emerged in the fifteenth century and dramatically shaped the interactions between Europeans and Africans. Religious divisions drawn by Europeans, between followers of Christ and heathens, helped define the meaning of race. "European" or "English" meant "Christian" and "white." "African," by contrast, meant "heathen," despite the fact that many Africans had been Christianized and large portions of

North and sub-Saharan Africa had fallen under the sway of Islam. Regardless, for European Christians, Africans were heathens, and black. In short, the categories of religion and race intertwined, each helping to define the other. Religion helped to create and solidify modern notions of whiteness and blackness. In that sense, it led to common understandings of white and black people. Religion created race, and race thereafter shaped religion.

From the perspective of European slavers, traders, and colonizers, Africans did not have a religion. Instead, they merely possessed "pagan" or "barbaric" customs. Even Europeans who lived and worked in regions of Africa heavily influenced by Islamic and Catholic missionaries generally could not see their subjects as practicing religion. Indeed, the very process of enslavement virtually *required* Europeans to place the victims outside the category of humanity. In theory, non-Christians could be enslaved; Christians could not. The earliest process of racializing diverse peoples involved ignoring, denying, or denigrating their religions. This held true both for Christian and Islamic enslavers.

The onset of the international slave trade in the early sixteenth century brought this diverse array of African religions to the New World. African peoples brought with them a variety of gods, ritual specialists, and religious practices. Followers of Orisha religions, practicing Muslims, and Catholic Kongolese were all part of this mix. Muslim slaves found little support to keep African Islam alive in North America. African Orisha religions could not survive as religious *systems*, either, for they were dependent on particular geographies, sacred spaces, kinship groups, and family/tribal relationships. In other words, African religions did not constitute a discrete set of religious beliefs that could be carried anywhere. Instead, they involved ritual practices intimately tied to social groupings set in particular natural geographies. When slave traders wrested Africans from their homes and threw them into the hellish cauldron of the Middle Passage, they also destroyed their ritual social systems, which were based on venerating localized spirits. The same held true for Christianized Africans, whose sacred practices also depended on geographically specific gods and social clans.

One of the basic questions European colonizers posed was whether Africans, Indians, and others could be brought into the Christian fold. For the Indians and Africans, who were colonized and enslaved, the question was very different; they understood that religions were to be respected, but they did not necessarily perceive proselytization as respect. In other words, the European, North African, and Middle Eastern religions of Protestantism, Catholicism, and Islam preached messages that their adherents believed applied to all mankind everywhere. Moreover, Protestantism, Catholicism, and Islam competed avidly, sometimes violently, for souls, including those in West and Central Africa. However, African peoples held to highly localized religions that varied widely by region and had little experience with religions that insisted on saving the souls of converts. When the aggressively expanding religions of Christianity and Islam met the localized practices of millions of African peoples, misunderstanding and conflict quickly emerged.

The destruction of African religions as *belief systems* was especially evident among enslaved Africans taken to the northern colonies of British North America. Their small numbers, their geographic dispersal, and their placement on small plantations and farms away from larger groupings of other Africans tended to undermine African religious systems. In contrast, on the West Indian islands and in Brazil, the higher numbers and greater concentrations of slaves in smaller locales allowed for greater survival of African religious traditions. In these regions, a different religious history emerged as a result.

The early slave trade to North America brought people from the African continent who came from widely differing societies, languages, and religions. Slave ships brought them to scattered settlements along the eastern seaboard of the colonies of North America. A handful of slaves made it as far north as New England, where many of them became involved with commercial seafaring ventures. They were "black jacks." Slaves in New York tended to be "Atlantic creoles," men (usually) and women who often had lived in various regions of the Atlantic world—in Africa, Europe, the Caribbean, and North America—and thus had acquired cosmopolitan knowledge of geographies and languages.

Slaves brought to the Chesapeake beginning in 1619 usually had some experience in the British Caribbean first, and they entered a world where their ambiguous status as "servants" was not altogether different from the English indentured servants whom they joined. An early death met most settlers in the Chesapeake, white and black, but those Africans who survived sometimes scrabbled upward to a free status. On occasion, they became landowners and even purchased servants themselves. Later in the seventeenth century, colonists established sizable plantations in the Chesapeake, resulting in the importation of large numbers of Africans. It spelled the decline of indentured servitude as an intermediary status between slavery and freedom. Virginia started to import African slave labor rather than English indentured servants or Caribbean blacks to meet its labor needs. Indentured servants from England had become more expensive, while the supply of slaves increased (and therefore the price of purchasing African humans decreased) as English ships brought more Africans to the Americas. As a result, "unseasoned" Africans began arriving in Virginia in large numbers. Most of them came from regions of Africa that had had little or no contact with Christianity, leading the colonial elites to conclude that it was "impossible to make any progress in their conversion."[1]

Initially, early colonizers in the Americas wondered whether Indians and black slaves could be Christians. The answer required, in part, deciding on whether Native people, Africans, and African Americans were fully human. The debate raged for several centuries, dragging on into the post–Civil War era of scientific racism. If only Christians were truly human——and Christians were white——then where did that leave people of African descent? And what was the status of Indians, people who never appeared in the biblical texts and whose origins were simply unknown? English settlers in Virginia debated these questions and by the 1660s codified their answers in law in ways that set the pattern for other English colonies.

Nonetheless, some Africans converted to Christianity and as a result claimed their freedom. Colonial assemblies in Maryland (1664) and Virginia (1667) responded by dissociating baptism from freedom. From that point on, Christianity and slavery seemed compatible. Children born of slave women, even Christian slave women, would be bondspeople for life.

In the late seventeenth and early eighteenth centuries, as a growing number of slaves converted to Christianity, Anglo-Americans once again faced the question of whether baptism made men white. The early advocates of slave Christianization, accordingly, had to conceive of Christianity apart from whiteness and freedom precisely for the purpose of defining "blackness" as a state of perpetual servitude. Slavery would continue beyond one's potential conversion to Christianity. It would extend beyond one's own life into the lives of one's children and grandchildren.

As slavery took hold in the Chesapeake, Virginians clarified further the status of "free and Christian" by legally defining precisely what constituted its opposite: unfree and heathen. The English solidified their own identity as Protestant and free by enumerating what constituted the status of unfreedom. By the early eighteenth century, they legally defined Christians and condemned non-Christians to slavery.[2] Baptism, a 1705 law stated, did not affect a person's status as slave or free. Some lawmakers, convinced of a Christian duty to preach the gospel among the slaves, hoped that the act would encourage the propagation of Christianity among Africans by assuring masters that baptism did not result in freedom.

Nonetheless, many European colonists remained convinced that blackness was incompatible with Christianity. For them, blackness conjured images of savagery, which were also evident in the way slaves practiced their religions.

The Reverend Morgan Godwyn, who ministered in seventeenth-century Virginia, charged that "nothing is more barbarous and contrary to Christianity, than their . . . *Idolatrous Dances*, and *Revels*."[3] Most Anglican planters did not provide for Christian preaching to slaves. It simply was not in their interest to do so. Many planters felt no duty to spread Christianity among slaves, and nearly all feared the possible consequences of slave conversion. The true cause of the lack of Christianization, one contemporary noted in the 1680s, was the "want of zeal in Masters, and the *untoward haughty behavior* of those Negros who have been admitted into the fellowship of Christ's religion."[4]

In New England, Puritan attempts to reach their relatively small black population also met indifference or resistance from whites, who were unconvinced that blacks had souls of equal value to God. By the early eighteenth century, a Puritan justification for racism already had arisen. John Saffin, a Massachusetts jurist and slaveholder, enunciated an argument that took hold in proslavery circles. The Bible sanctioned slavery, he insisted, and pointed out that the great patriarch Abraham owned slaves. Thus, Puritans simply imitated him, claiming that "any lawful Captives of Other Heathen Nations may be made Bond men." Beyond that, Saffin explained, God had "set different Orders and Degrees of Men in the World," which meant that God had made some men to be slaves.[5] Saffin also articulated another point dear to the heart of proslavery theorists: it was not evil to bring Africans out of their heathen homelands to a land where they could learn true Christian knowledge and be saved from eternal damnation.

While Puritans advocated Christian conversion, that argument failed to work in the British colony in South Carolina, which featured one of the earliest and most brutal plantation systems in North America. In South Carolina, importations of slaves began later in the seventeenth century and brought in large numbers of men and women directly from Africa, especially from the Kongo region, where many of them would have had exposure to Christianity via the Portuguese missionaries. Slavemasters in South Carolina, often Englishmen who came from the Caribbean seeking their riches with lands being distributed by the English monarch to encourage settlement on the continent, often vigorously opposed slave Christianization. The English paid little attention to the religion of the large number of slaves working in their rice fields. For the most part, they saw Africans as heathens, lacking any religion at all, which made them perfect candidates for enslavement.

By the 1730s, in Virginia as in South Carolina, very few planters showed any interest in imparting Christianity to the slaves. Missionaries who made it their task to do so generally met resistance from slave owners and indifference among the slaves. It was not that much different proselytizing among whites. Many parishes lacked ministers or churches. Others had widely scattered churches, often located too far away for ordinary folk to attend. In the eighteenth century, Anglican missionaries sought to implant Christianity more firmly among whites. Anglican elites sought to use Christian ritual to define their Englishness. For them, Christianity was a religion for whites. Elaborate Anglican ritual practices carried on through the liturgical year reminded Anglican families of their place in the social and heavenly order.

In 1701, responding to the embarrassing lack of "zeal in Masters," English Anglican idealists funded the Society for the Propagation of the Gospel in Foreign Parts (SPG). Its mission was to bring the gospel to Indians and blacks in the New World, though most SPG missionaries preached among whites, particularly in the South. They attempted to instill a stronger institutional structure for Anglicanism in the southern agricultural colonies. However, some SPG missionaries also did their best to convert slaves. These SPG emissaries found much the same response that others had complained about previously—lack of zeal among masters and "untoward haughty behavior" among slaves. Some white masters, SPG emissary Francis Le Jau exclaimed in exasperation in 1712, resisted his conversion efforts among their slaves. There seemed to be no reason for this opposition, he thought, other than the excuse that baptism made the slaves "proud and Undutifull."[6] Le Jau attempted to persuade whites otherwise by pointing to examples of slaves who were obedient and humble after being admitted to Communion. Seeking to reassure planters, Le Jau made black converts declare that they asked for baptism not to free themselves from their duties to their masters, but for the good of their souls.

At other times, Le Jau wondered about the safety of his project of proselytization, as his converts drew their own conclusions from visionary biblical passages, such as those from the Book of Revelation. One slave's dire visions of a religious apocalypse especially troubled the missionary. This convert, an honest and sober man in Le Jau's estimation, possessed learning that Le Jau feared would sow confusion among slaves. In Revelation, this slave had read descriptions of God's judgments at the end of time. Those biblical passages "made an Impression upon his Spirit, and he told his Master abruptly there wou'd be a dismal time and the Moon wou'd be turned into Blood, and there wou'd be dearth of darkness."[7] He further claimed that an angel had spoken to him and given him a book with special divine instructions. Since many slaves who had heard the man claimed that he had seen great visions of the impending end of the world, Le Jau wondered if it would be better if slaves were denied access to troublesome Bible passages that foretold an overturning of the social order. In addition to apocalyptic messages, slave masters were troubled by slave literacy, even in the service of slave Christianization. It was little wonder that colonies legislated against teaching slaves to read.

While Anglican missionaries anguished over the fact that planters resisted slave Christianization, claiming that it made the slaves too proud, white masters had good reasons for their opposition to conversion. Some Christianized slaves sued for freedom and asserted that Christianity contradicted slaveholding. In 1723, a group of Christian mixed-race slaves in Virginia pled their case for freedom in a letter to a newly installed Anglican bishop. They were brought up in the Christian church, they wrote, and followed the rules of Anglicanism. In all likelihood, they had learned limited reading and writing skills in church. Nonetheless, the laws of the land made them lifelong slaves, and their masters prevented them from their duty of observing the Sabbath. In their letter, these slaves compared their masters to the Egyptians who cruelly exercised rule over the Israelites in the Old Testament. They concluded with an explanation of why they did not sign their names: If their masters discovered their identities, they feared that they would soon be swinging from the gallows tree.

These slaves and others like them retained an older, more radical view of Christian conversion. Their religious status, they insisted, gave them rights to freedom and respect. They spoke the language of power precisely because they knew the language of power. They expressed that language in courtrooms, in letters to government officials, and, as a last resort, in acts of resistance. In 1751, when white authorities condemned a Christian slave to death for her part in poisoning her masters, she appealed to the reverend presiding over her execution. She hoped to be spared death because of her belief in Christ. A white contemporary scorned her testimony as a convenient protestation designed to shield her from the consequences of her acts, suggesting the extent of white suspicion that blacks would manipulate Christian rhetoric to their advantage.

By the early eighteenth century, African slaves in North America lived among English settlers, but also among Spanish and French colonizers. They sometimes forged alliances with Native American people and formed "maroon colonies" comprised of runaway slaves and Indians. They prayed to African orishas, drew on elements of Native American religions, and staged guerrilla attacks against white settlers. Others used alliances with Christian colonizers to win their freedom. However, a majority of them lived and died without any knowledge of Christianity.

While some African slaves embraced Christianity, others bitterly resisted Christianization, such as those slaves brought from Senegambia to Louisiana and the Mississippi River Valley. Led by Samba Bambara, a slave interpreter for the French, Afro-Louisianans formed alliances with Natchez Indians. Together, they fought fiercely against the French and their Native allies, the Choctaw. As a result, there were few black Catholics in the Louisiana territory. Most black Catholics in the territory resided in and around New Orleans, where they learned French and lived as part of a small colored elite. Many were the offspring of the liaisons of white masters and slave women. They included some African and African American women educated in academies begun by the Ursulines, who had been established in 1727 as the first female order in the United States. The Ursulines educated a select contingent of blacks in colonial Louisiana in Catholic Christianity. Beyond New Orleans, many slaves in the bayou country and Mississippi Valley resisted European power by forming maroon colonies either on their own or together with members of Native nations with whom they intermarried. They invoked the orishas in their fight against slavery and against Christianity.

While maroons resisted slavery in part by rejecting Christianity and European civilization, Spanish slaves in Florida used Catholicism and their service to the Spanish Crown to pursue lives of relative freedom. The Spanish imported slaves to Florida in the mid-seventeenth century, where they deployed them as soldiers to defend Spanish claims in North America and to harass the British settlement of South Carolina. In 1693, the Spanish Crown offered freedom to all South Carolina fugitives who converted to Catholicism and served the Spanish king's military. Word of the Spanish offer turned Florida into a magnet for black South Carolinians seeking to escape slavery. A number of Africans manned Fort Mose, a settlement built in 1738 near St. Augustine and led by an African soldier named Francisco Menendez. Catholic priests required the Carolina fugitives to be baptized anew and to receive additional religious instruction upon their arrival in Florida. One Spanish official observed that the slaves wanted to be Christians but that their English masters sought to prevent them from learning Catholic doctrine.

By 1746, blacks constituted about a quarter of St. Augustine's population of 1,500. These included Africans imported directly by the Spanish, as well as fugitives from the Carolinas and other English colonies. Catholic priests sanctified marriages among the slaves and fugitives and baptized their children. Membership in the Church and the militia created common bonds for these Atlantic creoles who served the Spanish Crown in exchange for their freedom. These promises of freedom were not always kept; some who tried to claim freedom were shipped to Havana and re-enslaved in Cuba.

Despite the fact that not all South Carolina fugitives gained their freedom, English colonists rightly feared the possible effects of slave Christianization in Spanish-controlled Florida. The Spanish employed religion to foment discontent among slaves in the British colonies of North America. The results were soon evident in South Carolina and New York, where slave rebellions betokened the potentially dangerous consequences of Christian conversion. In both cases, Christianized slaves took the lead in the revolts, adding to English fears about the effect of Christian preaching among people who lacked freedom but desired liberation. Had English colonists inquired more closely into the religion of their subjects, they might have discovered the influence of Kongolese Catholicism and foreseen it as an internal enemy. It proved so during the Stono Rebellion of 1739.

On Sunday morning, September 9, 1739, an enslaved man named Jemmy, originally from the Kingdom of Kongo, gathered a group of slaves near the Stono River in South Carolina. The group may have been inspired by recent runaways who had made it to Spanish Florida. The very date of the rebellion may have held a specific religious meaning for Kongolese Catholic rebels who believed September 8 to be the day of Nativity for the Virgin Mary. Kongolese Catholics believed that Mary protected those who venerated her. The slaves also may have known about the recent South Carolina law that, weeks later, would require all Englishmen to carry firearms to church on Sunday to prevent the possibilities of slave revolts. Beating the deadline, Jemmy and the rebels broke into a store, secured firearms, and killed twenty-one whites. The next morning they marched "in a Daring manner out of the Province, killing all they met and burning several Houses as they passed along the Road."[8] Many of the rebels were likely trying to flee to freedom in Florida. Proud of their Catholicism, the Kongolese welcomed the Spanish offers because this would allow them to gain freedom and practice their Catholicism free from the Protestant oppression of their South Carolina masters. However, their hopes were squashed when a posse of whites killed thirty of the rebels.

Similar to the Anglican slaves who had petitioned for their freedom in 1723, the Stono rebels understood the connection between Christianity and freedom. The rebels considered themselves to be Catholic Christians from an independent political kingdom. Some of them may have known how to fight based on their military experience with militia orders in the Kongo kingdom. Like the English, they understood that violence sometimes was necessary to defend one's freedom and one's faith. The Stono Rebellion shook the colony of South Carolina to its core. The idea that propagating Christian belief would inculcate order and obedience into an otherwise unruly slave population had failed.

A second incident, the "Great Negro Plot of 1741" in New York City, speaks more ambiguously to the role of religion, Christianization, and rebellion. In New York as in South Carolina, skepticism about religion and slave conversions and concerns about slave plots ran strongly among the white populace. Protestant white New Yorkers especially feared the presence of Catholic slaves and priests who seemingly threatened their dominance and supremacy, although no evidence exists linking the slaves in New York to Spain or Spanish plots.

In 1664, when the English won New Amsterdam from the Dutch, New York City had a small black population consisting of three hundred Africans who had come from all over the Atlantic world. By the early 1740s, enslaved people numbered about two thousand and comprised about 20 percent of the city's labor force. In the bitterly cold winter and spring of 1741, a burglary plot involving a white tavern owner and two slaves, along with a series of fires of obscure origins, set into motion the Great Negro Plot of 1741.

To this day, it is not clear whether there was any such plot, but New Yorkers of the time drew from a familiar set of stories about rebellious slaves and evil Catholics turning the world upside down. These formulaic narratives convinced New Yorkers that slaves had indeed planned to rebel. Allegedly, a group of "Spanish Negroes," freemen who had been captured from Spanish vessels and then sold into slavery in New York, were conspiring with Catholic priests to stage a revolt. Slaves rounded up as part of the conspiracy were self-professed Christians. One so-called Spanish Negro, a Portuguese-speaking slave possibly from Angola who had worked in the Spanish colonies, insisted on his innocence, praying and kissing a crucifix at his execution. Some jailed slave conspirators had worked with Anglicans who had instructed them in Christianity. Still other slaves had heard the word of God in the early years of the great Protestant revivals of the mid-eighteenth century. Authorities in New York browbeat suspects with Christian theology, threatening them with visions of the fires of Hell if they did not confess and repent. Despite the clear evidence of slave Christianization, however, authorities from the British Crown assumed that all slaves involved in the plot were heathens, for how else could their actions be explained?

By the end of the plot, New York authorities had arrested 172 people (152 blacks, 20 whites), executed 34 alleged conspirators (30 blacks, 4 whites), and exiled 84 slaves from the colony. One jailed slave committed suicide. Fearful of slave rebellions, real or imagined, whites clamped down further on slaves' religious practices. They sought to eliminate any vestige of slave autonomy by restricting meeting places, occupational choices, and avenues of redress for grievances. As part of this tightening of control, religious exercises came under closer scrutiny. White men with firearms kept watch over black assemblies and discouraged slave religious expressions. In New York as in South Carolina, Christianized slaves seemed to be the most dangerous, hence the concern with black religious assemblies.

The brutality of the Middle Passage, the spread of slavery throughout colonial North America, and the repression that met uprisings, real or imagined, such as those in South Carolina and New York, all speak to the obstacles Africans faced in adapting religious practices to their harsh new environments. In North America, slaves attempting to create communal cultures in their new worlds drew on their African past and their diverse variety of religious traditions, including Orisha practices, Islam, and Christianity. Their experiences in the New World either limited, drove underground, or transformed their religious practices.

Older African religious expressions survived in North America, but without the system of rituals that had supported them in African societies. Particular religious practices continued, but African religions as systems of practice tied to local geographies, spirits, and ancestors could not be transported to the Americas. Religious systems based on communal notions of space, geography, and sacred objects could not withstand the displacement caused by the Middle Passage.

Although Islam lacked any institutional structure in North America, Muslim slaves continued to practice individual forms of belief. They prayed to the East, chanted Qur'anic passages, ate food items that marked the end of fasting during Ramadan, and played melodic lines on instruments that had been derived from Islamic musical patterns. But for Muslim slaves, there were no formal calls to prayer, mosques, or public Islamic customs to sustain the faith in something other than an underground or privatized form.

Finally, the Christianity that was part of the religious culture of some enslaved Africans was a very different form of Christianity than the Protestantism that predominated in the English colonies of North America. Indeed, many English settlers assumed that Africans were simply heathens, for they could not see Orisha religions, Islamic customs, or Kongolese Catholicism as religion at all. However, that began to change in the mid-eighteenth century, when a series of evangelical revivals swept the colonies and attracted converts among the slaves. These Protestant evangelical revivals resulted in the birth of African American Christianity, which became a significant force in black American life.

The explosion of Protestant fervor in the colonies affected some slave owners who attempted to convert their slaves, but it also revived fears among other planters about the potentially dangerous consequences of slave conversion. Uneasiness about black Christianization, and the uncertainty of whites about whether slave conversion would undergird or undermine the social order, plagued the white slave-owning class. Meanwhile, Christian bondspeople, basing their beliefs on the biblical promise of equality and justice, employed the liberating potential of evangelicalism to challenge the premises that underlay slavery and white supremacy.

CHAPTER TWO

~

The Birth of Afro-Christianity in the Slave Quarters and the Urban North, 1740–1831

For much of the fifteenth through seventeenth centuries, the well-developed worldwide Catholic mission network dominated international Christian missions. Protestants came late to the game, but in America, where Protestants predominated, they took control of preaching Christianity to slaves. In the transatlantic Protestant revival movement of the eighteenth-century Great Awakening, itinerant ministers, including laypersons as well as ordained clergymen, questioned the established clerical hierarchy. The "New Lights," as colonial Americans called them, flaunted their salvation. They taunted the "Old Lights," who fired back with salvos questioning the sanity of the so-called awakened. Evangelical religion in eighteenth-century America was countercultural. It challenged the dominant religious establishment everywhere: Congregationalism in New England, Presbyterianism in the Middle Colonies, and Anglicanism in the South.

In the midst of this religious upheaval, which spread from New England and New York in the 1740s down to the Southern colonies by the 1770s, African Americans joined the evangelical movement. The Old Lights used the black presence in the Awakening to disparage the colonial revivals. If children, women, and slaves assumed religious authority, the critics of the Awakening declared, then surely the world must be turned upside down. But many white ministers who conducted missions among the slaves assured white authorities that Christianity had the potential of creating obedient, humble, and respectful servants. The results justified both the hopes of the missionaries and the fears of their critics. The expansion of Christian churches among the bondspeople allowed African Americans places of communal gathering and fellowship, while it assured whites that slaves were being "civilized" and taught biblical notions of a proper social order. In the nineteenth century, as white authorities increasingly took control of missionary work among slaves, they limited the opportunities for independent or unsupervised religious activity among African American ministers and churches. Evangelical doctrine taught spiritual brotherhood and equality, but evangelicals patterned their churches and institutions after the larger social hierarchy of white authority and black subordination.

Nonetheless, the coming of Protestant Christianity to African Americans was a seminal moment in black American history. A small minority of blacks converted to Christianity, but they established a religious culture and a set of institutions that defined much of African American religious life to come. From the 1740s to 1831, African American Christianity took on three forms, as black Americans adapted, shaped, and changed it to match their beliefs and circumstances. In the South, whites and blacks attended biracial churches with white ministers and segregated seating. A second formation took root in the North and in some Southern urban areas prior to 1831. There, free black churches such as the African Methodist Episcopal (AME) Church, organized in 1816, provided an independent religious denomination for black Christians. A third kind of black religious expression was covert. Separate and apart from the official churches, slaves conducted secret religious ceremonies in the slave quarters and in "brush harbors," the name given to small gathering spots in the backwoods protected by canopies of tree branches. In these secluded places, which slaves sometimes referred to as "hush harbors" because of their secrecy, black ministers preached in a manner they could not display in front of whites.

African American Christianity developed within the severe limitations required under the slave regime. Regardless of the rhetoric of Christian freedom and equality, there was an obvious power gulf between free whites and enslaved blacks. Slaves simply could not "make" their own world. Slaveholders held the power. In the eighteenth century, many slaveholders had discouraged the propagation of the Christian gospel, fearing its implications of equality. Nonetheless, a pioneering generation of slaves adopted Christianity enthusiastically, and some used their Christian faith to challenge the premises that underlay the slave regime. In the nineteenth century, slave rebels employed biblical reasoning to instigate uprisings. That history culminated in the actions of Nat Turner, whose religiously inspired visions compelled his furious and murderous resistance to the prevailing order of the South. Slaves who could not, or would not, engage in overt acts of rebellion found other ways to use the Christian message subversively.

The writings of African Americans who converted as a result of the Great Awakening constitute some of the earliest black American literature. The narrative of John Marrant illustrates the effect of evangelical preaching on a small but significant minority of black Americans, who served as a charter generation of black evangelicals in spreading black Christianity throughout North America.

Born free in New York in 1755, Marrant moved while still young to South Carolina, where he found a free black community that offered him economic opportunity. There, he became an apprentice musician, devoted himself to "pleasure and drinking," and became, as he later recalled, "a slave to every vice suited to my nature and to my years." In 1770, he came to Charleston, where he had heard that a "crazy man was hallooing" in town. This "crazy man" was the famous colonial evangelist George Whitefield, whose circuit of preaching tours through the colonies drew huge throngs.

The young prankster Marrant intended to disrupt Whitefield's service by blowing his French horn. Instead, Marrant fell under the preacher's spell. The message came with such force that Marrant recalled being literally struck down by Whitefield's words. Lying on the ground, those words felt like swords being thrust into him. He lay on the floor until Whitefield came and said to him, "Jesus Christ has got thee at last." For three days, Marrant fasted and prayed for salvation, and at last he felt that the Lord had given him eternal freedom. A black loyalist during the American Revolution, he later ministered to a group of black émigrés in Nova Scotia, Canada. After his death in 1791, about 1,200 of his black parishioners emigrated to Sierra Leone in Africa, where they established a Christian presence and carried on his work.[1]

Marrant was a product of the first Great Awakening, which began around 1740 in New England. The intellectual minister Jonathan Edwards and a cohort of evangelicals, the New Lights, spread a new message. A sovereign God, they proclaimed, required deliberate acts of repentance and obedience from His followers, and this had to come from one's own heart and soul. Being a good person and church member did not ensure salvation. Instead, a palpable and instantaneous act of grace within the soul marked the movement of God's spirit. Bodily expressions, such as singing, crying, dancing, and fainting or "falling out," signified this channeling of the spirit of God. One's social status did not matter, the Awakeners preached. The only thing that counted was one's personal relationship with God.

That message obviously appealed to ordinary whites at a time when religious institutions had defined and reinforced a colonial social hierarchy that was characterized by the rule of the "better class" of people. But the message of the New Lights was also appealing to African Americans as evangelical religious expressions that mirrored practices familiar to Africans. The evangelical appeal of rebirth, to be "born again," as well as baptisms by immersion in water and emotional communions, had clear parallels in African-based religious practices. The rebirth rituals of African secret societies, for example, could be compared with evangelical initiation ceremonies such as conversions and baptisms.

The Great Awakening first arrived in the South in the mid-eighteenth century when the English Anglican Whitefield, the great evangelist of the period, came to Charleston. Initially, he was a critic of slavery, believing it to be contrary to biblical teachings. By the 1750s, though, he was happy to be a slaveholder himself, as it relieved him of work and freed him to evangelize. Increasingly, he adopted the views of Southern slaveholders, assuming that men and women were born into social stations and should remain obedient in that role. Even then, he preached his message for whites and blacks alike, including slaves and free people of color such as Marrant.

His exhortations also reached a small group of planters in the low country of South Carolina, who responded to Whitefield's call to save the souls of their bondspeople. One of them, Hugh Bryan, had a powerful religious conversion experience that led him to proclaim prophecies of the destruction of Charleston and the freeing of blacks from bondage. The South Carolina Assembly punished Bryan for his insurrectionary outburst, but his sentence did not settle the matter for angry planters. They worried that white evangelicals were filling the heads of slaves with "a Parcel of Cant-Phrases, Trances, Dreams, Visions, and Revelations and something still worse," referring to Bryan's visions of the "Deliverance of the Negroes from servitude."[2]

Evangelicals such as Whitefield were intent on converting souls, not challenging or overturning the social order. Yet, as some whites perceived it, evangelical preaching harbored dangerous ideas, as could be seen in some of the advertisements for runaway slaves during that era. In 1793, slave owner Thomas Jones advertised for his fugitive slave, Sam, in a Maryland newspaper. The runaway slave had been raised in a family of evangelical churchgoers, the ad suggested, and lived with them virtually as an equal. He had been engaged in "exhorting his fellow creatures of all colors in matters of religious duties."[3] Like other early black evangelicals, Sam had preached a gospel of religious equality. He and others went further and used the Bible to advocate civic equality. In 1800, a black preacher compared the cause of slaves to that of the Israelites. In the Bible, he said, God had promised that a small number of believers could conquer a much larger number of enemies surrounding them. The slaves could do likewise, he implied. A planned slave rebellion that year failed when a flood washed out a creek the slaves had planned to cross into Richmond and a group of white slave patrollers discovered the rebels. Despite being squashed, the planned revolt heightened suspicions of black evangelical preaching.

Awakeners reprised the familiar argument that the slaves' Christianization would ensure obedience and good order among the servants. The enthusiastic behavior of converted blacks often failed to reassure critics of the Awakening. The New Light minister Samuel Davies, who preached to slaves in Virginia in 1757, reported to his benefactors that, when the slaves found a few moments of leisure, they came to his house. Davies led them in praying and singing, and some of the slaves stayed all night in his kitchen. Davies awoke at two or three o'clock in the morning to find that "a torrent of sacred harmony poured into my chamber, and carried my mind away to Heaven"; such singing lasted all night. Davies knew that the great majority of blacks in the Chesapeake remained non-Christians, like their African forebears, but he took heart at his success when one African-born man addressed him, saying, "I am a poor slave, brought into a strange country, where I never expect to enjoy my liberty. While I lived in my own country, I knew nothing of that JESUS I have heard you speak so much about." He was now determined to learn of the Savior, he said.

Such teaching, Davies also pointed out, could have good effects in terms of ensuring the safety of the white population. During the French and Indian War (1756–1763), Catholic and Indian enemies of the British Empire harassed Englishmen on the frontier. Making matters worse, Davies wrote, English settlers feared "Insurrection and Massacre" from the slaves living among them. Responding to this dangerous situation, Davies urged slaveholders to bring slaves under the restraints of the pacifying "Religion of JESUS," which would teach them proper behavior within their social role and ensure the safety of colonies fighting their external enemies.[4]

White evangelical attempts to appease masters who opposed the conversion of slaves were not fully persuasive. Regardless of the laws separating baptism from freedom, the implications of conversion remained ambiguous, hence the perpetual uneasiness of whites about slave conversion. White evangelicals faced an uphill battle in persuading planters to support substantial efforts to convert African American slaves.

The Great Awakening, which first reached a substantial number of black Americans in the 1760s and 1770s, reversed the earlier failures to teach

Christianity to African slaves in America. By the time the evangelicals reached the slaves, only a small minority of African Americans had converted to Christianity. Most slaves continued to follow traditional African religious practices, most particularly the large number of newly enslaved Africans who arrived in the new republic between 1783 and 1808, the year the international slave trade ended. Nonetheless, the Awakening fundamentally shaped African American religious practices, eventually making Christianity a primary form of African American religious expression.

As the Awakening spread, more people of African descent gravitated toward a gospel message that emphasized equality of men before God. After the American Revolution, the Awakenings in the South crested. A second Great Awakening arose in the early 1800s, inspiring many more Americans, white and black, to adopt evangelical Christianity. Evangelical revivalists during those years had to confront questions of slavery and race. After all, many of them preached in places where more black than white people lived. And for some idealistic evangelicals, the enthusiastic response of slave converts suggested the power of the word of God to overcome the obstacles imposed by human institutions.

During the Great Awakenings in the South, a brief moment of opportunity for a biracial religious order seemed to present itself. Whites and blacks in backcountry congregations worshipped together. They called each other by the respectful evangelical titles "brother" and "sister" and wept to each other's exhortations. White ministers tutored black protégés for missionary work, occasionally even setting these ministers free. Some white Baptist ministers in Virginia declared slavery a sin, freed their slaves, and advocated lifting restrictions on black men who wished to preach the gospel in public. But this apparent moment was illusory, for whites quickly learned to accommodate slavery with their desire to spread evangelical churches.

Methodists struggled with the issue in the era just after the American Revolution. In 1784, the Methodists had passed a church law requiring emancipation of slaves by white church members. Just six months later, recognizing the impossibility of enforcing such a rule among their Southern parishioners, the Methodists suspended that church edict. In 1801, when a few Methodists published a pamphlet denouncing slavery, residents of Charleston torched all the copies of the text and assaulted a minister they believed had circulated the offensive material. Just a few years later, in 1804, the Methodist denominational rules exempted churchgoers in several Southern states from ecclesiastical rules that discouraged slaveholding. Methodist leaders determined that converting slaves, not freeing them, best ensured the spread of Methodism into areas of the country that were experiencing explosive population growth. White Methodists made their peace with slavery.

Baptists in Virginia made important arguments on behalf of religious freedom, but slavery was another matter. In the 1790s and early 1800s, local Baptist associations raised a firestorm of complaints about antislavery statements made by foolish evangelical idealists, countering them with proslavery statements of their own. One planter in 1807 complained to the governor of South Carolina that the state housed numerous religious "Enthusiasts" who preached "very dangerous Doctrines and excit[ed] in our black populations Sentiments that must lead to fatal results."[5] Most planters wanted nothing to do with a religion that suggested anything about equality of souls. As a result, the antislavery sentiment expressed by some early Southern Baptists and Methodists did not survive into the antebellum era.

Over the course of the nineteenth century, the alliance between the ministerial establishment and the master class strengthened. They discouraged black independent religious expression, which threatened good order, but encouraged white-supervised religious instruction. The Christianization of the planter class, the introduction of slavery in the interior of the new nation, and the adoption of an ideal of the planter patriarch as "Christian steward" increasingly fed into planter support for missionary work among the slaves. So did the lessening of the original evangelical antislavery impulse. Since the success of churches in the South depended on converting slaveholders as well as ordinary white men and women who desired to become slaveholders, the vast majority of white Southern Christians erected a wall of separation between the realms of spiritual equality and social inequality. In South Carolina, Baptists in the early nineteenth century worked feverishly on a Christian proslavery argument, even making trips to the North to debate abolitionists. In their view, God watched over humanity as husbands provided for and protected their wives and children and masters provided for and protected their slaves. In return, good husbands and masters expected respect and obedience. By the 1830s, this view of a divinely ordained organic family hierarchy, with God at the top and slaves at the bottom, reigned as a virtually unchallenged orthodoxy among white Southern evangelicals.

Besides the evangelical revivals of the eighteenth and nineteenth centuries, a second major factor in the rise of African American Christianity was the mass movement of peoples from the eastern seaboard to the southern interior, including Kentucky, Tennessee, and parts of Georgia, Alabama, Mississippi, and eventually Texas. In this vast territorial expansion of slavery, which began at the time of the signing of the Constitution and ended with the Civil War, whites moved around a million black Americans from the eastern seaboard states, especially Virginia, to the interior of the country. The stimulus for the mass migration was the decline of the tobacco lands of the Chesapeake and the simultaneous rise of cotton, which became a lucrative crop following the introduction of the cotton gin in 1793. The prospect of cotton and profits enticed many Americans to resettle with their slaves in the newly opened territories and emerging states.

Evangelical institutions quickly took root in these new communities. The opening event of the Second Great Awakening occurred during the great camp meetings held in Kentucky between 1801 and 1805. Some historians see these gatherings of thousands of people on the bluegrass frontier, and the emotionally releasing exercises that accompanied the religious conversions, as the real birth of Southern evangelicalism. These revivals brought a powerful message of egalitarian evangelicalism to whites and blacks alike.

A final factor in the expansive spread of evangelicalism among both whites and blacks was the system of itinerant and circuit-riding preachers employed by evangelical groups such as the Methodists and Baptists. The Methodist churches first arose as a renewal and reform movement within the Church of England in the mid-eighteenth century. They combined a centralized system of church hierarchy with a decentralized system of circuit-riding ministers whose mobility allowed for the rapid spread of Methodism. The Methodist churches also featured weekly classes, the originators of contemporary Sunday schools, in which people learned Christian doctrine, confessed sins, and shared deeply felt personal religious experiences with one another.

Baptist churches, which first came to America from England early in the colonial era, defined themselves by an emphasis on baptism by complete water immersion as symbolic of salvation and by the independence of local congregations from any higher authority. Any group of Christians could start its own Baptist church and call a minister, who needed no higher qualification than being "called" by God. This local congregational independence and the freedom of people to start churches and call a pastor made Baptist churches especially popular among African Americans, who lacked the educational institutions to produce credentialed ministers.

Circuit riders for Methodists and independently operating preachers among Baptists carried the evangelical message energetically and successfully throughout the South. In a sense, they were some of the most successful traveling salesmen in American history.

These three developments combined—the Great Awakenings, the territorial expansion of slavery, and evangelical itinerancy among Methodists, Baptists, and other evangelical groups—transformed a relatively "unchurched"

South into the Bible Belt from the revolutionary era to the Civil War. Slaves and free people of color were a vital part of this process of the Christianization of the South. Thus, the Awakenings ultimately democratized religion in the region, and the Christian doctrine that planters hoped would create submissive slaves instead unsettled a regime uncomfortable with any idea of equality, even spiritual equality. Charles Ball, a fugitive slave from Maryland, later observed that blacks developed revolutionary ideas as a "corner-stone" of their religion—which is precisely what skeptical planters feared would happen.[6]

The Great Awakenings also inspired the founding of the first independent black denomination: the African Methodist Episcopal Church, first organized in the 1790s and legally incorporated in 1816. The church originated from the labors of Richard Allen (1760–1831). Born a slave in Delaware, Allen purchased his freedom in 1780. Shortly thereafter he moved to Philadelphia, which had become a haven for blacks seeking freedom in revolutionary-era America. Despite the city's reputation as a place of opportunity, however, former slaves and free people of color who migrated there often found themselves forced into dirty and physically exhausting jobs as dockworkers, domestic servants, and night-soil haulers. Allen himself collected dead bodies during a yellow fever epidemic in the city.

In 1786, Allen joined the St. George's Methodist Church in Philadelphia. He collaborated closely for a time with Francis Asbury, the white organizer of early American Methodism. Allen's message of Christ's love for all found a receptive audience among the struggling black population of the City of Brotherly Love. Together with his friend, Absalom Jones, in 1787 Allen formed the Free African Society, the first mutual aid group for African Americans in the United States. The society provided aid to black widows and children, opened schools for black Philadelphians, and provided medical care for sick black residents of the city.

Allen believed blacks should have their own church, and he wanted it to be Methodist. Sometime in the early 1790s, while praying at the altar of St. George's, white parishioners ordered Allen and his black colleagues to occupy segregated seats at the back of a gallery until whites had finished their prayers. Jones, Allen, and the others in the black contingent "all went out of the church in a body, and they were no longer plagued by us," as Allen tartly wrote later.[7] They raised money for their own congregation and opened Bethel Methodist Episcopal Church. Bethel belonged to the Methodist Episcopal order, but it was a church intended for African Americans, just as Allen had wished. Over the next twenty years, the church frequently found itself at odds with white Methodist authorities. Angered by the actions of their former black members, leaders of the original St. George's Methodist congregation did everything they could to gain legal control over Bethel. It was to no avail, though, as Bethel's membership grew to about 1,300 by 1813.

The black Philadelphians began corresponding with black Methodists elsewhere and developed close relationships with fellow worshippers in Baltimore, where Daniel Coker, a native of Maryland and an escaped slave, led adherents to the Methodist faith. In 1810, Coker had published *Dialogue between a Virginian and an African Minister*, a fictionalized conversation in which a goodhearted but misguided Virginia slaveholder comes to understand the fallacies of his own proslavery views through the reasoned discourse and well-informed biblically based arguments of a black minister. Coker's work included an appendix listing examples of accomplished African American churches and churchmen, illustrating his point about black capabilities.

In 1816, decades of work and legal petitioning by Allen, Coker, Jones, and others culminated in the formation of the first black denomination in America. That year, black churchmen from Pennsylvania and neighboring states convened to incorporate themselves as the African Methodist Episcopal (AME) Church. Six years later, African Americans in New York organized a rival federation, the African Methodist Episcopal Zion (AMEZ) Church. James Varick, a black New Yorker resentful of Richard Allen's intrusions into his territory, insisted on the black Methodists in New York forming their own group. Both black denominations, the AME and AMEZ churches, portrayed themselves as restoring the simplicity and purity of the old Methodist order, when all parishioners were welcomed as God's children. They adopted the *Doctrine and Discipline* of the American Methodist Church largely as their own. Unlike the white Methodists, however, the black Methodists prohibited their members from holding slaves, following the rule of John Wesley, the English originator of Methodism.

The organization of the AME church coincided with a move among some whites to remove blacks entirely from the United States. In 1817, a year after the formation of the AME Church, a group of elite Southern and Northern whites formed the American Colonization Society. Its purpose was to provide for the emigration of black Americans to Africa, thereby "solving" America's intractable problem of slavery and race. Soon thereafter, black proponents and opponents of colonization began debating the relationship of black Americans to the African motherland, a controversy that engaged black thinkers, including African Methodists, over the next century.

Most African American Christians claimed America as their true home, but a minority advocated colonization of blacks back to Africa. This philo-

Photo 2.1. A group illustration of many of the leading bishops of the African Methodist Episcopal Church in the nineteenth century. Courtesy of the Library of Congress.

sophical dispute about the destiny of African Americans split AME church-men. This rift was evident in the election of the AME's first presiding bishop, the highest office in the church. Richard Allen won the election, in part because some of the black Methodists felt that Baltimorean Daniel Coker, born of the union of a black male slave and a white servant female, was too light-skinned to head a black church.

But Allen and Coker also disagreed about colonization. Coker strongly urged African Americans to return to Africa. Moreover, he and his follow-ers believed that God would use the evil of slavery to prepare a group of Christianized African Americans to bring the Christian gospel to Africans who remained mired in heathen customs. Shortly after the formation of the AME Church, Coker became a missionary to Africa, where he died in 1820.

Allen and a majority of AME leaders, on the other hand, denounced colo-nization. While Allen and his AME congregants had organized a separate black denomination marked by the title "African," they also insisted on the full citizenship rights of black people as Americans. Allen and Absalom Jones already had put their philosophy into practice. In 1797, Jones authored one of the first African American petitions to Congress on behalf of four runaway slaves who had been kidnapped by slave catchers. Two years later, Jones penned an antislavery petition signed by seventy other free blacks, including Allen. If the Bill of Rights and the Declaration of Independence meant anything, Jones insisted, blacks should enjoy the same citizenship privileges as whites, including the right to petition for the redress of grievances.

Jones, Allen, and the early black Methodists fused ideas of Christian universalism, universal equality, citizenship rights, and black separatism. It was a delicate balancing act, one which thereafter defined the role of black Christian churches. They claimed their African heritage, yet they understood that black churches were necessary in the struggle for African American rights. They also insisted on their status as free Americans, subject to every protection under the laws. In short, they sought to be Africans *and* Americans, conscious of their heritage but securely placed as American citizens.

The original congregation of black Methodists in Philadelphia organized at a time of high hopes and revolutionary aspirations. By 1816, when the African Methodist Episcopal Church formally incorporated, it also was evident that black rights in the young republic would be imperiled and that black independent institutions would be required to advocate for those rights. The AME church's twenty-year legal battle with the Methodist Episcopal hierarchy, fought over whether blacks could organize their own church in Philadelphia, taught African Americans that their assertions of independence, what they called "manhood," would meet white resistance. The African Methodist historian Benjamin Tanner later reminisced that the "great crime" committed by AME founders "was that they dared to organize a Church of men, men to think for themselves, men to talk for themselves, men to act for themselves . . . men who prefer to live by the sweat of their own brow and be free."[8]

This "crime" was too much to bear for whites in Charleston, South Carolina. In 1822, five years after African Methodists there had struggled against great odds to form their own congregation, white authorities seized control of the church property. They charged that the Charleston AME congregation, under the leadership of Denmark Vesey, had been responsible for an alleged slave conspiracy that year. Vesey was rumored to have used the church as a cover to organize secret societies to foment the rebellion. To this day, it is not entirely clear how much truth there was in those charges. Some scholars have argued that the Vesey conspiracy was a figment of overheated white imaginations, created by whites who manufactured threatening stories to exert control over the sizable free black population of the port city. Scholars continue to debate the issue. Nonetheless, the fate of the AME congregation in Charleston shows that whites perceived black religious independence as a real danger. Crushed, its congregation scattered, the AME Church would not be allowed again in South Carolina until after the Civil War. Only a few AME congregations remained in the region, usually located in border towns of the Upper South such as Baltimore. But even there, AME ministers consistently proclaimed their loyalty and their desire to preach about Christ and not instigate rebellions that challenged the social order.

The works of black Methodist pamphleteers further accentuated white fears of the democratic religious ideas of freedom prevalent among black Christians. In the early nineteenth century, black writers, including Daniel Coker, had tried to convince whites of the clear relationship between American Protestantism and American freedom. They sought dialogue with white Christians, hoping they would see the injustice of slavery. During the 1810s and 1820s, the assumptions of a universalist Christianity put in the context of a free and democratic republic kept black Christian writers imbued with visions of imminent freedom. In subsequent decades, this kind of polite dialogue gave way to polemically powerful attacks on slavery and slaveholders, culminating in David Walker's *Appeal to the Colored Citizens of the World* (1829).

A free man of color originally from North Carolina who then resettled in Boston, Walker was an African Methodist who believed that the biblical message contained revolutionary antislavery sentiments. Unlike Coker, who tried to sway white Christians with his words, Walker advocated violent revolt against the slave system. "Are we MEN!!—I ask you, O my brethren! are we MEN?" he exclaimed. God had not made any men to be slaves, Walker argued, for all were but as "dying worms" in the eyes of the Creator, and whites too would have to appear before the Lord's judgment and account for their deeds.[9]

Christian messianism—the idea that Christ soon would come and establish a righteous order on earth—deeply influenced Walker. His *Appeal* showed whites that there was no telling how black Americans might understand the message of the evangelical revivals. Walker and others mixed a rational appeal about the injustices of slavery with desperate exposes of the hypocrisies of America as a Christian civilization. Vehemently rejecting the ideas of the American Colonization Society and critical of those who had chosen repatriation to Africa, Walker insisted that there were no truer Americans than black Americans. Who else possessed a deeper understanding of what freedom meant?

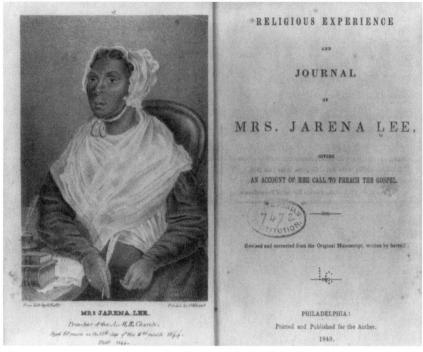

Photo 2.2. Jarena Lee, traveling female evangelist for the African Methodist Episcopal Church in the early nineteenth century. Courtesy of the Library of Congress.

Democratic ideas of evangelicalism also questioned authority within the churches. Female preachers emerged from AME and other black congregations to further challenge the gender barriers raised by the evangelical world of the early nineteenth century. The best known of these was Jarena Lee, a freeborn domestic servant who joined Richard Allen's Bethel congregation in Philadelphia in 1804. Tormented that her conversion was "incomplete," she sought further purifying experiences from the Holy Spirit. She became one of the early exponents of the Holiness movement. Holiness believers sought an infusion of the Holy Spirit following conversion. This second rebirth, Holiness believers exclaimed, would cleanse and perfect the soul in preparation for Christian work on earth. The antebellum Holiness movement primarily drew in middle-class white women in large Northern cities. But Lee, Julia Foote, and, later in the century, Amanda Smith and Rebecca Cox Jackson were African American women who operated outside of any conventional boundaries. Instead, they responded to profound personal stirrings, attracting sizable audiences through the nineteenth century. They felt the call to preach the gospel, and they hit the itinerant circuit, sometimes forsaking family and children in doing so.

African Methodist ministers challenged Lee and her female comrades. The male leadership respected the women's spiritual power and call to exhort, but they refused to recognize their call to the ministry. According to standard evangelical ideas, *exhorters* were informal itinerants who preached extemporaneously as the spirit moved them, while *ministers* were *men* ordained to the ministry. Exhorters could proclaim their calling and begin their work, while ministers had to be sanctified men called by God and tested by church authorities. According to Allen, they had to be educated men, prepared to serve their people as upstanding pastors, and not uneducated itinerant preachers. Lee saw it otherwise. "Did not Mary *first* preach the risen Saviour?" she asked in defense of her gospel ministry.[10]

For three decades, from about the early 1810s to the 1840s, Lee traveled across the land, imploring Christians to Holiness and inviting the movement of the Spirit among the poor and uneducated as well as the educated. However, male Church leaders soundly defeated attempts in the AME General Conference to recognize women as licensed ministers. In many ways, the entire philosophy of the AME Church was at stake. Whereas the AME leadership insisted on education, propriety, respectability, and decorum, the female Holiness proponents invited spontaneous outpourings of the spirit, questioned the value of education, and rejected respectable domesticity. They favored following the call of God wherever it took them. Lee and her fellow "sisters of the spirit" thus defied conventional notions of propriety and respectability. This was not to be the last time that spiritually empowered free Northern black women challenged the male black church hierarchy.

While free black Northerners in the AME Church struggled with gender issues, black Southern converts to Christianity were organizing the first black Baptist churches in and around Savannah, Georgia, and were soon extending into South Carolina. Many of the black Christians who founded these Baptist churches had been converted by the white evangelical planters Jonathan and Hugh Bryan or by slave preachers who came from the Bryan plantation. Leaders of the Great Awakening in the Lowcountry region, the Bryans had converted a slave named George Liele in 1773. Liele, a native of Virginia originally, became a leading force in spreading the Baptist gospel among slaves. In 1775, he began a preaching career with the blessing of his master who, two years later, freed him. In the late 1770s, he organized a Baptist congregation in Savannah, where he converted David George and Andrew Bryan. George was a runaway slave who had been re-enslaved by

Native Americans and later ended up as the property of George Galphin of Silver Bluff, South Carolina, across the river from Augusta, Georgia. Liele's exhortations converted George, who in the 1780s helped to form the black Silver Bluff Baptist Church, which was one of the first black Baptist congregations in the country.

Andrew Bryan, another Liele convert, was a former slave who first began to exhort near Savannah until city authorities arrested, jailed, and whipped him for violating a city ordinance. City laws mandated that black Christians, slave or free, worship only between sunrise and sunset to prevent African Americans from using religious gatherings for the purpose of organizing slave revolts. Nonetheless, Bryan's master was a devout Christian who believed in evangelizing slaves. In the late 1770s, he licensed Bryan to preach, a Baptist method of informally recognizing an individual as a legitimate gospel minister. After his master's death, Andrew Bryan purchased his freedom and eventually became a slaveholder himself. In 1788, Bryan organized his fledgling congregation into what became known as the First African Baptist Church of Savannah. This church and the Silver Bluff Church in South Carolina were the first two regularly constituted black Baptist congregations in the country. After his death in 1812, Bryan's nephew, Andrew Marshall, took the pulpit at First African Baptist and became one of the best known black ministers of the antebellum era.

In addition to being home to the first black Baptist churches, the region around Savannah also served as a fertile ground for small, independent black churches that catered to the large black population, including recently imported African slaves, who worked tending rice, gathering indigo, and growing cotton for the extraordinarily wealthy planters of the Lowcountry. These black congregations, often with free ministers but slave parishioners, sometimes were allowed a quasi-independent existence from their Baptist and Methodist parent churches. Blacks established more than 150 separate black churches, many boasting their own buildings, pastors, and deacons. Whites maintained a vigilant watch over them, though, fearing potential opportunities for subversive preaching. Nonetheless, African American church members used these quasi-independent institutions to train leaders and foster a communal life. The churches were not independent, but they nurtured independent spirits.

Although some black slave Christians in the South worshipped in these quasi-independent black congregations, such as First African Baptist in Savannah, many more attended church with their masters and sat in segregated galleries. Many Southern white churches claimed a substantial membership of enslaved people. During the early nineteenth century, the number of black

Methodists doubled, to about forty thousand, representing approximately one-third of the membership of American Methodism nationally. In South Carolina, blacks made up nearly 60 percent of the membership of the state's Baptist churches; the First Baptist Church in Charleston reported that 697 of its 862 members were black. Presiding white ministers often took the opportunity to address the slave congregants, solemnly recounting biblical injunctions to obey their masters. Nonetheless, black members were considered part of churches, even if only their first names were recorded in the roll book. Blacks participated in church decision making and testified in church disciplinary actions against white defendants. Thus, whether in independent churches or white congregations, African Americans embraced Christianity for its promises, both spiritual and earthly, but were fully aware of institutional inequalities within the church.

The experience of a devoutly evangelical sect of German immigrants, the Renewed Unity of Brethren, commonly called the Moravians, illustrates both the egalitarian promise of Awakening evangelicalism and the tragedy of America's religious capitulation to racist structures. The Moravians in the western Piedmont region of North Carolina provided a promising setting for egalitarian idealism, but ultimately a similar story of spiritual equality and increasing temporal inequality unfolded there as it did elsewhere in the South with the other evangelical groups.

The Moravians practiced close physical fellowship with other believers, which included love feasts characterized by the "holy kiss" and by washing the feet of fellow worshippers. Their theology, stemming from an intensely felt connection to Christ's blood shed on the cross, gave Moravians a strikingly egalitarian view of Christian brotherhood. When faced with morally fraught decisions, Moravians drew lots—pieces of paper from a container they thought contained divine answers ("yes," "no," or "empty," meaning that the wrong question was asked) to difficult queries. Forced to decide whether to purchase a slave named Sam in 1769, they drew lots. At that fateful moment, they felt that God instructed them to purchase Sam and become slaveholders.

Over the next two generations, Moravians often converted and integrated into their communities the slaves who worked for them. At the same time, they developed a theology that justified slavery. They gradually created separate "mission" churches for black Moravians and withdrew from the kinds of physical contact that maintained social harmony between believers. Thus, by the early nineteenth century, white Moravians offered a handshake rather than a holy kiss to black members of the church. Intent on expanding their economic base, white Moravians purchased increasing numbers of slaves. By the early 1820s, the children of Sam, the original Moravian slave, sustained the separate black Moravian churches initially established as mission outposts. Upon death, black Moravians took their final rest in separate cemeteries, segregated in death as in life. The inherently inegalitarian social order of slavery had overcome the original vision of the Moravians, the most radically egalitarian of eighteenth-century evangelicals.

The Moravian experience set a broader course for the hierarchy of race within American Protestant churches. Despite the biblical admonition that in Christ there was neither Jew nor Gentile, slave nor free, American evangelicalism reinforced and policed racial boundaries in American society. The Great Awakening, with its message of equality and its success at attracting white and black believers who worshipped together, produced an American-style evangelicalism that had the potential of undermining the nation's racial system. Ultimately, however, evangelicalism defined and undergirded that racial hierarchy. Southern evangelicals declared that the American social order reflected the will of God and that God expected men and women to perform their duties within their social stations. African Americans responded by adapting Christianity for their own purposes. Within their religious institutions, they adhered to an egalitarian version of evangelicalism, and at times they challenged the racially inegalitarian social order with violent revolts.

Perhaps the most notorious incident illustrating the revolutionary implications of African American Christianity was Nat Turner's slave revolt in 1831. In his younger years, Turner experienced intense personal visions of his self-proclaimed God-given mission to purge the land with blood. From his original master's son, he learned to read, and his reading of the Bible persuaded him that the same Spirit of biblical days had come to him. In 1828, after hearing a loud noise in the sky, Turner claimed that the Spirit appeared to him and said that the "Serpent was loosened, and Christ had laid down the yoke he had borne for the sins of men, and that I should take it on and fight against the Serpent." Turner felt inspired by divine direction, which he interpreted through natural signs such as a solar eclipse and drops of blood mixed with dew he saw one morning on corn plants.[11]

On August 21, 1831, Nat Turner instigated a short, violent, bloody rebellion in Southampton County, Virginia. He led a small posse of rebels who axed, smothered, and choked to death about sixty whites. The next day, a white militia rebuffed the rebels' attempt to attack the town of Jerusalem and captured Turner's small band. Turner himself escaped and hid out until October 30, when a local slave stumbled on him. Afterward, when his lawyer asked him if he still considered himself right, given his imprisonment and impending execution, he responded simply, "Was not Christ crucified?"

One month after the uprising, an anonymous report published in a local newspaper, probably authored by Turner's lawyer, laid a considerable portion of the blame for the insurrection on egalitarian religious fanaticism. Evangelical doctrines and preachers full of "*ranting cant* about equality," the report held, confused spiritual and temporal freedom. Evangelical ranters, the report concluded, had thrown Virginia into turmoil.[12] Black preachers filled their audiences with dangerous ideas about liberty and equality, and they stirred up fervor and excitement among blacks who believed that God spoke through them.

The governor of Virginia conveyed similar sentiments about the perils of democratic religious thought. The white populace, he said, ignored the dangers of black religious ideas until Turner's rampage. The governor was convinced that all the black ministers in the area had been involved in the conspiracy. They had gotten word of Turner's plans through the abolitionist and Northern press, he alleged. The governor further claimed that black churchmen were prepared to lead the slave masses in a revolt based on the idea of equality and emancipation.

By November 11, Nat Turner had been tried and executed, and his body subsequently skinned. The state of Virginia also put to death fifty-five other black men suspected of collusion in the plot and banned some free people of color from residence in the state. White mobs put to death around two hundred additional slaves, most of whom probably had nothing to do with the plot. The mob lined fence posts along one road with the heads of these victims, graphically demonstrating the consequences of defying white authority.

For white Virginians, Turner's bloody revolt represented the climax of the spread of democratic religious ideas that would revolutionize social and racial hierarchies in the United States. Turner's religious visions, drawn from messages he derived from the Bible and the natural world, were chilling to all whites—even to abolitionists. Turner's slave revolt compelled evangelicals to redouble their missionary efforts among the slaves and to spread a safer form of Christianity among the bondspeople.

Black evangelicalism in both North and South had proven dangerous, and whites sought to control it more firmly. They tried, but never fully succeeded. Although only a small handful of slaves took the dire route of Turner, the Christian message of freedom appealed to all of them. Many slaves found in Afro-American evangelicalism a faith that provided them with the sustenance to fend off the worst psychological abuses perpetrated by whites. Black Christian beliefs and rituals shielded them from the system of racial subjugation supported by their "white brethren" as God's plan to Christianize the heathen. Slave preachers and, especially, slave music and religious rituals kept alive a message of freedom in ways that sustained generations through the storm and through the night of the antebellum years, when cotton was king and slavery's expansion seemed unstoppable.

CHAPTER THREE

~

Through the Night

African American
Religion in the Antebellum Era

The Great Awakenings helped to establish Christianity as a significant presence in African American life. During the antebellum era, from the 1830s to
the Civil War, black Christianity assumed its full form in both the South and
North. Enslaved African Americans might have attended white-sanctioned
and supervised services and listened to white ministers who advised them to
be obedient, patient, and humble. But black Christians developed a religious
culture that brought together elements of their African past and their American evangelical training, resulting in the creation of a unique American
religious culture. This faith took shape partly under the suspicious eyes of
devout whites, but more importantly, it developed in the sacred spaces the
slaves created for themselves. In these private gatherings, the deepest desires
for freedom found expression among people who were otherwise compelled
to fake contentment and obedience in front of white masters. Before the
Civil War, black religious life manifested itself most clearly in black religious
rituals, which included "ring shouts," spirituals, and chanted sermons.

In the antebellum years, as evangelicalism spread throughout the South,
white slave owners often brought slaves to church with them. These biracial
churches provided religious instruction to many African Americans within
a context that was "safe," as perceived by whites. In larger congregations,
whites sat on the main floor, slaves in the balcony (except for slave nannies
responsible for nursing white children). In some cases, especially in urban
centers such as Richmond, Virginia, and Charleston, South Carolina, black
congregants formed a majority in "white" churches. In others, blacks were

allowed to attend their own churches, provided that whites remained in a supervisory capacity. Since slaves could not hold property, white trustees held and managed their church buildings and often dictated the selection of pastors and deacons. In this environment, unsupervised backwoods services took on greater significance to the slaves—and seemed a greater threat to whites.

In the antebellum North, by contrast, independent churches assumed central places in African American social life. These churches grew from the efforts of converts from the Great Awakenings, such as Richard Allen and Jarena Lee. Independent black denominations and black churches within the major American denominations expanded in the states north of the Mason-Dixon Line. They were north of slavery, but they were not north of Jim Crow. In some cases, they were not even north of slavery, which died an agonizingly slow death over a period of decades. Abraham Lincoln's home state of Illinois, for example, only abolished slavery in its 1848 constitution, an indication of the antipathy whites in the Old Northwest held toward African Americans.

The informal religious practices of slaves and the visible presence of biracial churches in the South and North provided spiritual sustenance and institutional homes for black Christians who lived through the night of oppression. In some instances, such as the story of Harriet Jacobs, black Christianity provided inspirations for flights to freedom.

Growing up in Edenton, North Carolina, Jacobs (1813–1897) was a favored child of urban slaveholders and attended Methodist class meetings and other religious services. When she was eighteen, Nat Turner's revolt, in a nearby Virginia county, led to a crackdown on religious exercises among the slaves. Slaves in the country, she later recalled, had sought to restore their privilege of meeting in their backwoods church: they had "no higher happiness than to meet there and sing hymns together, and pour out their hearts in spontaneous prayer." However, whites demolished the church and apportioned galleries in white churches for the use of slaves. When Jacobs's original owner passed away, she willed her to a niece, a toddler whose father became Jacobs's guardian and de facto master. "Dr. Flint," the pseudonym Jacobs used for him in her narrative, was a sexual predator who relentlessly pursued his light-skinned house slave. At last, she decided to escape what had become an unbearable situation.

During her harrowing journey to freedom, as Jacobs described it, the rebellious spirit of Nat Turner and the spirits of the ancestors invoked in slave religion stayed with her. Before she left her master's home, she visited her parents' graves in the cemetery near the demolished church. Slaves often considered cemeteries to be gathering points for spirits and ancestors. Jacobs heard her father's voice, "bidding me not to tarry till I reached freedom or the grave. I rushed on with renovated hopes. My trust in God had been strengthened by the prayer among the graves."[1] For seven years, from 1835 to 1842, Jacobs stowed herself away in the attic of a family member. Eventually she made her break for Philadelphia and then New York, where she became an abolitionist.

Like others, Jacobs differentiated between "true Christianity" and the false Christianity practiced by slaveholders; and, like others, she noted the dark irony that when her master joined the Episcopal Church, his cruelty toward his human property only grew worse. Jacobs herself maintained her faith in true Christianity, believing it would open the hearts of Americans to the evils of slavery. A generation of enslaved Americans and oppressed free people of color before the Civil War did much the same.

Slave Christianity combined a range of religious traditions such as African Orisha practices, Africanized Christianity, Islam, and folkloric beliefs drawn from European, African, and Native American stories and medicines. Indeed, one planter-preacher condemned slave religion as "a jumble of Protestantism, Romanism, and Fetishism."[2] The importation of tens of thousands of Africans just prior to 1808, the last year of the slave trade, and the illegal importation of some fifty thousand slaves thereafter, ensured the continued infusion of African religious traditions into American slave culture. These traditions continued to influence slave religious expressions.

Whites found the spiritual practices of black members sometimes difficult to control, even in the seemingly safe confines of white-directed churches. For example, in one North Carolina church, a black woman named in the records only as "Aunt Katy" felt the spirit in the midst of a Methodist revival service in the 1810s. She made "many extravagant gestures" and "cried out that she was 'young King Jesus.'"[3] Black worshippers knew that she was filled with the spirit and channeling the voices of ancestors through the language of Jesus. Aunt Katy's spirit was captured by Jesus in ways derived directly from African conceptions of soul transformations.

The blending of African beliefs and Christian symbols was evident not only in slave testimony but also in material culture, as Jesus appeared amidst objects designed to guide souls into the afterlife. For example, Harriet Powers, born in 1837 into slavery in Georgia, later produced quilts with multiple religious meanings stitched into the fabric. In her work, Christian and Kongo symbols merge into a classic product of Afro-Americanized Christianity. In the quilt shown in the photo, Jesus' crucifixion is depicted in the lower right panel, over a small sun. The quilt mixes the cross of Jesus and the cross of

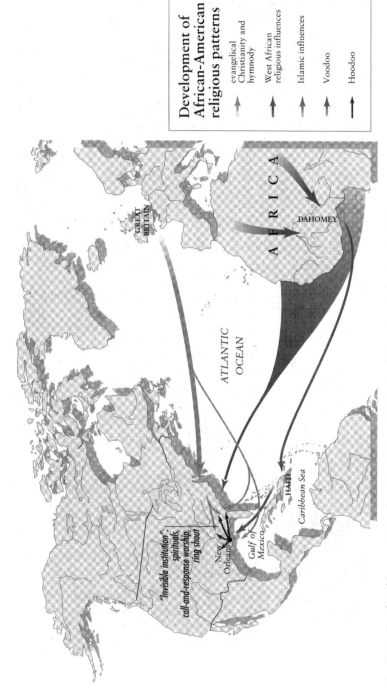

Development of African-American religious patterns

↑ evangelical Christianity and hymnody

↑ West African religious influences

↑ Islamic influences

↑ Voodoo

↑ Hoodoo

GREAT BRITAIN

AFRICA

DAHOMEY

ATLANTIC OCEAN

HAITI

Caribbean Sea

Gulf of Mexico

New Orleans

"Invisible institution", spirituals, call-and-response worship, ring shout

Map 3.1. Reprinted by permission from Bret E. Carroll, *The Routledge Historical Atlas of Religion in America* (New York: Routledge, 2000).

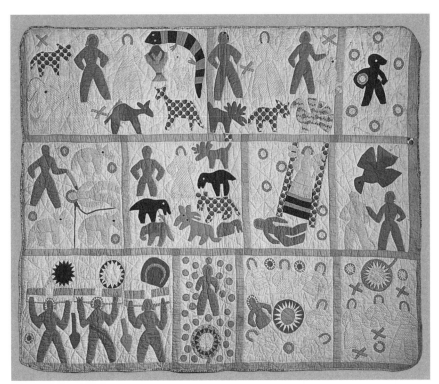

Photo 3.1. A quilt, with sections showing biblical parables and depicting Christ's crucifixion, by the well-known African American female artist and quilter Harriet Powers, from the 1880s. Courtesy of the National Museum of American History, Smithsonian Institution.

Kongo symbolism, signifying western Christian and Central African understandings of religious experience.

The baptismal ritual did much the same. Its symbolism of cleansing and rebirth came from, and spoke to, a variety of traditions at once, both African and American in origin. African and New World influences also shaped funeral and burial practices. Slaves often decorated graves with the objects of the deceased, including saucers, bottles, pipes, and pieces of pottery, much as their forebears had done in Africa. The living set free the spirit of the deceased by breaking objects and scattering them around gravesites, enabling the souls to escape this world into the realm of the spirits and ancestors.

The importation of African Muslims shaped the religious practices of many slaves, too. Descendants of these slaves, interviewed by the Works

Progress Administration in the 1930s, frequently recalled observing recognizably Muslim practices, such as praying at particular times, bowing to the East, seeking out certain foods and shunning others, and chanting Qur'anic verses. One Muslim slave, Omar ibn Said (1770–1864), was taken from his home region in present-day Senegal at the age of thirty-seven. In his early sixties, he penned a fragmentary memoir, written in Arabic and translated for an American audience. Said recalled that as a "Mohammedan"—the nineteenth-century term for Muslim—he prayed in these words: "Thanks be to God, Lord of all worlds, the merciful the gracious, Lord of the day of Judgment, thee we serve, on thee we call for help. Direct us in the right way, the way of those on whom thou hast had mercy, with whom thou hast not been angry and who walk not in error. Amen." After his conversion to Christianity, he prayed to "'Our Father', etc., in the words of our Lord Jesus the Messiah."[4] But even then, he carried on many of his Muslim practices, and he wrote a dedication to Allah in his Bible.

Southern missionaries observed Muslim slaves who insisted that the Christian God was the same as Allah and that Jesus Christ was simply a different name for Muhammad. They participated in Christian slave gatherings at night and then prayed at sunrise by bowing to the East. In this way, Muslim forms persisted in slave communities, even among some slaves who claimed Christianity as their religious faith.

Christian planters and whites who advocated missionary work among the slaves expressed grave concern about the inadequate degree to which the slave population had been "Christianized." The continued presence of African practices such as shouts, grave decorations, spirit possessions, visions of "King Jesus," and a belief in magic and "superstition," befuddled them. The complete absence of Christianity or churches on many plantations and the persistent influence of Islam troubled them. And the unorthodox interpretations slaves placed on Christianity convinced whites that they had to take firmer control of the slaves' religious expression. The fear of black religious autonomy, heightened by Nat Turner's revolt, spurred this drive, which led to white missionary efforts among the slaves in the 1840s.

Perhaps the leading white missionary to slaves was Charles Colcock Jones, who became known as the white "apostle to the slaves." Jones was a well-educated Presbyterian minister and slaveholder in Georgia who worried about the relatively small proportion of slaves who were Christians, as well as their "heathenish practices." They were, he said, inclined to value "excited states of feeling. And true conversion, in dreams, visions, trances, voices."[5] Jones met with concerned white Southern evangelicals, urging them to step up efforts toward reaching the slaves with a proper version of the Gospel.

Jones and other missionaries were particularly troubled by the slaves' continued practice of "conjure," or "black magic." They commonly referred to it as superstition; slaves frequently called it "hoodoo." The practice of conjure, a form of healing and counter-harming that drew from both Christian and African-based religious elements, was particularly common among slaves. Although slaves were its primary practitioners, whites formed a substantial clientele base. Among poorer blacks and whites alike, fears of unseen powers compelled frequent recourse to conjure men. Belief in conjure—or at least a willingness to suspend disbelief—pervaded much of the Deep South. Many Southern black and white Christians also kept one foot in the world of spirits invoked by conjurers. Whites in the South's backcountry also consulted the conjure men, for Euro-American folk beliefs often paralleled that of Africans and African Americans. In an age of ineffective and at times harmful professional medicine, ordinary Americans sought relief from illnesses and ailments wherever they could.

Slaves commonly consulted the services of a conjure man, a sort of folk priest who claimed special powers and knowledge of the spiritual potentials of natural materials. The conjure man had access to forces that could provide protection or harm one's enemies. Many slave families believed that children born with a "caul" covering their heads, or otherwise physically marked, possessed special access to the spirit world, and that God destined these children to be conjure men. The masters of hoodoo assembled bags of natural or manmade materials, containing roots, toads' feet, snake teeth, the tails of rabbits, snails' shells, rusty nails, flannel, and human hair, fingernails, or toenails. The African connection here is clear from the contents of these bags, which closely resembled the African *gris-gris*. The bags could be placed under the pillow of an enemy, who would then experience some calamity, or near a cabin of a person seeking protection. Conjure bags also resembled Kongo *minkisi* in that they served as focal objects for ritual beliefs and practices.

Folk beliefs that imparted spiritual meanings to objects in the natural world remained a resilient part of Southern folklore. Studies of the mutual relationship between religion and magic show how these different ways of thinking about the supernatural world interact, collide, complement, and supplement one another. For white and black religious reformers, Christianity and conjure were inherently contradictory. But for many black Southerners, they were complementary, allowing them to address different spiritual needs at different times. For enslaved people, conjure supplemented Christianity. They were two ways of accessing the spirit world. Conjure provided certain pragmatic benefits that Christianity did not, while Christianity provided reassurance about the fate of human souls in a way that the pragmatic manipulations of conjure men could not.

Conjure men might have been respected and feared, but the foremost spiritual leaders of slave communities were slave preachers. In the early twentieth century, W. E. B. Du Bois aptly described the complex figure of the slave preacher as "the most unique personality developed by the Negro on American soil," someone who was a "leader, a politician, an orator, a 'boss,' an intriguer, an idealist."[6] Slave preachers carefully balanced their varied roles as emissaries to whites, counselors to blacks, and competitors to conjure men and other alternative sources of religious and spiritual authority.

Under the leadership of slave preachers who ministered to the needs of the people in their quarters, slave religious services took shape. In many cases, slave religious practices cultivated a sense of obedience or humility in the presence of whites, while expressing deeper longings for freedom and hatred of the slave regime once white observers left. "I been preaching the gospel and farming since slavery time," an elderly black minister named Anderson Edwards recalled in the 1930s. He had joined the church as a slave and was baptized in a spring near the plantation where he lived. When Edwards started preaching, he was illiterate and "had to preach what Master told me." He told his listeners what the slaveholder wanted him to say: that if they obeyed their master, they would go to heaven. At the same time, he said, "I knowed there's something better for them, but daren't tell them 'cept on the sly. That I done lots. I tells 'em iffen they keeps praying, the Lord will set 'em free."[7] Edwards represented a generation of slave preachers in the antebellum era who learned to preach a secret message of freedom while living in the shadow of slavery.

African Americans developed religious rites that merged African cultural practices and evangelical belief patterns. In the backwoods, in brush harbors sometimes sanctioned by plantation owners, slaves created a religious culture that sustained them throughout slavery. Enslaved Christians assembled out of the reach of slave patrollers, signaling to each other privately when and where they would meet. The first one to arrive would break the boughs from trees and point them to a meeting spot. Once gathered, the slaves sang and preached. They would shore up each other's spirits, shaking hands and reassuring themselves that enslavement and suffering on this earth was but a temporary condition en route to spiritual freedom. At these services or during small gatherings in slave cabins, slaves sometimes turned over wash pots to "catch" the noise from the meetings and thus provide protection from

Photo 3.2.   Lithograph from *Harper's Weekly* in 1872, illustrating how whites thought of rural religious meetings and religious rituals among Southern blacks. Courtesy of the Library of Congress.

the slave patrollers, whom the slaves called "paddy-rollers." Turning over the pots also allowed the release of the spirits contained within them.

Slaves recounted emotionally gripping conversion tales. Individual converts told of how a spiritual guide, usually described as a "little man," showed them the wonders of the spirit world and then brought them back to earth. Some converts recalled taking wing, their souls flying away from their bodies like birds. In these visions, conversion candidates were robed in white and rode on white chariots pulled by white horses. In later years, some African Americans worried over the frequent invocations of whiteness. They believed this signaled an acceptance of the symbols of oppression. Black artists deliberately portrayed black Christs in poetry and painting. For many slaves, though, whiteness seemed more symbolic of purity and salvation than of skin color.

And conceptions of the brightness of Christ in no way hindered identification with a Jesus who seemed to have a heart that naturally empathized with slaves and all those who suffered on earth. Slaves spoke of a "little me" inside a "big me," and Jesus often appeared as a "little" or "small" man, a gentle guide to the soul represented by the little me. This was a Jesus who communed with slaves in their covert Christianity practiced in the brush harbor settings and in their private visions of salvation. In these visions, Jesus' smallness made him visible. It also made him akin to a trickster, for in the trickster tales, such as "Brer Rabbit," smaller but crafty animals always outwitted their larger, clumsier competitors.

According to slave theology and conversion experiences, Jesus intervened actively in the everyday lives of ordinary people, including the lowliest servants of the South. More than a spirit, he was seeable, touchable, tangible. He walked on earth like a man, a suffering servant who channeled God's power. Jesus listened to the agonies of sinners who passed through the iron gates of spiritual death to the other side of salvation. Jesus' personal power overwhelmed any other on earth. White folks might have been afraid of true religion, one South Carolina slave explained, adding: "I stays independent of what white folks tells me when I shouts. . . . Never does it make no difference how I's tossed about. Jesus. He comes and save me everytime."[8]

Jesus' power during abusive encounters between bondspeople and white masters marks many slave narratives. Jesus was said to have appeared in the midst of whippings and beatings, restraining unjust punishers and soothing wounded bodies. James Watkins, a slave in Maryland, was one of many who recounted his conversion experience at a camp meeting, where the white minister spoke to whites and slaves alike about how Jesus restored sight to the blind. Watkins yearned to encounter and come to know this Jesus, explaining that "if I could but find out this great man I should be free from slavery as well as from sin." But when Watkins returned to the slave quarters, his master accosted him, saying: "You infernal black ghost, you have got no soul."[9] Intending to whip Watkins, the master instead succumbed to Watkins's prayers and pleadings. Watkins attributed his rescue to the intervention of Jesus.

Without an opportunity to develop truly independent churches, and often discouraged by indifferent or hostile masters from practicing any spiritual tradition, slaves nonetheless managed to develop a religious culture that sustained many bondspeople through the storm and through the night of slavery. In services held in slave cabins or in the woods at night, African Americans developed a religious culture that brought together elements of their African past and their exposure to American evangelicalism. The rise of the black spirituals as a primary form of African American religious music suggests much about the blending of the African past and the American present.

Emerging from the slave quarters, scarcely noticed by whites until after the Civil War, African American spirituals still stand as one of America's most profound contributions to theology and culture. The spirituals came from a mixture of white evangelical hymnology, African traditional song and dance, and Southern black folklore. Many spirituals have some base in the white popular evangelical tunes that were making their way to the churches in the newly settled areas. But the slaves also brought their own images and literary devices into the songs; these derived as much from their African heritage as from their white Christian training. The spirituals cannot be attributed to individual authors, but instead they emerged as a communal voice of slave believers. Some lines of the spirituals clearly derived from folk tunes and hymns from the Anglo-American tradition, while others originated from African American interpretations of biblical stories.

Spirituals incorporated countless variations of the stories of Moses, King David, and King Jesus and also offered ways for slaves to think about evil. "Moses, Moses, don't get lost," one lyric went, "in that Red Sea / Smite your rod and come across / in that Red Sea." Likewise, Jesus was a conqueror and a mighty warrior, as in this adaptation set to a compilation of older verses:

> Ride on, King Jesus.
> No man can a-hinder me. . . .
> King Jesus rides on a milk white horse.
> No man can a-hinder me.
> The river Jordan he did cross.
> No man can a-hinder me.

The devil as portrayed in the spirituals bears a striking resemblance to the conjuring shyster of West African folklore, more so than the unambiguously evil Satan of the Western Christian tradition. The Devil became "a liar and a conjurer" in many songs. He was a humanlike figure who attempted to deceive humans, more than to overpower them with terrible evil. At times, the Devil became a conjure man—crafty, deceptive, untrustworthy, but a little bit alluring at the same time:

> Old Satan is a liar and a conjurer, too;
> If you don't mind, he'll conjer you.

Much debate about the spirituals has focused on the degree to which their lyrics contained encoded messages. To what degree was the spiritual freedom referred to in many songs a code for freedom from slavery? In times of turmoil and war, when the very future of slavery was in doubt, freedom could take on more obvious meanings. Not surprisingly, enslaved blacks drew on Old Testament stories and in their spirituals exalted heroes such as Moses.

They also turned New Testament figures such as Jesus into avenging heroes. One favorite was "Steal Away to Jesus," with its obvious connotation of stealing oneself away from the slave master into freedom: "Steal away, steal away home / I ain't got long to stay here." Finally, the remarkable rapidity with which slaves took up the story of the enslaved Israelites in Egypt as their own, despite the attempts of slavemasters to prevent these passages in the Bible from being taught, shows that many slaves had to be aware of the various potential meanings of what they sang. "Go Down Moses," with its exhortation to tell the Pharaoh to release the captives in Egypt, obviously contained multiple layers of meaning.

One of the remarkable attributes of the "sorrow songs," as W. E. B. Du Bois called the spirituals, is the characteristic hope and jubilation even in this world of woe. A profound theology of triumph characterized the sorrow songs. Spirituals expressed the deepest religious longings of enslaved African Americans and rarely spoke of individual sin and wretchedness. Instead, they looked to communal triumph.

Slaves recognized that Southern whites used the Bible to justify slavery as God's predestined fate for black people. They countered this view with their songs, which contained powerful images of self-worth and transcendence. The spirituals recognized that this was a world of woe, in lines such as "Sometimes I feel like a motherless child," "This world is not my home," or "I've been in the storm so long, been in the storm so long." Moreover, songs such as "I Know Moon-Rise" envisioned the peace for believers at death: "I'll lie in de grave and stretch out my arms; Lay dis body down." And yet, even in "I Know Moon-Rise," the lyrics attest to the conquering of death, as the individual was still able to gaze at the canopy of the night sky. Even in one of the darker spirituals, "Sometimes I Feel Like a Motherless Child," lines such as "Sometimes I feel like an eagle in de air. . . . Spread my wings and / Fly, fly, fly" interrupt the sorrowful mood of the lyrics. The spirituals recognized the evanescence of human power: "Did not old Pharaoh get lost, get lost, get lost. . . . get lost in the Red Sea." The slaves knew they would not be lost or drowned in that sea, for they would soon be home with Jesus: "I ain't got long to stay here."

The lyrics of the spirituals generally came from biblical stories, but the rhythm and sound of the songs emerged from a mixed African and American musical heritage. The call-and-response pattern of the spirituals, as well as their complex rhythmical structure, drew from roots in African and African American music. The common practice in antebellum American singing of "lining out" hymns, with a leader calling out verses and congregants responding, reinforced the call-and-response style. Folklorists and nineteenth-century musicologists despaired at ever being able to transcribe the music of the spirituals into conventional Western notation. Slaves sang at pitches "between" the notes on a conventional Western scale, what later would be called the "blue note." Their melodies sounded irregular and untranslatable to the ears of white recorders. Further, slave spirituals involved much improvisation in the melody, rhythm, and lyrics, meaning they would be sung differently depending on the time and situation. Rhythmically and sonically, African song styles transformed Protestant hymns into black spirituals.

The African contribution to the spirituals is mostly clearly demonstrated in the ritual accompanying the singing: the moans, shuffles, dances, foot stamping, and hand clapping central to African American religious expression. In slave cabins or in other secluded settings, slaves formed a circle around a song leader who called out the main lines of the songs. The group sang the chorus and refrain in call-and-response form. Gradually the slaves began a slow shuffle, clapping their hands and moving rhythmically counterclockwise, circling the leader. Because evangelicals prohibited dancing, Christian slaves shuffled around the circle without crossing their feet, as feet crossing was the barrier between sexually suggestive "dancing" and perfectly acceptable forms of religious expression. Sometimes after hours of singing, the ring shout grew in intensity, as song leaders picked up the tempo with successive verses and refrains of familiar tunes. Participants called out new verses, adding local names and locations to the more universal themes of the lyrics. By such means, slaves replaced stock phrases with new material, some of which found their way into the versions of the spirituals recorded by observers. Eventually, the intensity of the ring shout would wane, and the informal services finished with slower and more solemn spiritual tunes. Slaves used the religious expressions such as spirituals to assert their humanity and worth in the midst of their dehumanizing life.

Alongside the slaves' informal religious practices, many semi- or fully independent black Christian churches served the spiritual needs of African Americans. By the mid-nineteenth century, there were more than two hundred black Baptist churches, two-thirds of them in the South, and almost three hundred AME congregations, about two-thirds in the North and the rest located in cities of the Upper South such as Baltimore, Louisville, and Richmond (see table 3.1). In addition, there were 329 white-supervised Methodist missions to the slaves. Whites generally monitored or oversaw the quasi-independent black churches of the South.

In addition, some African Americans worshipped in a variety of other denominations. In Maryland and Louisiana, blacks attended Catholic

Table 3.1. Number of Known Formal All-Black Churches in the Antebellum Period

Denomination	South	North	Total
Methodist Missions (white supervised)	329		329
African Methodist Episcopal (AME)	89	192	281
Baptist	130	75	205
AME Zion	3	46	49
African Union (Methodist Protestant)	1	29	30
Presbyterian	1	21	22
Catholic	3		3
Disciples of Christ	4		4
Society of Friends (Quakers)	1	3	4
Episcopal	2	2	4
Total	563	368	931

Source: Mechal Sobel, *Trabelin' On: The Slave Journey to an Afro-Baptist Faith* (reprint, Princeton, NJ: Princeton University Press, 1997).

congregations in sizable numbers. White Catholics in the South supervised their own missions to the slaves. Over time, these "fathers on the frontier" became entrenched defenders of the slave regime, which they saw as symbolic of a godly hierarchy and an orderly society.

In the North, black church members in urban areas cultivated some degree of independence in sizable evangelical congregations, but they encountered numerous obstacles to a free life. Northern states invented formal systems of state-sanctioned segregation, writing the kinds of laws Southern states copied in the late nineteenth and early twentieth centuries. They denied black men the vote, or else restricted it to a very few who could prove their worth through literacy and property ownership. They mandated segregation on streetcars, in stores, in waiting rooms, in eating establishments, and even at the cemetery. Some states attempted to deny residency to newly arrived free blacks to prevent labor competition and to deny a place for the expansion of slavery.

In the midst of this formidable array of legal restrictions, cultural degradation, and social ostracism, free black churches in the North provided havens of relative freedom and autonomy. Black Northerners who organized churches, conventions, fraternal orders, and self-improvement societies adopted the dress and behavior of the white middle class when they could afford it, preached a gospel of temperance and uplift, published newspapers, and demanded propriety in their churches. Nonetheless, they continued to care and feel a kinship for their enslaved Southern brethren. This explains why Northern black churches rejected colonization: They felt that the United States was their home country since their labor had played a central role in constructing it.

Whereas in the South slaves practiced emotionally, rhythmically, and sonically expressive forms of communing with the spirits, free people of color in the antebellum North developed a religious culture that situated them as respectable members of a free republic. Northern black churches, especially those affiliated with the African Methodist Episcopal (AME) and African Methodist Episcopal Zion (AMEZ) churches, sponsored publications that encouraged African Americans to articulate their religious strivings. First published in the 1850s, the *Christian Recorder*, the AME Church's official newspaper, served as a central repository of African American religious thought. Later publications, including the *A.M.E. Church Review*, provided African American ministers with a forum to discuss theological issues. Other African American churches and denominations founded similar publications.

These Northern black churches also sponsored schools to educate children, insurance and burial societies to help people prepare for the passing of family members, and lecture halls for black adults to hear addresses on subjects of public interest. They also hosted conventions at which black men and women expressed their opposition to slavery and their demands for black citizenship rights. In this sense, Northern black churches already were centers of political activity during the antebellum era and helped prepare the way for Southern black churches to serve a similar role after the Civil War.

The black churches in the North afforded crucial spaces for the powerful voices of black abolitionists, including those of women. Two icons of black freedom were Sojourner Truth and Harriet Tubman. Both were empowered by deeply felt religious callings, premonitions, and visions. They seemed to represent spiritual female Old Testament heroes.

Born into slavery in late eighteenth century New York, Isabella Baumfree adopted the name "Sojourner Truth" in 1843. It was a reflection of her Methodist calling to preach abolition on the itinerant circuit. "The Spirit calls me, and I must go," she told friends. Her commanding voice drew admirers, detractors, and the curious alike, as she became perhaps the best known female antislavery speaker.

Harriet Tubman, born into slavery in Maryland in the early 1820s, escaped to Philadelphia in 1849. She learned Bible stories from her mother, who influenced her strong religious convictions and visions. As a young woman, she sustained a severe head wound, collateral damage from an abusive overseer's attack on a slave standing nearby. In all likelihood, the epilepsy initiated by the vicious blow to her head accentuated her intense religious visions. Following her escape, Tubman traveled to the South thirteen times to conduct seventy slaves, including several of her family members, to freedom in the North and Canada. Admiring her daring determination and reflecting

I Sell the Shadow to Support the Substance.

SOJOURNER TRUTH.

Photo 3.3. Sojourner Truth, famous female abolitionist and orator from the mid-nineteenth century. Courtesy of the Library of Congress.

her well-known religious reputation, African Americans nicknamed her "Moses."

The best known black female author of that time, Maria W. Stewart, defended African American rights with a "holy indignation." Stewart condemned whites who professed to be Christians while embracing race prejudice. Drawing on the Old Testament, Stewart compared Americans to King Solomon, who got credit for building a temple even though he did no labor on it; white Americans likewise claimed credit for black workers' achievements. "We have pursued the shadow," Stewart said, while "they have obtained the substance; we have formed the labor, they have received the profits; we have planted the vines, they have eaten the fruits of them."[10] White Americans were like biblical Babylonians, thinking themselves exalted while they sold the souls of men into slavery.

Stewart, Truth, and Tubman were not the only black religious voices that challenged slavery. In the antebellum years, black Christian pamphleteers also pressed the cause for freedom. Picking up on David Walker's *Appeal to the Colored Citizens of the World*, they often employed religious rhetoric. Among the most famous African Americans who used the pen to condemn slavery was Frederick Douglass. Following his flight for freedom in the 1830s and ordination as a minister in the AMEZ Church, Douglass served as a powerful propagandist for the antislavery cause. In the 1850s, while residing in Rochester, New York, where he published the black abolitionist newspaper the *North Star*, he attacked the slave system and the so-called revivalism that accompanied its spread. As Douglass told an abolitionist gathering:

> Revivals in religion, and revivals in the slave trade, go hand in hand together. The church and the slave prison stand next to each other, the groans and cries of the heartbroken slave are often drowned in the pious devotions of his religious master. . . . While the blood-stained gold goes to support the pulpit, the pulpit covers the infernal business with the garb of Christianity.[11]

Slaveholders, for example, financed the mission to the slaves by stealing the labor of bondspeople to fund Christian preaching among them.

Douglass ridiculed and parodied the hypocritical piousness of white Southern preachers. Their orations made a mockery of true Christianity, he claimed. After preaching to slaveholders in the main part of the church, Douglass told riveted audiences, the slaveholding preachers gazed up at the gallery and, with comical hypocrisy, urged slaves to "labor diligently." Then they exclaimed with false piety that God had given slaves strong bodies to perform hard labor, while God had endowed the white master class with delicate physical constitutions but intellectual talents, so that they could do the thinking. This gospel, Douglass scoffed, "more than chains, or whips, or thumb-screws, gives perpetuity to this horrible system."[12]

While Douglass relied on biblical passages to condemn slavery rhetorically, the black Northern Presbyterian minister Henry Highland Garnet advocated violent resistance. In 1843, Garnet outlined his religiously based argument in his famous "Address to the Slaves of the United States," which he presented at a national convention of black clergymen, authors, and abolitionists in Buffalo, New York. While at first considered too inflammatory to publish, it appeared in print five years later. Recounting the history of the forced migration of African Americans to the land of slavery, Garnet claimed that God had "frowned upon the nefarious institution, and thunderbolts, red with vengeance, struggled to leap forth to blast the guilty wretches who maintained it."[13] Combining Christian piety with calls for resistance to slavery, Garnet insisted that it was sinful to submit to the slave power and urged the black churches to use every means at their disposal, including violence, to make clear their hatred of the degrading system. Black Americans should take as their motto "RESISTANCE!" he proclaimed, for that was the only way to implement God's will, which was to secure their liberty.[14]

Douglass and Garnet argued in terms that set the stage for much debate to come among black religious intellectuals. The antebellum black conventions, often led by or disproportionately attended by black ministers and activist churchpeople, served as training grounds for religious and political leaders in the black community. A majority of black ministers and leaders attending the 1843 convention opposed Garnet's call for violent resistance. Douglass insisted that it would be suicidal for slaves to follow such a course. He consistently articulated universalist ideals of black integration into the American Republic and his opposition to all forms of colonization, which was part of his faith in the American Constitution, the Bible, and true Christianity.

Black conventions, often led by black ministers, continued to serve as a platform for the struggle against slavery. Speakers there acknowledged that the white pulpit had been "prostituted" to serve slavery.[15] In the conventions, black clergymen such as Garnet and other black nationalist authors and orators pressed the case for resistance and separate black institutions. The "determined aim of the whites," minister and black nationalist Martin Delany said, was to "crush the colored races wherever found"; only an active resistance could forestall "this work of universal subjugation."[16] Garnet, Delany, and other pioneering black nationalists called on black churches to lead the fight against that subjugation. Nonetheless, as the debate between

Douglass and Garnet demonstrates, black Christians disagreed on whether the Bible condoned violence in the fight against injustice. Their philosophical differences shaped future debates about how to resist oppression and racism in America.

By and large, black religious organizations took the position of those, like Maria Stewart and Frederick Douglass, who condemned violence to end racial oppression. Seeking integration into American society remained the predominant position of black churches after the Civil War. Most black Christians interpreted their faith as encouraging unity and equality among God's people and freedom from the sins of oppression and injustice. However, in the twentieth century, there was a countercurrent of support, sometimes arising within Christian denominations and other times from black religious traditions outside Christianity, for ideas that black separatism, or black nationalism, remained the best response to American racism. For advocates of this position, black churches themselves served as the perfect example of why separate black institutions were essential. Only separate black institutions, such advocates argued, provided a space for African Americans to flourish as a people. Furthermore, some black theologians suggested that black spirituality, arising from African rather than European traditions, was fundamentally different from that of whites, and that African American religious leaders should be responsible for cultivating it.

These contrasting ideas between integrationists and separatists about the meaning of African American religious ideas and institutions, which had developed during slavery, reverberated in future decades. Yet all the resolutions by Northern black churches and religious organizations seemed to have little effect on the great majority of white Americans—until war in 1861 forced the issue. It was then that black Christian faith became a weapon for freedom. During the Civil War, black soldiers, sometimes recruited by figures such as Douglass in black churches, fought for freedom of body and soul.

CHAPTER FOUR

~

Day of Jubilee

Black Churches from
Emancipation to the Era of Jim Crow

When the Civil War ended in April 1865, nearly four million former slaves gained their physical and spiritual freedom. At the war's conclusion, former slaves in Richmond, Virginia, greeted the arrival of President Lincoln as tantamount to the coming of Moses. The day of Jubilee had come, and hopes ran high that freedom meant civil equality.

Black believers saw in the war the fulfillment of prayers for emancipation, education, and the right to worship freely in their own churches. After the war, independent churches and denominational organizations sprang up quickly in black communities, including thousands of small local congregations and major national organizations. Within a decade after the war, only a few black parishioners continued to worship in white-dominated churches.

During Reconstruction, churches provided an indispensable public forum where African American men and women could advocate, organize, and agitate in their own defense. For the former slaves, who reshaped Christianity for their own purposes, freedom meant that they would no longer submit to white Christians for spiritual guidance. "We act toward them as brethren," a black Baptist missionary said of white churchgoers after the Civil War, "but never shall we again let them rule us as masters."[1]

Black churches served as community institutions that provided spiritual sustenance, mutual aid, educational facilities, and a venue for political dialogue. But black church leaders also faced new challenges, such as the merging of the informal religious practices of the former slaves with the more formal worship style of black denominations. Moreover, by the late nineteenth century, they confronted an elaborate set of segregation laws, a series of tragic Supreme Court decisions that provided legal cover for those laws, and, worst of all, a horrific upsurge of hanging, burning, and torturing African Americans (usually men) in public lynching spectacles. From the advent of emancipation in 1865 to the coming of Jim Crow by the end of the nineteenth century, black Christians had to grapple with the quandary of how God's purposes in the war, emancipation, and Reconstruction could have been so undermined by the human evil of white supremacy. In responding to the rise of the legal proscriptions and terrorist violence of this segregated America, African American churches and denominations represented the initiative freedpeople took to carve out separate cultural spaces, including churches, schools, clubs, political organizations, and fraternal orders.

In his second Inaugural Address, in March 1865, President Abraham Lincoln described the results of the Civil War as "fundamental and astounding." With the deaths of 626,000 soldiers, the maiming of hundreds of thousands of others, and the anguished response to this vast machinery of death and destruction, many Americans saw this revolutionary struggle in providential terms. They sought to understand God's will, even after Lincoln reminded them that God had his own inscrutable purposes. Black soldiers understood God's purposes perfectly clearly, for they knew this was a war about freedom long before whites generally had seen it as such.

During the war, slaves in South Carolina were jailed for singing what many whites deemed to be subversive lines, such as "We'll soon be free." Recording these lines, Thomas Wentworth Higginson, a white Army officer who commanded a black regiment in South Carolina, wrote that "though the chant was an old one, it was no doubt sung with redoubled emphasis during the new events." As one of his black soldiers told him, they thought "*de Lord* mean for say *de Yankees*," and that the "final river to cross" was not the Jordan River of biblical times but the Potomac River, into Washington, D.C. Higginson recounted how the words of the spiritual "We'll Soon Be Free" took on a special meaning as emancipation neared:

> We'll soon be free [× 3]
> When de Lord will call us home.
> My brudder, how long, [× 3]
> 'Fore we done sufferin' here?
> It won't be long (*Thrice.*)
> 'Fore de Lord will call us home.[2]

"Home" was freedom, and the suffering would give way providentially to a day of Jubilee.

A few months before the end of the war, African American ministers from the Georgia low country asked Union officers to assist the approximately 15,000 refugees freed by Gen. William Tecumseh Sherman during his famous "March to the Sea." After taking Savannah, Sherman and other Union leaders, such as Gen. Oliver O. Howard, soon to be head of the Freedmen's Bureau, met with a delegation of black ministers led by Garrison Frazier, a longtime black Baptist pastor. Frazier told Sherman that blacks in his region saw the famous general as an agent of Providence. Indeed, the black delegation led by Frazier and the Union officers under Sherman met at a time of revolution. In February 1865, the Thirteenth Amendment to the Constitution put a permanent end to slavery.

Frazier spoke for tens of thousands of former slaves in the Georgia low country when he told Sherman that "freedom" meant that blacks could fend for themselves best by taking ownership of and working their own land, providing for themselves and their families, and lending support to a government to which they had been loyal. Frazier also suggested that blacks preferred to worship among their own race rather than in white-controlled churches. However, other members of the black delegation disagreed with Frazier. Methodist James Lynch argued that African Americans and Southern whites should learn to live and worship together. In his Special Field Order no. 15, Sherman set aside, for temporary occupancy, some land in the Georgia and South Carolina low country and Sea Islands. The decision soon made its way into the prevailing folklore that the government had promised to provide "forty acres and a mule" to the freedpeople.

Ironically, during slavery, whites had wanted black slaves to attend their churches. In freedom, whites soon insisted on segregated churches. Following emancipation, white Southern Christians initially expected a continuation of the religious services they had enjoyed during slavery. African Americans, they envisioned, would attend white-run churches but be seated in segregated areas, preferably in the rear or in balconies. For Southern whites, this arrangement symbolized the proper spiritual and racial hierarchy. Instead, black congregations withdrew from Southern white-dominated churches. For freedpeople, the creation of separate churches and denominational institutions was an act of cultural autonomy. It was not segregation, but voluntary separation, that would allow them to create black-controlled institutions.

These churches also provided ample opportunities for ambitious freedpeople. Political leadership for freedpeople came mostly from the ranks of men who had been free people of color. They were generally literate and skilled in artisanal or professional trades. Religious leadership, by contrast, was open to anyone with charisma and perseverance. Baptist churches, which could be formed by any group of congregants who agreed to establish an individual church, drew by far the greatest number of freedpeople. Local Baptist congregations operated independently of any higher church authorities. Their independent governance allowed for entrepreneurial spirits to create churches with strong local followings. Long-established churches such as the First African Baptist Church of Savannah spun off scores of new congregations when it sent preachers to evangelize among the freedpeople in the Georgia low country. Other churches did the same and, as a result, numerous new black congregations sprang up throughout the South.

In the last third of the nineteenth century, black church membership grew rapidly. Overall, church membership among African Americans rose from 2.6 million to 3.6 million between 1890 and 1906. Independent black churches and denominations claimed the vast majority of black churchgoers. By 1906, the National Baptist Convention, a nationwide organization of black Baptists that had been created in 1895, claimed more than two million communicants, comprising 61 percent of all black churchgoers. That same year (1906), the African Methodist Episcopal (AME) Church numbered some 500,000 communicants, the African Methodist Episcopal Zion (AMEZ) denomination about 185,000, and the Colored Methodist Episcopal (CME) church approximately 173,000. Predominantly white denominations also claimed some black members, but most of them worshipped in separate black congregations within the white-led denominations. For example, the Methodist Episcopal Church (MEC) encompassed about 60,000 black adherents. Catholics in 1906 included around 38,000 African American worshippers, while the Presbyterians and Congregationalists had a combined membership of 30,000 African Americans.

Many of the large, independent black congregations originated with some degree of white cooperation. Richmond's historic First African Baptist Church had started in an old building whites had donated to slave members of their congregation in 1841. The Reverend Robert Ryland, its white pastor, ministered to the slave congregation until 1867, when, recognizing that his members preferred black leadership, he resigned. His protégé, James Henry Holmes, a former slave who had worked in Richmond's tobacco warehouses, replaced him. Holmes pastored the church until 1901, as it grew to a membership of several thousand.

Throughout the South, urban black congregations such as First African Baptist in Richmond served not only the spiritual but also the social needs of the freedpeople. Moreover, black congregations became centers of black political and economic power. For example, during Reconstruction, First African served as the home to many black political meetings, where freedpeople

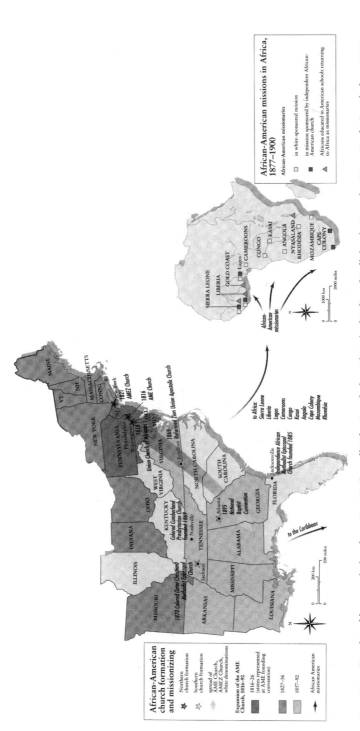

African-American church formation and missionizing

- Northern church formation
- Southern church formation
- spread of AME Church, AMEZ Church, white denominations

Expansion of the AME Church, 1816–92

- 1816–26 (states represented at AME founding convention)
- 1827–56
- 1857–92
- African American missionaries

Bethel African Methodist Episcopal Church
1870 Colored (later Christian) Methodist Episcopal Church
Jackson

Nashville
Colored Cumberland Presbyterian Church founded 1869

Kelmar
1895 National Baptist Convention

Jacksonville
Independence African Methodist Episcopal Church founded 1885

New York
1821 AMEZ Church
1816 AME Church
Union Church of Africans 1813
Wilmington
Philadelphia 1815
Boydton Reformed Zion Union Apostolic Church 1869

to the Caribbean

to Africa:
Sierra Leone
Liberia
Lagos
Cameroons
Congo
Kasai
Angola
Cape Colony
Mozambique
Rhodesia

African-American missions in Africa, 1877–1900

African-American missionaries

- ☐ in white-sponsored mission
- ■ in mission sponsored by independent African-American church
- ▲ Africans educated in American schools returning to Africa as missionaries

African-American missionaries

SIERRA LEONE
LIBERIA
GOLD COAST
Lagos
CAMEROONS
CONGO
KASAI
ANGOLA
NYASALAND
RHODESIA
MOZAMBIQUE
CAPE COLONY

Map 4.1. Reprinted by permission from Bret E. Carroll, *The Routledge Historical Atlas of Religion in America* (New York: Routledge, 2000).

Photo 4.1.   Illustration of the interior of the largest black Baptist church after the Civil War, the First African Baptist Church of Richmond, Virginia. Courtesy of the Library of Congress.

collectively composed petitions to be sent to city and state officials demanding equal citizenship rights. Black religious leaders generally tried to protect their autonomy from white intrusion, which resulted in virtually complete racial separation of Southern churches.

In the face of the rapid move to racial separatism in religion, some white and black believers rejected the general practice of racial separation in church life. The history of Methodism and Catholicism in New Orleans presents a striking example. The Crescent City was unique in the way that Creole people of mixed African and French descent, free blacks, ex-slaves, and white Southern members of the MEC interacted. The particular racial history of New Orleans, which boasted a large community of free people of color and of French-speaking Creoles, made religious life in New Orleans different than almost anywhere else in America. Methodist and Catholic parishioners in New Orleans developed a tradition of interracial religious organizations that lasted almost until the end of the nineteenth century, long after most Southern churches were separated by race. In a major exception to the usual pattern of racial ecclesiastical separation, Methodists and Catholics in New Orleans supported racially integrated church organizations as important symbols of a society not yet divided by race. However, they soon encountered difficulties that ultimately proved to be insurmountable.

As was typical of congregations everywhere in America, churches in the historic Louisiana city diverged by class and color. Despite such divisions, politically radical and racially desegregated Methodism found a home in New Orleans. The MEC, with a membership of about three thousand white and black parishioners in New Orleans by the 1880s, attracted whites seeking respite from the Confederate religion of the Southern Methodist churches, as well as African Americans who objected to the racialist bent of the AME Church. The MEC supported Republican politicians who emphasized racial equality and equal citizenship rights, including the racial integration of public institutions.

Black church people used their institutions to blunt racial terror and state-sanctioned segregation and to advance the living, working, and legal conditions of their congregants. In doing so, they were often intimately involved in the politics of the time, particularly during Reconstruction. In the years after the Civil War, black churches insisted that freedpeople were equal citizens under the law. To white supremacists, this was subversive preaching. Even more upsetting to them was the fact that the black churches were the prime recruiting grounds for the Republican Party. At black church services, observers witnessed fervent prayers being offered up for Republican candidates. Lincoln's party was God's party.

Black ministers played a prominent role in Republican politics. More than 230 black clergymen held local, state, or national office during Reconstruction. The first African American to win election to the U.S. Senate, Hiram Revels of Mississippi, was an AME cleric. The postwar constitutional convention in Georgia included nine ministers of that church. The same held true for Mississippi, where six of the sixteen black men attending the 1868 state constitutional convention were clergymen. Ministers made up some 40 percent of the founders of the Union League, an organization of Southern supporters of the Republican Party that eventually helped to organize militias to protect black voters at the polls.

During the tumultuous years of Reconstruction, black citizens and voters needed all the protection they could get from churches, ministers, and religious organizations. As new citizens, they depended on Republican Reconstruction regimes and religious faith as God's instruments to protect their precarious rights. Christian freedpeople circulated harrowing tales of harassment and savagery. The Ku Klux Klan in Texas perpetrated some terrible deeds during Reconstruction days, an ex-slave recollected. Her response: "But I just built a wall of the Lord 'round me so they couldn't get at me." When Klansmen heard anything black preachers said about politics, another former bondsperson recounted, they took the "radical" ministers out for whippings and beatings. As a result of this white vigilante violence, black clergymen had to be extraordinarily careful about what they said in their sermons. One former slave most succinctly expressed the view of black Christians about freedom's coming after the Civil War and the turmoil of Reconstruction: "That was about equalization after freedom. That was the cause of that."[3] Contending religious visions of equalization after freedom shaped the evolving political struggle in the South through the end of the nineteenth century. Black churches and religious organizations played central roles in that struggle.

Blacks used white Northern allies in that struggle when possible, and some white churchmen viewed the cause of the freedpeople as the cause of Christ. For example, the official organ of the Louisiana Conference of the MEC, the *Southwestern Christian Advocate*, was an outspoken proponent of racial equality. Its editor, a white Methodist named Joseph Hartzell, was a native of Illinois who came to New Orleans in 1869. He pastored the Ames Methodist Episcopal Church, whose parishioners included the white state governor and other notable white and black Republicans. Since white Southerners resented Republicans, it is not surprising that the church faced opposition from wealthy local whites, some of whom remained Confederate sympathizers and all of whom feared black equality. Conflicts between the interracial church and white supremacists intensified when Hartzell hired Aristides Elphonso Peter (A. E. P.) Albert as assistant editor of the *Southwestern Christian Advocate*. Albert was born in St. Charles Parish, thirty-five miles from New Orleans, where he grew up as a French-speaking Catholic slave. After the war, he converted to Methodism. Albert demanded resistance to segregation in any form. Emphasizing the necessity of protecting rights of citizenship, including equal access to public accommodations and voting privileges, Albert entertained the possibility of using violence against white supremacists in self-defense, an early example of how the political positions of black churchmen could leave whites uneasy, including white allies of the freedpeople.

In the 1870s, succumbing to pressure from white Methodists who were uneasy about integrated churches and black ministers who were eager to maintain autonomous black churches, the MEC granted its members the right to establish all-black and all-white churches. When Hartzell resisted the racial segregation of Methodist conferences, national leaders removed him from his post at the *Southwestern Christian Advocate*. Nonetheless, in Louisiana some black and white Methodist ministers continued to lead integrated congregations, seeking to prove that they would not yield to prejudice. Over time, however, even those churches became racially separated due to the strong social pressures that pushed whites to avoid social contact with blacks and the determination of blacks to organize separate institutions for their own self-protection and to cultivate their own leaders.

After placing great hope in the Methodist Episcopal Church as a beacon of Christian interracialism, Albert and Hartzell expressed frustration at the powerlessness of African American believers to gain the appointment of a black bishop or shape any major decision at the denominational level. In the 1890s, just prior to the ominous *Plessy v. Ferguson* decision that ratified the constitutionality of racial segregation in public transportation, Albert formed alliances with Creole Catholics in civil rights organizations, which landed him in trouble with increasingly conservative white Methodists.

By the early twentieth century, the MEC decreed the Louisiana Conference as a separate organization for black Methodists in that region. In other words, white Methodist church leaders placed black members of the predominantly white national MEC into a segregated Methodist jurisdiction. Elsewhere, attempts to create a biracial Methodist polity met the same fate. White Methodists succumbed to the theological racism that was characteristic of American church bodies as a whole. Moreover, many African American Christians preferred to support black-controlled churches. For many blacks, the experience simply demonstrated that separate churches were necessary if African American rights were to be protected within church hierarchies that tended, even if unintentionally, to reflect the white supremacist order.

Black denominational institutions such as mission societies and publishing boards grew along with black independent churches. In the 1890s, for example, black Baptists established the National Baptist Publishing Board, which sprang from the work of Richard Henry Boyd. Born a slave in Mississippi and educated at a black Baptist college in Texas, Boyd was an early advocate of all-black Baptist organizations. In 1895, Boyd moved to Nashville, Tennessee, where he became a successful religious entrepreneur. The following year, he established the National Baptist Publishing Board, which distributed millions of pieces of Sunday school literature to black churches. He exemplified the spirit of resistance to Southern racism and Northern paternalism. As he said of his efforts, "The Holy Spirit come to us and forbid the Negro taking a second place."[4] By the time of his death in 1922, Boyd had turned the small Nashville-based company into the largest black-owned publishing house in the nation. Boyd's other business ventures included the Nashville *Globe*, a black newspaper he launched with his son Henry Allen Boyd in 1906; the One-Cent Savings Bank and Trust Company, established in 1904; and the National Negro Doll Company, created in 1911.

Boyd's business career personified the racial advancement strategy of Booker T. Washington, the nation's leading black spokesman. In 1895, Washington had advised African Americans to stay in the South and forgo political rights and social equality in exchange for the chance to pursue economic self-sufficiency with the assistance of sympathetic whites. However, unlike Washington, Boyd challenged racial segregation publicly. In 1905, for example, he helped organize a black boycott of Nashville streetcars, founding the short-lived Union Transportation Company. Moreover, he used the *Globe* to articulate black opposition to segregation.

The stories of two black ministers, missionaries, and newspaper editors—William Jefferson White (1832–1913) and Henry McNeal Turner (1834–1915)—suggest much about the connection between religion and politics for the first generation of freed African Americans. Their lives almost perfectly trace the arc of African American Christianity from the nineteenth into the early twentieth century. Both men were ministers whose careers arose in part from independent incomes derived from artisanal work. Both also headed independent black churches and published newspapers. They fought furiously for civil rights and equal access to education after the Civil War and against the rise of segregation laws in the nineteenth century.

White, the son of a white planter and a mother who was probably of mixed Native American and African American ancestry, was an ambitious Georgian who, because of his light skin, could have passed as white but self-identified as black. In the 1850s, as a free man of color, he had worked as a carpenter and cabinetmaker, thus securing the economic base that funded his postwar career as a minister and newspaper editor. At the first meeting of the Georgia Equal Rights and Education Association, held at Augusta's historic black Springfield Baptist Church in early 1866, White's eloquent address drew the attention of Gen. Oliver O. Howard, director of the Freedmen's Bureau, who assured White of his assistance. The following year, with the help of Howard, White opened Augusta Baptist Institute, a school to teach black youngsters the basics of a primary education and also to provide more advanced training for those capable of high-school-level work.

Despite hostility from opponents of black education in the town, the Augusta Baptist Institute trained some talented students who left a significant mark on black Georgia, including Emmanuel K. Love, who became the pastor of Georgia's largest black Baptist church and a founder of the National Baptist Convention. In 1879, the school moved to the rapidly growing and more centrally located city of Atlanta, where it eventually took the name of Morehouse College, honoring the white Northern Baptist educator Henry Morehouse. The college later served as a base for the twentieth-century educator John Hope and trained Martin Luther King Jr. and other civil rights leaders. Today it stands as one of the strongest historically black colleges in the United States.

White not only created one of the leading historically black colleges and universities but also launched the *Georgia Baptist* in 1880. With its masthead reading "Great Elevator, Educator, and Defender of the People," the *Georgia Baptist* was one of the most widely distributed black newspapers in the late nineteenth-century South. He used the paper to defend black rights amidst the growing racial turmoil. After he publicly denounced a local lynching and defended its victim, local whites threatened his life. His black friends took up sentry posts outside the paper's offices. Seeking to spare his life and career in Augusta, White withdrew an editorial condemning the action of local whites, but privately he feared the meaning of this turn of events. "We seem to be standing on a volcano," he wrote to his son. White's paper also lent vocal support to a streetcar boycott that blacks in Augusta organized in 1898 to protest newly enacted segregation laws. "The colored people of Augusta are keeping off the street cars because of the revival of Jim Crowism on them, and some of the white papers of the city are howling about it," he exclaimed. "They howl if colored people ride on the cars and howl if they stay off of them. What in the name of high heaven do the white people want the colored people to do?"[5]

In 1906, White joined W. E. B. Du Bois and other race leaders to establish the Georgia Equal Rights League. The bloody Atlanta riot of that year, which caused three days of mayhem in the supposed capital of the "New South," dashed black hopes for a racial truce. By the time of his death in 1913, White's religiously inspired hopes of equal rights for all were a distant memory.

From economic independence to vigorous work in church organizing to disillusionment in the era of Jim Crow, Henry McNeal Turner's life followed a similar trajectory to that of White. Turner was born free in 1834 in South Carolina. In the 1850s, Turner moved to White's home state of Georgia, where he made his name and career. There, biracial crowds eagerly gathered to hear his powerful preaching. Indeed, Turner's masterful oratory persuaded some incredulous whites that he was a white man in disguise.

Following his Civil War service as a Union Army chaplain, Turner became a prominent African Methodist Episcopal churchman, missionary, legislator, and newspaper editor. Turner's major achievement was the establishment of the AME Church in the South after the Civil War. The AME Church and its competitor, the AMEZ Church, sent black missionaries to evangelize the freedpeople. Turner and his fellow black missionaries

Photo 4.2. Portrait of Henry McNeal Turner, African Methodist Episcopal bishop, Reconstruction-era legislator, and fiery advocate of emigration to Africa in the late nineteenth century. Courtesy of the Library of Congress.

envisioned their religious work as being essential to securing full citizenship rights for the freedpeople. Civil rights, church organization, and racial uplift, he believed, went hand in hand. Turner expressed this sentiment when he defended the continued use of the word "African" in the AME denominational title. He believed that by claiming their African descent, African Americans honored themselves as a people. This rhetorical move, he insisted, was essential given that African Americans lived in a country where whiteness was tantamount to godliness, while blackness stood for "ignorance, degradation, indolence, and all that is low and vile." Turner urged African Americans to "honor black, dignify it with virtues, and pay as much respect to it as nature and nature's God does." In his most succinct phrasing, he said simply, "Respect black."[6]

Turner also served as a delegate to the postwar constitutional convention in Georgia. In 1868, he was elected to the legislature, but the white Democratic majority expelled him and his fellow black legislators, arguing that men who came from servile backgrounds were not eligible to serve in the state government. In other words, white legislators staged an illegal coup against the black Reconstruction legislators. Black lawmakers such as Turner often came from the church or were ministers themselves. Many of them incorrectly assumed that their religious credentials would save them from attacks such as the one they experienced in the state legislature. After appealing to federal authorities, Turner was reinstated, but his efforts at winning over potential white adversaries failed because he was perceived as a "Radical." White lawmakers knew Turner would defend black citizenship rights. By 1871, however, the Peach State had been "redeemed" from "Black Republican" rule, something white state residents perceived as contrary to the will of God.

With his political career terminated, first by a coup and later by Democratic victories over Republicans at the polls, Turner settled into three more decades of ceaseless work for the AME Church in the South. He traveled constantly, edited the official denominational hymnal, and in 1880 was elected a bishop. He fought internal church battles with Northern bishops over the degree of education necessary for ministerial ordination and the place of women in the church. In both cases, Turner argued for democratizing the church polity by extending opportunities to those historically excluded from church leadership positions.

When race-based segregation and disfranchisement laws swept the South in the 1890s, Turner blasted American hypocrisy. As editor of the *Voice of Missions* from 1892 to his death in 1915, Turner served as a public advocate for black emigration to Africa, thinking that the movement of a select group of talented African Americans back to the home continent would fulfill God's destiny for black people. His advocacy of emigration to Africa angered many fellow AME leaders, who, like Richard Allen, rejected colonization or emigration, insisting instead that the United States was the home of African

Americans. During the late nineteenth century, Turner traveled to Liberia, Sierra Leone, and South Africa, publicizing the economic and religious opportunities available for black Americans on the home continent. His work in South Africa, where his preaching tour in 1898 drew much attention, was especially significant, and the AME Church there became a home base for what evolved into the African National Congress—the organization that later, under Nelson Mandela, defeated the system of racial apartheid in the country.

Even as he traveled through southern Africa exploring the possibilities for emigration, Turner blasted the implicit and explicit racism that underlay the religious conceptions of most Americans. Turner articulated what later would be called "black theology," religious thinking that identified the oppression of African Americans with the sufferings of Christ on earth. By 1898, Turner had concluded that God was black, for only God could comprehend the suffering of African Americans. He urged black Christians to adopt religious symbolism appropriate to express pride in their race. Black people had every right to believe that they had been created in the image of God. "We have as much right biblically and otherwise to believe that God is a Negro, as you buckra, or white, people have to believe that God is a fine looking, symmetrical and ornamented white man," he exclaimed in 1898. "For the bulk of you, and all the fool Negroes of the country, believe that God is white-skinned, blue-eyed, straight-haired, projecting-nosed compressed-lipped and finely-robed *white* gentleman sitting upon a throne somewhere in the heavens."[7] Turner's evolution exemplified the hopes so many African American Christians placed in Reconstruction, their vigorous church and denominational organizing in the South after the Civil War, and finally the disillusionment and search for providential answers that came with the rise of Jim Crow in America.

Black theologians and intellectuals such as Turner and a host of African Methodist writers in that era produced a genre of "race histories" that explained the origins and destiny of the race to African American readers. These race writers collectively disputed the racist notions of inherent inferiority. For example, African Methodist minister Lorenzo Dow Blackson's *The Rise and Progress of the Kingdoms of Light and Darkness* (1867) traced the history of "the race" from the ancient world to the present, giving black Americans an identifiable and honorable history and heritage and countering white racist assertions that African Americans lacked culture. Contrary to common views held by many white Americans and Europeans in the nineteenth century, Africans were a people of history; they were not, as the German philosopher Hegel infamously asserted, a "people without history."

African American religious thinkers challenged the creation of blackness as a synonym for inferiority and shame. They sought to influence the discussion of race in America by imparting to blacks a dignified history and a respectable present. But few white Americans listened. Black Americans might develop a sterling character, acquire property, foster a vigorous church life, start their own schools, and improve their homes, but none of this would bring about respect for the race, numerous black ministers noted during the era. Indeed, black Southerners were restless, ready to move from a land of Southern oppression from which there seemed no escape other than migration. This restlessness soon spurred one of the largest migrations in American history.

Class and regional differences in African American society, which emerged prominently in the years after the Civil War, also took root in the religious culture that arose during the late nineteenth century. African American churchpeople might gain the respect of whites, many black church leaders felt, if they cultivated a style of worship decorum in their churches that closely resembled that of whites.

Since the early nineteenth century, Daniel Alexander Payne (1811–1893) had spearheaded this movement in the African Methodist Episcopal Church. Born into the free black elite of Charleston, South Carolina, Payne believed that education, social progress, and upward mobility were the keys to African American success. As he traveled through the South after the Civil War, he tried to transform the worship style of the freedpeople. He insisted that the kinds of practices slaves had developed in the brush harbors would have to be changed if African Americans were to gain the respect of whites. Payne advocated racial uplift through education and cultural refinement. The black elites, who were educated and culturally refined, should take the lead in bringing civilization to ordinary freedpeople who had been denied access to education and culture, he believed. As a member of the culturally educated black elite, Payne condemned the enthusiastic black worship styles prevalent among the former slaves. The different worship cultures, rooted in class distinctions, increasingly divided black churches.

Not only black church leaders like Payne but also white clergymen condemned many of the religious customs prevalent among Southerners as uncivilized adaptations of African religious traditions and holdovers from slave styles of worship. Payne and his fellow church leaders were particularly troubled by the music and spiritual dancing of black worshippers. Most specifically, they denigrated the ring shout, which they justifiably suspected to be an African rite grafted onto a Christian form. The "shouts"—also called

Photo 4.3. Negro Revival in the South. Courtesy of the New York Public Library.

"Egypt walking," "patting Juba," or "rings"—were most frequently observed in black services in the Lowcountry and Deep South. They fascinated many observers but also embarrassed white and black church leaders.

The ring shouts involved dances originating from traditions of worship practice that developed during slavery. Secret black societies often oversaw shout ceremonies held outside the regular services. They enforced the rules of sacred movement: no crossing the feet (meaning, no dancing), no sexually suggestive motion (or "cake-walking"), and a prescribed order of song style from slow tempo to double-time. The dances varied according to the songs and different rhythms derived from traditional slave shouts. Sometimes a stick or other homemade instrument provided the drumbeat. Practitioners would "heel & toe tumultuously, others merely tremble & stagger on, others stoop & rise, others whirl, others caper sidewise all keep steadily circling like dervishes," with congregants "falling out" or "walking the pews" during services. As described by a contemporary, after one prayer service, the room was cleared and a ring of six dancers formed. A chanting singer stood off to the side. The most skillful dancers moved about gracefully and quietly, making little noise except through the movement of their feet. They danced in a circle as a chanter on the side called out lines, with the dancers responding with refrains such as "Oh Lord, yes my Lord" to the chanter's line "Pray a little longer, Jericho, do worry me."[8]

Convinced that the ring shouts deviated from proper religious practices, Payne embarked on tours after the Civil War to teach dignified worship to the Southern members of his church. Despite the efforts of Payne and others, many black Southerners held onto their traditional religious ceremonies. At one brush meeting, he witnessed congregants forming a ring after the service, stamping their feet, clapping, swaying, and dancing "in a most ridiculous and heathenish way."[9] When Payne asked the congregants to sit down and worship more sedately, they responded by walking away. A leader of the congregation told Payne that unless there was a ring, the sinners would never convert, but Payne refused to accept the old folkways of worship as true manifestations of the spirit of God and criticized those who encouraged them.

Like Payne, many other black religious leaders encouraged public decorum during worship. They vilified practices such as vision quests, dreams, ecstatic conversion experiences and testimonies, spiritual dancing, ring shouts, and songlike sermonizing. The religious rites the freedpeople had developed during slavery, they insisted, had to be transformed. On occasion, they found success in this mission. One missionary in the late nineteenth century recounted a baptismal service where, when a few ex-slaves raised a shout, they were shushed by a female worship leader who was enforcing worship respectability. A white minister who would not permit shouting found some approval for his sermon, even from those used to older ways of worship. But, as one elderly congregant commented, "It most killed me to hold in them shouts."[10] Such attempts at self-control demonstrated the gradual internalization of the ideal of public respectability.

Ultimately, despite the efforts of Payne and other worship reformers, many black worshippers still attended secretive ring shouts, and the black churches continued the practices of singing and shouting during their services. Bodily expressions of possession by the spirit remained central to African American spirituality. Parishioners expected to hear dramatic conversion tales from young people captured by the spirit. The embodiment of religious expression accorded with African rituals and with evangelical notions of how the spirit worked in one's soul, even if it contradicted middle-class respectable notions of decorum and propriety in religious behavior.

Payne and his fellows believed firmly that respectable worship would lead to the acculturation of blacks into American society. They were wrong. Black respectability did not dampen racism. On the contrary, it only helped to fuel white anger and violence. Even those whose lives perfectly exemplified the cultivation of education, personal decorum, and rigid respectability could not escape the degradation of American racism that followed the demise of Reconstruction.

Payne, like his Methodist ministerial colleague Turner, encountered personally how little respectability would mean to white racists. On a train traveling to a religious conference in Jacksonville, Florida, in the 1880s, the conductor ordered the elderly AME bishop to move to the Jim Crow car. Payne responded that he would not dishonor himself by doing so and demanded that he be left off the train rather than switch train cars. The conductor ejected him five miles from his destination. Payne, the elderly paragon of propriety, walked the rest of the way while carrying his baggage. Upon his arrival in Jacksonville, black Methodists indignant at the treatment accorded Payne organized a protest meeting. Because legal cases had been filed on his behalf, Payne determined not to file suit himself. God would judge the perpetrators, he decided. Payne's experience posed a profound challenge to his lifelong faith that religion would lead to universal brotherhood. Despite his troubles, however, he fared much better than the untold numbers that white Southerners cheated, beat, and murdered during the Jim Crow era.

For black Christians, the coming of freedom in 1865 held far less promise by 1900. The hopes for equal rights that had characterized the Reconstruction era dimmed in the harsh reality of the segregated order white Southerners constructed in the late nineteenth and early twentieth centuries. Freedom, it became clear, would come only through a constant struggle. During the Jim Crow era, which lasted from the late nineteenth century to the 1950s, black churches prepared to play a part in that struggle.

~

CHAPTER FIVE

Jesus on the Main Line

Black Christianity from the
Great Migration through World War II

From 1900 to 1945, developments in African American Christianity mirrored the larger transformations in black life during the first half of the twentieth century. One of the most significant forces shaping the black experience was the Great Migration. A massive exodus of African Americans from the South to the North and the West shifted the center of African American religious life from the small towns in the South to urban areas outside that region. Detroit, Chicago, and New York rapidly became gathering places for tens of thousands of black migrants in the post–World War I era. Churches in those cities assumed central positions of community leadership and nurtured black talent that would explode onto the American social, cultural, and political scene in the mid-twentieth century. In the nineteenth century, First African Baptist Church in Richmond had been the largest black congregation in the country; by World War II, that honor went to Mt. Olivet Baptist Church in Chicago. Career-oriented ministers who sought larger congregations, more extensive influence, opportunities to rise in denominational hierarchies, and higher paychecks often followed their parishioners northward and westward. These churches also fostered new musical styles, particularly black gospel music, which took black religious expression in new directions over the course of the twentieth century.

Just as significant as the sermonic and musical styles pioneered by black Christian migrants was the emergence of new churches and religious movements among African Americans in the urban North. These included

Holiness/Pentecostal churches, which contemporaries usually called "Sanctified" churches. These emerged from a movement of spiritual renewal and transformation in the early twentieth century emphasizing being "filled with the spirit" after conversion and expressing their rapture through bodily trances, speaking in tongues, and enthusiastic music. Besides the emergence of Holiness/Pentecostalism, the new religious movements also gave rise to independent black religious groups that challenged conventional religious institutions, including the Moorish Science Temple, the Lost-Found Nation of Islam, the International Peace Mission Movement, and the All Nations Pentecostal Church. Some were Christian or quasi-Christian; others were outside the Christian tradition but nonetheless attracted black churchgoers. Other black secular groups, such as Marcus Garvey's Universal Negro Improvement Association in New York, developed religious rituals and auxiliaries that promoted alternative black religious ideas, including a "black Christ," which had been enunciated by Henry McNeal Turner in the late nineteenth century.

The Baptist and Methodist churches remained the dominant institutional and cultural force in African American Christianity. However, the new black religious movements did attract many black migrants, as well as considerable attention and derision from established black church leaders. For the first time since the Great Awakenings, alternative black religious movements posed a serious threat to black Christianity. Established black Protestant churches had to fight for attention and attendance in Northern cities. Meanwhile, Sanctified congregations took in black migrants seeking more spiritual enthusiasm than could be found in the respectable urban congregations. Derided as refuges for the dispossessed, these churches created musical forms that eventually transformed American popular culture.

Before 1920, the great bulk of African Americans continued to worship in Baptist and Methodist churches in the South. In 1916, black Baptists numbered three million congregants, 89 percent of whom were Southerners. Black Methodists, more than one million strong and divided up into three major denominational bodies, also represented a mostly Southern demographic, well over 80 percent. Black religious institutions ran the gamut from large urban churches and recent Holiness and Pentecostal congregations in cities to countless small rural churches that dotted the landscape throughout the region.

Both Southern and Northern black churches engaged in much community work. In so doing, they applied the ideas of the social gospel movement, which emphasized emulating Jesus' life in practical works of caring for people

Table 5.1. Membership in African American Denominations, 1906–1936

Number of African American members reported in specific denominations, compiled from U.S. Census of Religious Bodies, 1906 to 1936

Denomination	1906	1916	1926	1936
National Baptists	2,261,607 (7% Southern)	2,938,579 (89.0% Southern)	3,196,623 (84.3% Southern, 39% urban)	3,782,464 (72.9% Southern, 50% urban)
AME Church	494,777 (85.9% Southern)	548,355 (81.2% Southern)	545,814 (75.2% Southern, 50% urban)	493,357 (65.6% Southern, 58% urban)
AMEZ Church	184,542 (88.6% Southern)	257,169 (84.6% Southern)	456,813 (82.1% Southern, 42.5% urban)	414,244 (65.6% Southern, 52% urban)
CME Church	172,996 (98.6% Southern)	245,749 (95.5% Southern)	202,713 (88.7% Southern, 39.1% urban)	269,915 (92.4% Southern, 43% urban)
Methodist Episcopal	308,551	320,025	332,345 (45% urban)	193,761 (55% urban)
Roman Catholic	44,982	51,688	124,324 (85.9% urban)	137,684 (80% urban)
Baptists, Northern Convention	32,639	53,842	— (99% urban)	45,821
Church of God and Saints of Christ	1,823 (29.3% Southern)	3,311 (32.7% Southern)	6,741 (41.8% Southern, 89.9% urban)	37,084 (36% Southern, 94% urban)
Church of God in Christ	—	—	30,263 (64.9% Southern, 68.7% urban)	31,584 (55.5% Southern, 75% urban)
Episcopal	19,089	23,775	1,502 (89.7% urban)	29,738 (92% urban)
Church of Christ Holiness, U.S.A.	—	—	4,919 (70.9% Southern, 61% urban)	29,738 (92% urban)
Presbyterian Church in the U.S.	27,799	31,957	37,090 (72.4% urban)	2,971 (79.7% Southern, 48% urban) (92% urban)

Source: Milton Sernett, Bound for the Promised Land: African American Religion and the Great Migration (Durham: Duke University Press, 1997), appendix. The figures are from the four religious censuses in 1906, 1916, 1926, and 1936. Details on the classifications employed in collecting these statistics may be found in Sernett.

rather than focusing on the spiritual afterlife. The best example of a Southern black church committed to the social gospel was Henry Proctor's First Congregational Church in Atlanta. Seeking to serve the body, mind, and spirit of his congregants, Proctor took this pulpit in 1894. Historically, the church had been a biracial congregation pastored by whites. By Proctor's tenure, however, the congregation was all black. Proctor immediately doubled the church membership to four hundred, in part through his efforts toward making church activities more relevant to the everyday lives of congregants. By 1900, he had launched a local chapter of the Christian Endeavor Society, a nationwide organization of Christian youth, and a Working Men's Club, which sought to deter men from frequenting taverns and pool halls. Proctor stayed in Atlanta even during the riots of 1906, when white gangs attacked African Americans on the street and set fires to black neighborhoods. After the brutal melee, he served on the local biracial Committee on Church Cooperation, which tried to dispel rumors of race riots that could set tense Southern cities ablaze. He condemned the social and political apathy of white ministers and tried to align himself with progressive forces in the white community. However, in 1919, Proctor abandoned that strategy when he moved to Brooklyn to establish a church to service the needs of Southern migrants who had moved to the city during the Great Migration of the World War I era.

Like Proctor's congregation, numerous churches throughout the country fulfilled the progressive ideal of the congregation involved in every facet of believers' lives. Churchwomen led much of this work. During the Jim Crow era, black women in particular vigorously pursued evangelization and moral uplift, raising significant sums for benevolent endeavors and filling more pews in churches than black men. The ministry in the established denominations was confined to men, but African Americans recognized that women did most of the work that sustained congregations and church organizations. It was women's work that made black churches thrive.

Black Baptist women organized under the dynamic direction of Nannie H. Burroughs. In 1900, Burroughs proposed her idea for a Woman's Convention, Auxiliary to the National Baptist Convention, the largest black church organization in the country. Black Baptist churchmen at first rejected her idea, insisting that God designated men to lead religious endeavors, but she met resistance from convention churchmen with determined rhetoric. Burroughs spoke of the "righteous discontent" and "burning zeal" motivating black churchwomen to uplift black women who were oppressed both because of their race and their gender. African American churchwomen believed passionately, she announced in 1903, that black women throughout the country must "hear the gospel of industry and heed its blessed principles before they can be morally saved," illustrating her dual emphases on spiritual and moral regeneration. Racial segregation, Burroughs added, could be fought not only through political protests but also by "soap and water, hoes, spades, shovels and paint."[1]

Burroughs tirelessly sought to activate black women's mission societies and clubs to address specific problems in their communities, including demanding better city services from local governments, repairing decaying housing stock, picking up trash and garbage in neighborhoods, and teaching families to cultivate gardens in their own yards to improve their diets. She also aimed to put her philosophy into practice by building a school, owned and managed by black women, that would train young African American females in religious doctrine, moral behavior, and practical skills to take to the job market.

By 1909, Burroughs's Woman's Convention owned the only educational institution run by black women in the country, the National Training School for Women and Girls in Washington, D.C. At her training school, she taught young women the virtues of the "three B's": Bible, the bath, and the broom. As Burroughs saw it, cleanliness reflected a code of morality arising from Christian practice. Burroughs also stressed the importance of proper personal conduct as a means of racial uplift, continuing a point that African Methodist leaders, including Daniel Alexander Payne, had advocated in the nineteenth century.

Burroughs's emphasis on personal responsibility did not contradict her eloquent public voice protesting racial proscriptions. In 1903, she noted that black Southerners faithfully had followed every prescription for individual and collective success but still faced the wrath of fearful Southern whites. Burroughs urged women to cooperate with the National Association for the Advancement of Colored People (NAACP), the nation's leading civil rights organization since its establishment in 1909, and other groups working toward improving race relations. She blasted the ugly racial caricatures common in popular culture and history texts and implored black families and schools to teach their children to commit their lives to uplifting the race.

In the early twentieth century, Nannie Burroughs belonged to a network of black female religious reformers who formed missionary societies, clubs, and reform organizations. In Atlanta, for example, a group of black women led by Lugenia Hope, the wife of the president of Morehouse College, a black Baptist educational institution, formed a professional settlement house organization in 1908. Settlement houses were urban centers that Progressive Era women opened in larger cities to provide social services to immigrants from abroad and to poor urban migrants who needed assistance in establishing new lives. Gradually, Hope's settlement house expanded to include the entire range of social, spiritual, intellectual, and physical needs of black female migrants to Atlanta. Worried about the lack of playground facilities for black children, Hope started Gate City Free Kindergarten Association in 1905. By 1917, Hope ran an organization called the Neighborhood Union, sponsored by black churchwomen and operating in affiliation with other civic organizations. It helped to house, clothe, and educate three thousand children. The union also pressured for better salaries for teachers, paved streets, reduction of exorbitant rents, and the removal of foul privies in black neighborhoods.

Other black churches and religious organizations joined in the work of religious progressivism and the social gospel. These movements harnessed the funds, energies, and piety of churchpeople toward improving the social and economic conditions of African Americans. For example, in Atlanta, Bethel AME Church offered an employment bureau for domestics, Wheat Street Baptist Church opened a home for elderly women and a school for black laborers, and Friendship Baptist Church built a house to care for the indigent and elderly. Black churchwomen thus realized the goal of the social gospel: harnessing religious idealism to improve the everyday lives of ordinary citizens.

In addition to urban churches, clubs, and missionary societies that provided essential assistance to black migrants, other new religious movements pioneered forms of spiritual expression that enticed black worshippers in search of renewed religious experiences. In the late nineteenth and early twentieth centuries, Pentecostalism arose as such a revitalization movement among ordinary white and black churchgoers. It was a national movement, but among blacks it originated in the South and later spread to the North. Pentecostals believed in the "third blessing." The Holy Ghost, they claimed, descended on those Christians who sought a higher spiritual life, who came in search of deeper states of spiritual experience. They believed that, once the Holy Ghost entered them, they started to speak in tongues. Most early black believers in the South were refugees from Baptist and Methodist churches. When they migrated North, their religious beliefs did as well.

The Church of God in Christ (COGIC), founded in 1897, emerged as the largest and most influential expression of black Pentecostalism. Its founder, Charles Harrison Mason, was born in Tennessee to parents who had been slaves. Mason intended to become a minister but was also filled with dreams, visions, and premonitions. Stricken with tuberculosis at an early age, he interpreted the disease as God's punishment for ignoring his call to preach and his healing as a miraculous reprieve and divine message to pursue his spiritual duty. Following a short stint at a Baptist college, Mason became a Baptist minister. He then teamed in evangelistic efforts with Charles Price Jones, an early pioneer of the Black Holiness movement and author of numerous songs and hymns. Mason and Jones preached throughout the Mississippi Delta region. In the 1890s, they felt called to pursue their spiritual quests outside the established Baptist denomination. They were not satisfied with the second blessing of sanctification, the standard Holiness doctrine of the infusion of the Holy Ghost following conversion. Like other early Pentecostals, they sought a more profound spiritual awakening.

In 1906, along with several hundred other people of all races from across the globe, Mason traveled to a small chapel in south central Los Angeles. There he hoped to receive a spiritual baptism from William J. Seymour, a black Louisianan whose preaching of the physical manifestations of the blessing of the Holy Spirit attracted believers of all races. During a night of intense prayer, Mason felt himself levitated from his seat. A light as bright as the sun enveloped him, he said, and when he opened his mouth to praise God, "a flame touched my tongue which ran down in me. My language changed and no word could I speak in my own tongue."[2] His experience of speaking in tongues confirmed for him his deep spiritual transformation. Mason described the kind of conversion vision quests that slaves often narrated in the days of the brush harbor. In this way and many others, Mason and groups such as COGIC revitalized black religious expression stemming from slavery. They took slave religious practices and gave them the doctrinal twist of speaking in tongues as evidence of the baptism of the Holy Spirit.

Mason's followers believed that he was supernaturally gifted. Some members of his congregations might have detected in Mason's preaching elements of conjuring traditions. One admirer wrote that Mason would pick up a stick "shaped in the exact likeness of a snake . . . or a potato shaped in the exact likeness of the head and ears of a pig," and then use the objects to preach with an authority that mesmerized his many listeners.[3] He appeared to be receiving the word of God by "reading" these newfound sacred objects, like gold diggers used divining rods to search for hidden treasures. Some blacks criticized him for importing conjure into the churches. Mason responded by pointing to the scriptures and explaining that Jesus employed the same kinds of healings and spirit possessions that he himself preached.

Mason's preaching skill garnered considerable attention among black as well as white Pentecostals. His COGIC became a significant force in American religious life as Pentecostal churches took root throughout the nation, including in Northern cities. Mason himself did not migrate North

but ministered to a growing congregation of ordinary rural black Southerners who were moving to Southern cities such as Memphis, Tennessee, where
COGIC was based. Many rural African Americans who moved to Southern
cities used those initial relocations as a way station on their journey to larger
Northern cities, where economic opportunity and greater personal freedoms
beckoned.

The most dramatic development affecting African American religious life
through the first half of the twentieth century was the Great Migration. Between 1910 and 1930, an estimated 1.5 million blacks moved from the South
to the North, 400,000 of whom moved during and just after World War I.
This massive movement of Southern people continued throughout much of
the twentieth century. The movement took black leaders, secular and religious alike, by surprise, and despite white Southern efforts to employ black
Southern ministers to urge people to "stay home," the migration continued
unabated. One black Georgia Baptist estimated that 69,000 black residents
of the Peach State disappeared in 1922 alone. Given the centrality of Georgia to the history of black Baptists, the shift in the center of gravity was stun-
ning and alarming to many ministers, some of whom faced empty churches.

Many of the migrants moved to Chicago, where the black population
tripled from 30,000 in 1900 to 90,000 in 1920. By the 1930s, Chicago's
black population had reached nearly a quarter million. Other Northern
cities mirrored Chicago's black population explosion. In Detroit, the black
population rose from 6,000 in 1910 to 41,000 in 1920 and to 120,000 by the
end of the 1920s. The migrants to all these northern cities not only were
the downtrodden poor but also included future literary luminaries, such as
Langston Hughes, and leaders of alternative black religious movements, such
as George Baker (better known as "Father Divine").

The reasons for the migration were many. Racial oppression and terrible
living and working conditions pushed black people out of the South, while
economic incentives and cultural opportunities pulled African Americans to
the cities of the North. Migrants immediately interpreted the movement in
religious terms. They likened it to the Israelites escaping oppression in Egypt,
much like runaway slaves had narrated their experiences.

Despite this tremendous resettlement, the majority of African Americans
did *not* migrate to the North. On the eve of World War II, about three-
fourths of African Americans still lived in the South. But the very sizable minority who did move came so rapidly and in such numbers that they attracted
close attention. A nation accustomed over centuries to equate "black" with
"Southern" soon learned to associate "black" with "urban."

Everywhere migrants went, they sought places of religious refuge. In many Northern churches, revivals sprang up, as new migrants celebrated their arrival in the Promised Land. In some cases, when a sufficient number of migrants from a Southern town or church arrived in the North, they reestablished their congregations. At times, their pastors even followed them to the North.

As the Great Migration peaked during and after World War I, there was even more demand for faith-based institutions to minister to men and women who faced a daunting array of challenges in their new environments. In the North, the major black congregations, such as Chicago's Mt. Olivet Baptist Church, served as welcoming stations, relief agencies, and employment bureaus for migrants. They provided immediate help for people in distress and meeting places for groups such as the NAACP and the Urban League. Black ministers, moreover, served as political power brokers, promising to funnel votes to candidates who delivered the goods. And in some cases, they operated as employment referral agencies, particularly when clerics developed close relationships with leading industrial employers. In Detroit, for instance, the Ford Motor Company worked with black churches and ministers to find suitable employment candidates among Southern blacks who wanted to escape low pay and social restrictions in the South. The pastor of the city's largest black Baptist church developed a personal relationship with Henry Ford, which he used to secure jobs for migrants at Ford's auto plant. Migrants who landed these well-paying jobs thanked the minister by joining his rapidly growing church.

In addition to the explosion of black churches in Southern and Northern cities, alternative black religious movements provided new options for those who were dissatisfied with the historic black Christian institutions. Many of the new black religious movements were quasi-Christian offshoots, and some explicitly challenged Christian doctrine. The development of Noble Drew Ali's Moorish Science Temple, Elijah Muhammad's nascent Nation of Islam, Father Divine's Peace Mission, and Lucy Smith's All Nations Pentecostal Church illustrate the kind of religious challengers to mainstream black denominations that emerged in Northern cities. Each of these movements was the product of Southern migrants who left the established Christian churches and set off on their own religious quests.

Among the migrant-led religious groups was the Moorish Science Temple established by Noble Drew Ali. Ali was born Timothy Drew in North Carolina in 1886, but historians know little else about his early life. In the 1910s, Drew arrived in New Jersey and began to preach that black Americans were derived not from sub-Saharan Africans but from North African Moors who traditionally had practiced Islam. Thus, Ali claimed, blacks were Muslims in their religious ancestry and needed to recover their Islamic roots. Ali also drew heavily from Western mysticism as well as unorthodox works published by eccentric American preachers. According to Ali, Jesus journeyed through India, Palestine, and North Africa, where he soaked up the wisdom of the ancients, and Jesus himself, Ali explained, was of Middle Eastern and North African origin. Ali's book *The Seven Circle Koran* (1927) purported to tell of the history of the Moabites, the ancestors of black Americans. Ali saw Jesus as a nonwhite prophet who prepared the way for Islam.

In the 1920s, Ali established the Moorish Science Temple in Chicago. At its peak, it had about 30,000 members in congregations in Chicago, Detroit, and Philadelphia. He financed his temples through dues, as well as the sale of a variety of consumer products, which both celebrated and commodified the Moorish heritage. Moorish Science men and women, for example, adopted Arabic and Turkish dress codes, such as wearing fezzes (Turkish hats). Moreover, they added suffixes containing "Bey" or "El" to their names. In Ali's view, these names signified the two original tribes of Moorish Americans. By rejecting the term "Negro" and insisting that they had North African and Islamic roots, Moorish Science members also denied the basis for America's racial classifications. Ali's teachings appealed to many black migrants who sought a clearer sense of their heritage in Northern urban environments where many white immigrants claimed a particular ethnicity as central to their identity.

One of Ali's followers, and his self-proclaimed successor, was Wallace Fard Muhammad. After taking charge of one of the Moorish Science temples in Chicago in 1929, Muhammad clashed with other followers of Ali and developed the Lost-Found Nation of Islam, also known as the Nation of Islam. While Wallace Fard's origin and life are obscure, his successor, Elijah Muhammad, proclaimed that Fard was a redeemer of Islam, sent to save the black man who had been corrupted by the white man's Christian religion. Born in Georgia as Robert (or Elijah) Poole, Elijah Muhammad adopted some of the doctrines of the Moorish Science tradition, including arguments about the Moorish origins of black people and that Islam was the "true religion" of the black man. He drew on Islam and various other theological and folkloric sources to create an institutional structure for Black Muslims. Muhammad later became best known for his mentorship of Malcolm X, who emerged as the preeminent spokesman of the movement in the early 1960s.

Ali, Muhammad, and others were practitioners of "black ethnic" religions. That is, they created religions that imparted to black people a sense of being an ethnic people—not just black, but of identifiable and traceable ethnic origins. The dominant white culture, they charged, had deliberately lied about black history. Henry McNeal Turner had made that claim in the nineteenth century, and a variety of black theologians reiterated his ideas during the first half of the twentieth century. They traced an African lineage for Jesus and resurrected the black story of the Bible.

For instance, W. L. Hunter's *Jesus Christ Had Negro Blood in His Veins: The Wonder of the 20th Century* (1901) claimed to have discovered four black women in Christ's genealogy. Hunter further argued that Noah's son Ham and many other biblical figures had African origins. He concluded that if Jesus, who was partly of African descent, lived in the United States, he would have to be called a black man.

In similar fashion, James Morris Webb explained that Jesus was descended from Africans. A native of Tennessee, the entrepreneurial minister Webb sold his book *The Black Man, the Father of Civilization* (1908) through widely circulated black newspapers such as the *Chicago Defender*. Through those venues, his works reached black migrants in Northern cities. In a sermon he recorded to advertise his book, Webb detailed how God had used black men and women in major scriptural events. Like the nineteenth-century black authors of "race histories," he rescued the biblical figure of Ham from being the subject of a curse and claimed him as the biblical father of black men.

Marcus Garvey's associate George McGuire further developed these ideas in the African Orthodox Church, established in the United States in 1921. A black Episcopalian minister originally from the Caribbean, McGuire created this new church as an informal religious affiliate of Garvey's Universal Negro Improvement Association (UNIA). The UNIA emerged in the post–World War I era, when decolonization movements gained popularity worldwide. Garveyites loved elaborate ceremonies and rituals, and McGuire's African Orthodox Church provided those as well as a narrative explaining the African origins and culture of Jesus. McGuire and his followers proclaimed that *all* biblical figures were black, a belief shared by many followers of the black religious movements. McGuire preached at UNIA mass assemblies in New York and elsewhere. Garveyites distributed images of a black Jesus to reinforce their belief that Christianity was an African religion in its origin. The African Orthodox Church was not officially part of the UNIA but was a separate black Episcopalian movement that continued to exist as a small organization even after FBI authorities arrested Garvey and deported him. By the time of McGuire's death in 1934, his African Orthodox Church counted about 30,000 members nationally. It has maintained a presence in the United States to the present day.

While some African Americans created separate black churches, Father Divine did just the opposite. In 1919, he organized his "peace missions" in celebration of human universalism and in opposition to all racial and ethnic distinctions. Probably born in Maryland as George Baker, the man who later adopted the moniker of Father Divine claimed that he was divinely called to erase race distinctions. Unlike the black ethnic religions that had emerged during the Great Migration, he rejected race as a category defining humanity. Instead, Divine hoped to unify all nations in a new world creed that emphasized love, community, and positive thinking. During the Depression, Father Divine oversaw the establishment of more than 150 so-called peace missions throughout the country, a quarter of them in New York. Divine's services, which drew in both white and black followers, included lavish banquets that catered to hungry worshippers during the Depression. He used his white followers to help him purchase property and feed poorer parishioners. Eventually he became the largest property owner in Harlem. At his feasts, he preached his doctrine of universal brotherhood and New Thought, the idea that one's own thinking patterns could shape reality in desired directions.

Photo 5.1. Illustration of one of the peace missions of George Baker, also known as Father Divine, which spread through Northern cities during the Great Depression. Courtesy of the Library of Congress.

After the 1930s, the end of the Depression and scandals within various national peace mission outlets led to the decline of Father Divine's movement.

More than any of these so-called black sects or cults, informal storefront Christian congregations shaped the religious life of a generation of black migrants in the early and mid-twentieth century. The "storefront" churches were so named because leaders of these groups rented storefronts to use as gathering places on Sunday. Their leaders, who usually lacked formal ministerial training or qualifications, developed a reputation for charlatanism and for fooling deluded followers out of their money. A large number of these storefront churches were Sanctified congregations. Congregants practiced enthusiastic religious rituals that looked a lot like the ring shouts a previous generation of black religious leaders had condemned as primitive. Ministers in these usually small churches preached lengthy, fiery sermons, and black gospel music filled the air. The storefront churches appealed to many of the Southern migrants because it offered them religious services that resembled those of rural Southern churches, where congregants worried less about proper clothing or respectable behavior than about communing with the spirit. A number of black musicians, authors, and artists grew up in this tradition and later reflected about its meaning in their work. Black author James Baldwin, who was a teenage preacher in a Pentecostal congregation in New York in the 1930s, later wrote with understanding but also bitterness about the "wellspring of despair" he perceived lurking behind Pentecostal "joy," in his novel *Go Tell It on the Mountain*.

Chicago was home to tens of thousands of migrants and numerous storefront churches to service their spiritual needs. One of these migrants, Elder Lucy Smith (1866–1952), opened a storefront church in 1916 that quickly blossomed into the All Nations Pentecostal Church. Hailing from Georgia, Smith's career as a religious leader was a product of the Great Migration. Her Southern birth and background, experience as a faith healer who dispensed medical miracles to her supplicants, and prominence as a female leader of a body of churches that were predominantly female in membership all defined her religious work. Like many other congregations of that era, Smith's All Nations Pentecostal Church mixed celebratory worship with social services. Her congregants sang joyously and danced ecstatically on Sundays and sought faith healings during special Wednesday evening services. When the Depression started, she attracted thousands of parishioners by offering food and other practical assistance to needy migrants. Beginning in 1933, she drew an even larger following by broadcasting a popular radio show, *The Glorious Church of the Air*, which reached audiences through the Midwest and as far away as Mexico. Her broadcasts featured the early stars of black

Photo 5.2.   Portrait of Elder Lucy Smith of Chicago, founder of the All Nations Pente-costal Church and pioneering radio broadcaster during the Great Depression. Courtesy of the Library of Congress.

gospel music and a hundred-voice choir. Black Chicagoans listened intently, hoping to catch the newest gospel hits.

Not all African Americans were as appreciative of these kinds of storefront churches and religious entrepreneurs, however. Contemporary black scholars and observers celebrated the traditions and heritage of black churches, but they also condemned what they characterized as the hopelessness and fatalism of many black congregations of the era, including the numerous small urban congregations that sprang up to service the migrant communities in Northern cities. Church services, said a generation of black scholars and religious reformers, allowed for emotional enthusiasm that "compensated" for the lack of any real social power in this world. Black religion, they charged, had been depoliticized. Like Daniel Alexander Payne before them, these scholars, including the pioneering historian Carter Woodson and the black Baptist educator and author Benjamin Mays, insisted that black congregations needed well-educated ministers who could advocate for better education, improved agricultural practices, practical job skills, and moral propriety in family life. The black church, they said, needed less emotion and more organization.

The black intellectual and activist W. E. B. Du Bois was familiar with these criticisms. He had voiced many of them himself. Although Du Bois had celebrated expressions of black religious culture, such as the spirituals, he attacked the wasted potential of the church. What were churches doing to raise the ethical standards of their congregants? How were they helping church members to improve themselves and their world? "The flat answer is nothing, if not less than nothing," Du Bois responded. The church, he explained, depended upon a "body of dogma and fairy tale, fantastic fables of sin and salvation."[4] Although Du Bois severely criticized the black church for its failure to engage in practical action, he also understood the cultural power of black religious rituals. Furthermore, critics such as Du Bois and Woodson often overlooked the services many alternative and mainstream churches provided to help migrants adjust to urban life.

Despite the popularity of alternative movements, the majority of African American churchgoers remained members of Protestant congregations. Black Baptist churches in the North especially benefited from the migration, as they expanded rapidly and soon had an enormous numerical advantage over all other black churches, including African Methodist Episcopal denominations. For example, by 1927, Chicago boasted fifty-five African American Baptist churches, numbering some 66,000 congregants. Black Baptists were the largest Protestant group in the city, and in total numbers trailed only Catholics, who attracted large numbers of white immigrants.

Nonetheless, the rise of Holiness/Pentecostalism fundamentally shaped not just African American religious expression but all of America's popular culture through a generation of pioneering ministers, gospel music singers, and broadcasters. Holiness and Pentecostal congregations reintroduced the music of slaves, such as spirituals and ring shouts. They encouraged the heavily syncopated and melodically enthusiastic music that characterized religious as well as popular secular sound in the late twentieth century. After all, Pentecostals asked, why should the Devil have all the good music?

Among the two most important individuals who introduced Baptist and Pentecostal celebratory sounds to the larger world of music were black gospel singer Mahalia Jackson (1911–1972) and musical innovator Thomas Dorsey (1899–1993). Their lives personified nearly all the major developments in African American Christianity from the night of Jim Crow to the dawn of the civil rights era. Both grew up in the South as the talented children of Baptist ministers, and both migrated to Chicago, which became home to many of the most important black musical innovations. Jackson and Dorsey drew on the black musical tradition from slavery and from Sanctified churches. Pentecostal churches accepted and nurtured the music Dorsey, Jackson, and the early generation of black gospel pioneers originated.

Jackson grew up in New Orleans. Although born into a family of Baptists, her musical influences came from listening to the music of the Holiness and Pentecostal churches that dotted her home neighborhood. These churches were largely composed of working-class African Americans who were alienated by the perceived stuffiness of the middle-class worshippers who dominated the established churches. As middle-class African American churches in the North embraced the norms of respectability, alternative religious traditions—especially storefront and Sanctified congregations—attracted a growing number of working-class and migrant churchgoers who sought out places where spiritual enthusiasm could be expressed freely. They found vibrant religious experiences, feeling direct contact with the Holy Spirit, in the powerful music of their churches. Their religious expressive culture recaptured African rhythms and motions, spirit possessions, shouting, and "holy dancing." These, of course, were exactly the "primitive" religious practices that reformers such as Daniel Alexander Payne had tried to discourage. Lacking elaborate musical instruments, members of the Holiness and Pentecostal churches turned to drums, cymbals, tambourines, triangles, horns, stringed instruments, and washboards. They sang with fervor and "stomped their feet and sang with their whole bodies," Jackson remembered. Their "powerful beat" was something "we held on to from slavery days, and their music was so strong and expressive it used to bring the tears to my eyes."[5]

In 1927, Jackson moved to Chicago, where she met Thomas A. Dorsey. A native of Villa Rica, Georgia, and like Jackson the scion of a Baptist family, Dorsey made a name for himself as the pianist for the great blues singer Ma Rainey. Dorsey's years as a musician took him to juke joints, blues haunts, and Holiness storefront churches as well as some of Chicago's largest and most respectable Baptist congregations. Gradually, he married blues feeling to gospel message. Unlike many other evangelicals, he did not reject blues as inherently ungodly, for as a musical form, blues was just another way of crying out to God, of expressing deep individual pain: "When you cry out, that is something down there that should have come out a long time ago."[6]

In the late 1920s, Dorsey's wife suddenly passed away, and he experienced a spiritual crisis unlike any he had known. When he heard the voice of God comforting him, he wrote his best known song, "Precious Lord, Take My Hand," to express his anguish and spiritual hope.

> Precious Lord, take my hand
> Lead me on, let me stand
> I am tired, I am weak, I am worn
> Through the storm, through the night
> Lead me on to the light
> Take my hand, precious Lord, lead me home.[7]

The song remains a classic of twentieth-century American music.

Dorsey's blues-influenced gospel music fit Jackson's powerful voice perfectly. But when the gospel duo introduced black Baptist parishioners to their music, they met rejection in Chicago and other cities. "They were cold to it," Jackson later remembered of those congregations. "They didn't like the hand-clapping and the stomping and they said we were bringing jazz into the church and it wasn't dignified."[8] But a sympathetic black minister and funeral home director began sponsoring Jackson's musical singing tours and also introduced Jackson to the radio, which proved an ideal medium for her talent. Throughout the 1930s and into the early 1940s, she sang in churches, at funerals, and at other black religious gatherings, spreading the new black gospel music. Meanwhile, Dorsey created the National Convention of Gospel Choirs and Choruses, where composers, performers, and church choirs gathered yearly to premiere new works and stage "battles" between aspiring composers and performers. Playing the piano, Dorsey often accompanied Jackson at these meetings, spreading her fame in the black church world.

After World War II, Jackson's recording of black Baptist minister and gospel songwriter William Herbert Brewster's "Move On Up a Little Higher" became an immediate sensation, eventually selling over eight million copies. Thereafter, gospel quickly established itself as one of the building blocks of American popular music. Dorsey's musical and organizational genius, Jackson's voice, and the wealth of talent that congregated in the growing urban churches throughout the country made gospel an irresistible force in American musical culture.

The prevalence of Pentecostal performers among gospel blues singers and musicians, and in other popular musical derivatives such as soul music, suggests the vital importance of the Sanctified church in twentieth-century black religious culture. Pentecostalism was a vital force in providing an outlet for new blues-influenced gospel music that took the black church world by storm beginning in the 1930s. During the interwar years, gospel and blues music emerged virtually simultaneously, competing for the allegiance of souls. Secular and gospel bluesmen performed on the radio and recorded for major companies such as Columbia Records. The most successful of their records sold tens of thousands of copies to black consumers who were eager to listen to the newest talents emerging from their communities.

The black female gospel pioneer Sister Rosetta Tharpe (1915–1973) kept alive the exuberant tradition of black religious music and took it to the world of stage shows, nightclubs, television, and records from the late 1930s to the 1960s. Like Dorsey before her, Tharpe infused black Protestant music with blues sounds. Born in Arkansas to a family active in the Sanctified church, at the age of four she stood on boxes and belted out the song "Jesus on the Mainline," which kicked off her career as a performer. Tharpe brought the rhythmically expressive music of her upbringing to the world of street and revival tent singing. Later in her life, she took this music to the commercial marketplace of recordings, nightclubs, and appearances at venues such as Carnegie Hall in New York City. Like many lyrics during this era, which often incorporated contemporary technological innovations such as airplanes and telephones, "Jesus on the Mainline" drew a spiritual moral through the use of modern technology. Singers urged listeners who were "part of His Kingdom" to call up Jesus on the "main line"—the central line of a telephone system—and "tell him what you want."[9]

Like blues instrumentalists, Tharpe picked her guitar with rhythmic intensity that accompanied a large variety of religious lyrics drawn from all eras of American sacred music. Her guitar playing pioneered early rock-and-roll styles, but her lyrics focused on Christian themes. Tharpe's transition from the world of Sanctified religion to religious recordings blazed a trail that introduced black religious music to the mainstream. She was a popular star who sold tens of thousands of records and influenced the rising generation of rock and roll and soul singers. Even more so than Jackson, Tharpe married black religious music to secular instrumentation and styles. She was the gospel blueswoman par excellence, with Jesus on the main line to racial freedom and personal success.

During the interwar years, a number of musicians combined the blues and religious music. They imported blue notes and instrumental virtuosity into spiritual songs, bringing the skills of charismatic soloists into what had been highly communal forms of sacred expression. Some performers, chronicling their personal struggles in song, wavered between their roles as blues performers and preachers, unable to settle into either one. The Mississippi Delta guitarist and vocalist Eddie "Son" House, one of the most important pioneering bluesmen of the 1930s, serves as a good example of the performer conscious of his own sin as he was torn between his desire to preach the gospel and his enjoyment of worldly delights, including alcohol and sex. When he bowed to pray in his room, according to one of his autobiographical compositions, the blues came along and drove his spirit into exile. House's struggles mirrored those of a generation of talented men and women who saw the church as an avenue for respectability but could not reconcile themselves to the self-denial required of evangelicals. House took his 1930 recording of "Preachin the Blues," a riff from blueswoman Bessie Smith's 1927 version of the song, and added his own autobiographical struggles:

Oh I have religion this very day,
But the womens and whiskey, well they would not
    let me pray. . . .
Oh I'm going to preach these gospel blues and
    choose my seat and sit down.
When the spirit comes sisters, I want you to jump
    straight up and down.[10]

Rural Southern singers such as Son House served as folk theologians. They explored the nature of good and evil, commented on the nature of human relationships, and lampooned the hypocrisies of supposedly respectable community leaders. The preachers and the blues singers offered two apparently contradictory but ultimately complementary versions of black folk spirituality. This closely paralleled the relationship between conjure and African American Christianity. In both cases, blacks variously employed the formal doctrine learned in churches and the informal tales and songs coming from conjure men and blues music to cope with a harsh and racist world. The church offered salvation and communal support; the conjure men and blues musicians suggested that other spirits besides God and Jesus, or even just random evil, might be in control of the world.

The visionary experiences of converts and blues singers both drew from a long tradition of African American folklore that told stories of how spirits guided individual lives. Robert Johnson, the great Mississippi Delta bluesman of the 1930s, sung of how "me and the devil was walking side by side." He personified the blues as "walkin' like a man," and expected his spirit to be laid by a roadside. Johnson lyrically embellished his version of his mythical deal with the devil at the crossroads, where he claimed to have received special power to play a guitar like no other man.

Besides blues and gospel music, black churchgoers also bought recorded sermons of black ministerial superstars. In the 1920s and subsequent decades, talented ministers in both the South and North discovered the art of recording their sermons and then selling them to the black community. The Reverend J. M. Gates, pastor of a sizable black Baptist congregation in Atlanta, pioneered the tactic in the 1920s, cutting three-minute sermonic classics combined with musical accompaniment such as "Death's Black Train Is Coming." Gates sold tens of thousands of records, and his church prospered even during the years of the Great Depression.

But the champion of sermons distributed on "race records" was Clarence LaVaughan (C. L.) Franklin. Originally from Mississippi, Franklin became best known as the pastor of a large Baptist congregation in Detroit. He mastered "the whoop," the rhythmic and ecstatically poetic style of black sermon delivery. Like other ministers who left the South, Franklin linked the whoop to the contemporary African American experience. His rhythmic, poetic sermons excited enthusiastic congregants and carried evangelical messages of sin and salvation, but his pulpit oratory also spoke to issues of migration, segregation, discrimination, and hopes for upward mobility. During the 1940s and 1950s, millions of listeners tuned into the live radio broadcasts of Franklin's evening sermons. His radio fame propelled his recording career, as fans bought scores of 45s and LPs of his sermons. Franklin's daughter, Aretha, developed her sensational talents as a piano player and singer in her father's church. During the height of her fame as a popular artist, she continued to perform gospel to enthusiastic audiences, melding gospel and pop music in ways that deeply influenced all of American music.

Other musicians and arrangers also integrated folk and popular cultural styles into sacred lyrics. Memphis-based Baptist minister and songwriter W. Herbert Brewster elevated the religious pageant, a miniature sacred opera set on the church stage, to national renown. During his illustrious preaching career at the East Trigg Baptist Church in Memphis, he published more than two hundred religious songs. He set many of his most loved tunes in religious theatrical productions depicting black history, including "From Auction Block to Glory." As he later reminisced, life in Memphis was "pretty rough on the Black Church."[11] To bolster the spirits of his parishioners, he wrote the tune "Move On Up a Little Higher," which exhorted listeners to use the power of God to succeed in every field of endeavor.

In the first half of the twentieth century, the culture developed in black congregations such as the Reverend Brewster's church, which exemplified the twin poles of black Christian life: protest and praise. Black churches gradually embraced gospel music and other forms of black inspirational music, even though some congregations in mainstream black denominations continued to follow the norms of respectability defined by their nineteenth-century founders and leaders. Black middle-class critics disparaged churches that conducted "otherworldly" services focused on reaching a world of spiritual enchantment through enthusiastic singing and shouting. But even in Northern cities, where black Pentecostals especially encouraged passionate religious theater in their services, the churches generally also provided an important way station for their largely working-class congregants. Many of their congregations provided precisely the kind of social services black church reformers and critics demanded.

Black ministers and churchpeople also continued to provide political leadership, much as they had during Reconstruction. In 1937, the Reverend Adam Clayton Powell Jr. took the reins of the Abyssinian Baptist Church in Harlem. He used the church as a power base to promote boycotts and pickets of stores that discriminated against African Americans and also forced the city to hire more black city employees at nondiscriminatory, equal wages. At the end of World War II, Powell won election to the U.S. House of Representatives as the first African American congressman from New York. Powell served as an early example of a black Northern minister who used the influence of the black pulpit and votes of migrants to establish himself as a significant political figure in American history.

Powell was not alone in his blending of religion and politics. In 1947, at a Pentecostal congregation in Washington, D.C., longtime independent Sanctified minister Smallwood Williams held a celebratory funeral for Mississippi's recently deceased racist Senator Theodore Bilbo. More than two thousand worshippers turned out at Smallwood's congregation to give the former lawmaker his proper wake. Williams felt called as a black minister to preach about Bilbo's death because it was African Americans who had lived under the senator's odious racial views. Williams claimed that, a year prior to Bilbo's death, he had prophesied his passing, and that the end of the senator's infamous career was an answer to his prayer: "Just as God dramatically removed Mr. Bilbo from the political scene, he is able to erase Bilbo-ism, and all that Bilbo stood for, from our country and from the face of the earth."[12]

Because of their faith in the imminence of Christ's return, Pentecostals developed a reputation, sometimes well deserved, for staying out of politics. Yet Williams's funeral services for Bilbo mixed secular and spiritual salvation. Other black preachers, combining praise and protest, also used the pulpit to claim citizenship rights. Not surprisingly, the black freedom struggle of the post–World War II era drew heavily on black churches for its leadership, and black churchpeople provided many of the shock troops who manned the front lines of the battle for the soul of America.

∼

CHAPTER SIX

Freedom's Main Line

African American Christianity, Civil Rights, and Religious Pluralism

Black Christians empowered the post–World War II civil rights movement. Churches served as meeting places for civil rights activities. A fundamentally Protestant imagery of Exodus, redemption, and salvation inspired the revivalistic fervor of the movement. Black Protestant thinkers and activists also deftly combined the social gospel and black church traditions, infused with notions of active resistance to social evil. They sought to harness the means of nonviolent civil disobedience toward achieving the end of biblical and racial justice in America.

At the same time, movement activists held a conflicted relationship with churches. Whether because of indifference, fear, theological conservatism, or white coercion, many congregations and denominational institutions avoided involvement. Civil rights organizers gave them plenty of heat for their apparent apathy. Moreover, the Christian-inspired movement's emphasis on nonviolently confronting the immorality of segregation fell short when forced to address more structurally ingrained inequalities in American society. To those stuck in poverty, the right to eat a hamburger at a lunch counter was not particularly meaningful. They needed economic resources more than maxims about moral justice.

As the 1960s progressed, rhetorically radical leaders emerged who often distrusted black Christian institutions, seeing them as too complicit with larger power structures. Others simply condemned Christianity as the "white man's religion." The Reverend Martin Luther King Jr. and his followers appealed to a nation's sense of Christian morality. Critics of King questioned whether Christian morality and nonviolence could address basic questions of power and economic justice.

Nonetheless, it is impossible to conceive of the civil rights movement without placing black Christianity at its center, for it empowered the rank and file who made the movement *move*. And when it moved, it demolished the system of legal segregation. Further, black religious music, adapted as freedom songs, inspired a movement culture that transformed a nation. The history of black Christianity in America made that transformation possible, even as it frustrated some of the deeper-rooted aims of some activists who sought to address issues of income and wealth inequality as much as the formal legal structures of "civil rights."

In the years since the civil rights movement, the black church has become even more diverse, with the arrival of new black immigrants (from African nations, the Caribbean, and elsewhere) in the United States and the growth of black megachurches outside of mainstream denominations. Yet many of the debates within black churches still reflect the paradoxes that have existed throughout the history of African American Christianity. Black churches continue to sustain their members spiritually against racism even as they struggle to maintain their relevance to younger people who enjoy a range of spiritual options much greater than that of their forebears.

The civil rights movement had legislative aims. To that extent, it was a political movement. But more than that, it was a religious crusade sustained by Christian imagery and revivalist fervor. It arose out of a religious culture steeped in the rituals of mass meetings, revivalistic preaching, and sacred singing. Black Christians in the movement espoused a vision of interracialism encapsulated in the idea of the beloved community, the idea that Christian nonviolent resistance to social evil could overpower social injustice and create human relations based on love and justice.

Many civil rights leaders such as black Methodist missionary James Lawson, a mentor to King, emerged from Protestant backgrounds and developed ideas of pacifism and nonviolent civil disobedience during the 1940s and 1950s. They borrowed from the ideas of Richard Gregg, a former Quaker and pacifist. Gregg's work *The Power of Non-Violence* (1934) taught a rising generation in the 1940s and 1950s about the "moral ju-jitsu" of nonviolence, meaning the way nonviolent civil disobedience could tie up an oppressor with the bonds of his own words. It was, he said, a force powerful enough to defeat the oppressor without needing to land a physical blow. They also took inspiration from the writings and actions of Indian nationalist Mohandas Gandhi, who staged a nonviolent revolution that overthrew the British colonial regime in India in 1947. Lawson and others observed nonviolence in action firsthand during visits to India after World War II. They introduced Gregg's message and Gandhian tactics of nonviolence as keys to overturning the American system of segregation.

In the postwar years, as activists embraced nonviolence as articulated by Gregg and others, black theologians explored the way Christianity in America historically had supported white supremacy. For example, Howard Thurman, a former Baptist turned Unitarian/Humanist who also mentored King and numerous other black religious and civil rights leaders, provided one influential explanation for Christianity's appeal to the oppressed in *Jesus and the Disinherited* (1947). In this work, he explained how segregation damaged the psyche of black Americans. The accepted behavior patterns of the South, he suggested, assumed "segregation to be normal—if normal, then correct; if correct, then moral; if moral, then religious."[1]

Like Henry McNeal Turner before him, Thurman critiqued the ways in which the white God of American Christian culture undermined black aspirations. Drawing on the exploration of white Christian symbolism pioneered by Turner, Thurman wrote that the American God "for all practical purposes" was "imaged as an elderly, benign white man, seated on a white throne, with bright, white light emanating from his countenance."[2] The devil's messengers, of course, were black. This religious color hierarchy symbolized the plight of those who lacked social status or protection. Historically, he concluded, religion in America had sanctioned and given divine approval to segregation. The implication was that if white Americans practiced true Christianity, they would not support segregation. Moreover, African Americans could draw strength from Christianity to resist discrimination. Thurman's work deeply influenced King and other civil rights leaders of the 1950s and 1960s as they mounted a campaign to redeem the soul of America.

In the 1950s, Lawson led an interracial group of idealists to Montgomery, Alabama, seeking to persuade King to adopt the philosophy of nonviolence. Initially, King was reluctant to do so. Every man in town owned a gun, he pointed out, and he should, too, since his family might be threatened. However, eventually he gave up his firearms and accepted nonviolence not just as a useful strategy for a political cause but as a way of life that demanded religious devotion.

Sitting in his kitchen during the evening of January 27, 1956, not yet two months into the 381-day-long Montgomery bus boycott, King was overcome with a vision. Discouraged by constant threats and setbacks, he pondered giving up leadership of the nascent movement, which was to consume the rest of his life. Early negotiations with the city of Montgomery had soured, and he increasingly feared for the safety of his family. As King later acknowledged, he had grown up in a religious family and the church was real to him, but he was a "cultural Christian"; he had inherited religious beliefs from family upbringing rather than personal experience. Having withstood dozens of threatening phone calls, King felt depleted by that January evening.

At midnight, the phone rang again: "Nigger, we are tired of you and your mess now, and if you aren't out of this town in three days, we're going to blow your brains out and blow up your house." At this moment, King called Jesus on the main line and discovered that "I had to know God for myself. And I bowed down over that cup of coffee. . . . I prayed out loud that night. I said, 'Lord, I'm down here trying to do what's right. I think I'm right. I think the cause that we represent is right. But Lord, I must confess that I'm weak now. I'm faltering. I'm losing my courage. And I can't let the people see me like this because if they see me weak and losing my courage, they will begin to get weak.'"[3] That night, he heard the voice of the divine spirit, urging him to keep fighting. Days later, when local thugs tried to destroy his home, King calmed an angry crowd with words of nonviolence. He felt strength for the battle to come as well as "strength to love."[4]

In his addresses and writings, Martin Luther King Jr. explained the relationship among Jesus Christ, freedom, and active nonviolent resistance to injustice. While Jesus taught the spirit, he said, Gandhi had captured the technique of putting the spirit into action. Indeed, Gandhi took the love of Jesus and distilled it into a great social force that transformed colonial subjects of the British Empire into independent citizens of India. From his study of black church history and the social gospel, King understood that Christianity could be a powerful tool for social reform. From his study of Gandhi, King had learned that nonviolence could be used as an effective tool to change society. King soon came to see that the "Christian doctrine of love operating through the Gandhian method of nonviolence was one of the most potent weapons available" in the black struggle for freedom.[5]

The young minister took those messages to his congregants and fellow bus boycotters in Montgomery. At the beginning of the boycott in December 1955, he told a cheering crowd, "If we are wrong, God Almighty is wrong. If we are wrong, Jesus of Nazareth was merely a utopian dreamer and never came down to earth. If we are wrong, justice is a lie."[6]

King and the male leaders of the Southern Christian Leadership Conference, the civil rights organization that emerged in 1957 after the Montgomery bus boycott as the primary instrument of King's civil rights leadership, garnered much of the media attention. However, behind their work lay the everyday efforts of generations of black churchwomen. Men led the civil rights movement in public, but women organized it behind the scenes. Black Christianity empowered and spiritually sustained them.

In Montgomery, JoAnn Gibson Robinson, an English professor at a local black college and loyal churchwoman, mapped out the day-to-day details of the bus boycott, including figuring out a transportation system to get those who had formerly taken the bus to places of employment. The organizational efforts of black Christian women such as Robinson arose from applying their spiritual beliefs to the social realm. The moment of freedom for black Mississippian Bee Jenkins came when facing down a group of state troopers. Forced to decide whether to join a civil rights march or stand back out of fear, she walked out of her house, prayed to God, and started marching. Despite her feeling that somebody would be killed, she knew "I had somebody there who was on my side. And that was Jesus; he was able to take care of me. That who I can depend on and put my trust in."[7] Jenkins became a key civil rights activist and organizer in Mississippi, the most violent and oppressive state in enforcing white supremacy. Another black Mississippian, Susie Morgan, joined the freedom movement one Sunday, recalling later that "something hit me like a new religion."[8]

The new religion was catching, and it led to the formation of the Student Nonviolent Coordinating Committee (SNCC). In the spring of 1960, in the wake of the widespread student sit-in movements to desegregate lunch counters, longtime activist Ella Baker convened a group of students at her alma mater Shaw College, a black Baptist institution in Raleigh, North Carolina. Baker's career as an agitator began in the 1920s when she protested overly restrictive dress codes at Shaw. The students at the 1960 meeting intended to form a youth wing of the Southern Christian Leadership Conference (SCLC), but Baker urged the students not to be co-opted by adults. She wanted them to push the movement forward in dramatic new directions. The students agreed with her logic and formed SNCC. The committee's initial goal was to organize and support the students who were staging nonviolent sit-ins throughout the South. The students applied the moral ju-jitsu of Christian and Gandhian nonviolence to fight white supremacy. Many in SNCC, who paid a heavy physical and psychological price for their involvement, conceived of their sacrifice in religious terms.

While Baker was personally a religious skeptic, ironically her words and example inspired a youth movement for civil rights that drew heavily from spiritual teachings. SNCC's language was deeply theological. In its original manifesto, written in 1960 by James Lawson, SNCC declared that it sought a "social order of justice permeated by love." Through disciplined nonviolence, the manifesto continued,

> courage displaces fear; love transforms hate. Acceptance dissipates prejudice; hope ends despair. Peace dominates war; faith reconciles doubt. Mutual regard cancels enmity. Justice for all overthrows injustice. The redemptive community supersedes systems of gross social immorality.[9]

The group's real impulse went beyond integration, one participant explained, for activists sought to achieve the "beloved community."[10] Martin Luther King employed that term in some of the founding documents of the SCLC, but SNCC activists took the phrase as a way of life. They saw civil rights as a means not only to achieve desegregation and political power but also to reclaim "personhood." They sought to undermine the fear that underlay the segregationist system, restore a sense of spiritual dignity to an oppressed people, and allow the oppressed to show love to their oppressors.

During the civil rights years, spiritual courage for the rank-and-file protestors often came from singing freedom songs. These were tunes adapted from traditional black religious music and set to new lyrics reflecting the experiences of the civil rights struggle. As was true throughout the history of black Christianity, music inspired new visions of freedom. Movement activists converted widely known spirituals, hymns, church anthems, and popular songs into versions of civil rights manifestos. Sometimes older traditional songs were infused with lyrics appropriate to the civil rights struggle. In other cases, song leaders playfully took up popular tunes from the era and transformed them into energizing freedom songs. For example, the calypso-tinged line "Daylight come and I wan' go home" in "Day-O," or the "Banana Boat Song," became "Freedom's coming, and it won't be long." The freedom songs remain some of the most politically potent ritual music in American history. They expressed the latent power contained in the spirituals and gospel music.

Freedom songs arose in a variety of ritual contexts. They rang out at the beginning and end of mass meetings, as crowds energized themselves with music. Traditional Protestant hymns familiar especially to older churchpeople often began the mass meetings. Newer lyrics, sometimes composed on the spot in specific response to frightening situations and then disseminated through word of mouth and traveling troubadours, increasingly took their place as the movement progressed. Participants propelled the music forward with singing, shouting, bodily movement, and rhythmic accompaniment of spirited hand clapping and foot stomping, all of which were legacies from the rituals of the antebellum era.

Freedom songs soothed congregants surrounded by hostile whites and fortified marchers as they tramped down streets. Freedom music gave energy to the black working men and women who stayed off the buses in Montgomery and sustained thousands of black citizens who faced incarceration for trying to exercise their constitutional rights. As protestors filled penitentiaries throughout the South, they sang to each other and to the sheriffs arresting them, following the example of the Apostle Paul and his traveling evangelist companion Silas in the New Testament. Dozens of new verses spontaneously arose in jail cells, during pickets, and in boycott lines.

In the spring of 1961, freedom songs accompanied an interracial group of thirteen members of the Congress of Racial Equality (CORE) as they set out on a fateful Greyhound bus trip from Washington, D.C., to New Orleans. As these "freedom riders" traveled the road to Mississippi, they struck up a renewed version of "Hallelujah, I'm a-Traveling," a song used in black protest movements since the 1940s:

> I'm paying my fare on the Greyhound bus lines
> I'm riding the front seat to Jackson this time
> Hallelujah, I'm a-traveling,
> Hallelujah, ain't it fine,
> Hallelujah, I'm a-traveling,
> Down freedom's main line.

When the riders arrived in Jackson, Mississippi, state authorities, who had cut a deal with the Kennedy administration, escorted them to jail. In some cases, this meant detention at Parchman Farm, a gigantic convict labor camp in the Mississippi Delta. The protestors sang throughout the evenings, and true to form, the jail authorities tried to stop them. When these jailed activists took up the old gospel song "I Woke Up This Morning with My Mind Stayed on Jesus," they changed the lyrics to "Woke up this morning with my mind (my mind it was) stayed on freedom." While in jail, one activist invented new verses such as "Ain't no harm in keep'n' your mind, in keepin' it stayed on freedom," and "Singin' and prayin' with my mind / My mind it was stayed on freedom."[11]

Freedom songs empowered civil rights protestors in many campaigns after the freedom rides. During SNCC's 1962 campaign to desegregate the city of Albany, in southwest Georgia, songleader Bernice Johnson Reagon and other churchpeople united the black citizens with song at the mass meetings held to discuss the progress of the campaign. Reagon remembered the power of singing during those meetings: "When we did those marches and went to jail, we expanded the space we could operate in, and that was echoed in the singing. It was a bigger, more powerful singing." At one meeting in Albany, Reagon struck up the song "Over My Head I See Trouble in the Air," but spontaneously substituted "freedom" for "trouble." She immediately took personal possession of the songs and felt a palpable sense of freedom. "What I can remember," she later said, "is being very alive and very clear, the clearest I've ever been in my life. I knew that every minute, I was doing what I was supposed to do."[12] She knew God was on her side, and at her side.

Early victories for the nonviolent movement proved hard to sustain in the brutally violent Deep South, and movement activists grew discouraged. Nevertheless, they heeded the call of a black Baptist minister from Birmingham, Alabama, named Fred Shuttlesworth, who had endured years of bombings, beatings, and racial harassment from Klansmen and policemen. The city's de facto boss was police chief Theophilus Eugene "Bull" Connor, who had been involved in repressing black city residents since the 1930s and would soon unleash the fire hoses and police dogs on peaceful protestors in Birmingham. Shuttlesworth encouraged King and the SCLC to put their faith in the dream of a beloved community to the test in his tough, industrial city.

King and the SCLC began to organize there early in 1963. That spring, the movement reached an impasse when boycotts failed to open up city stores. In April, King was arrested, and while he was in jail, eight local white "moderate" clergymen took out an advertisement in a local newspaper suggesting that the protests were "ill-timed." The authors reasoned that an imminent change of city government would soon take power away from Connor and place it in the hands of a more reasonable city council. King issued a masterful response in his "Letter from a Birmingham Jail," now a modern American literary classic. Noting that he had never been engaged in a "well-timed" campaign, King's letter explained the philosophy and methods of nonviolent civil disobedience. He defended civil rights leaders from charges of extremism by saying that Jesus was an "extremist for love." King's letter called on civil rights protestors to be "extremists for justice." Resistance to unjust laws, he insisted, was a Christian duty, for God called believers first and foremost to obey their higher calling as Christians committed to creating a just social order.

In Birmingham in 1963, freedom songs once again filled the air and gave people strength to continue their fight. As support from adults waned during the difficult campaign, organizers recruited hundreds of black schoolchildren to fill up the city's jails, creating a renewed crisis that forced the city to the negotiating table. The children sang "I'm on my way, to freedom land / Oh, yes, I'm on my way," while lining up to be carted off in police wagons:

> If my mother don't go, I'll go anyhow [repeated three times]
> Oh yes, Oh Lord, I'm on my way
> I'm on my way, to freedom land.

A few months later, on August 28, 1963, King delivered his most famous address. "I have a dream," he told a crowd of about a quarter of a million people gathered at the Lincoln Memorial in Washington, D.C. When King's speech culminated with "Thank God Almighty, we are free at last," he articulated a dream deeply rooted in African American religious history and culture. It was not yet a moment of fulfillment, as King searingly noted in his address, for in many places the bell of freedom had yet to toll.

At the mass march in Washington, the anthem of the freedom struggle and the best known of the freedom songs, "We Shall Overcome," captured the movement's religious, interracial, and nonviolent emphasis. The song dated from the antebellum era. South Carolina slaves sang a tune entitled "I'll Be Alright," which soon entered the black sacred music repertoire. In the early twentieth century, the pioneering gospel songwriter Charles Albert Tindley composed the hymn "I'll Overcome Someday," which drew from the traditional tune "I'll Be Alright." Another version, with the words "I Will Overcome," emerged from black workers picketing in Charleston, South Carolina, in the 1940s. During that decade, black tobacco workers and labor organizers picked up the tune and its compelling lyrics. In the 1950s, folksinger Pete Seeger introduced it to activists at the Highlander Folk School in Tennessee, an interracial training ground for civil rights workers. At Highlander, the tune became identified with the freedom struggle. Later in the 1960s, activists replaced the final words "some day" with the more insistent "today." New verses arose spontaneously, addressing the needs of specific situations, as when Birmingham residents in 1963 sang:

> We shall go to jail, we shall go to jail
> We shall go to jail, today.

Through song, protestors found both Jesus and freedom on their main line.

Black religious music also shaped popular music in the 1960s, and popular musicians joined their voices to the movement. An abundance of talented performers who had been honed in the gospel music world made recordings that became part of the freedom music of the era. Among them was Sam

Cooke, who was a member of the Church of Christ, Holiness, founded by the Mississippi black Holiness pioneer Charles Price Jones. As a teenager, Cooke sang in the Highway QCs, a group that served as a farm team for major black gospel groups. Later he became a lead singer for the Soul Stirrers. In the 1950s, he struck out on his own and became the famous crooner of doo-wop and soul classics, but in his classic "Change Gonna Come," he sang for a civil rights generation eager for change that had been "a long, long time coming."

Curtis Mayfield provides another example of the influence of the "beat" of the Sanctified church and the politicization of lyrics handed down in folk and commercial traditions. In his anthem "People Get Ready," written to celebrate the 1963 March on Washington, he employed gospel quartet harmonies to accentuate the image of the train taking people to freedom:

> People get ready, there's a train a-comin'
> You don't need no baggage, just get on board
> All you need is faith, to hear the diesels hummin'
> Don't need no ticket, just thank the Lord.[13]

Freedom songs and soul gospel classics such as "People Get Ready" empowered student activists. Many of them affiliated with the Student Nonviolent Coordinating Committee, which propelled civil rights struggles in some of the darkest corners of the South through the 1960s.

Meanwhile, segregationists defending their own sacred "Southern way of life" aggressively battled civil rights protestors. Violent racist groups, many drawing members from white churches, countered civil rights activists, whom they derided as "outside agitators." Ku Klux Klan leaders in Mississippi intoned that the white resistance movement should be full of Christian reverence, while more "respectable" ministers in the state's largest white churches simply defended the "purity" of the church against the outside agitators. Their words signaled that segregationists would not go down without a fight, fueled by their own religious visions of the "purity" of the white race and the sanctity of Southern social institutions. The drama of the civil rights movement came in part because of this conflict of religious visions.

In Birmingham, King's dream turned into a nightmare a little over two weeks after the March on Washington. On September 15, a group of nearly thirty black children sat in a basement of the 16th Street Baptist Church, awaiting the closing prayers of a sermon entitled "The Love That Forgives." Upstairs, adult black congregants gathered for the upcoming service. They had been through tumultuous times during the Birmingham campaign. And what they were about to see confirmed the worst fears of many about the consequences of nonviolence. The 16th Street Baptist Church in Birmingham was at the forefront of the nationally televised civil rights struggles, which included protestors' encounters with snarling dogs and pulsating fire hoses that shot streams of water powerful enough to strip the bark off trees. By opening their church to civil rights protestors, these black Baptists had made their sanctuary a target of white terrorists.

The evening before the September 15 Sunday morning service, a group of Klansmen placed more than a hundred sticks of dynamite outside the church building, ready to explode. At about 10:20 a.m., during Sunday worship, the explosives detonated, killing four girls. The impact of the blast destroyed the church's rear wall and steps of the structure and blew out all but one of the stained-glass windows. The sole surviving window frame featured a stained glass rendering of Jesus leading the children, an image the more poignant since that Sunday had been Youth Day at the church. While the frame and structure of the window miraculously survived, the window itself sustained powerful symbolic damage: the face of Jesus had been blown off. In a gruesome parallel, one of the girls had been decapitated by bricks that fell into the basement room where the children had been dressing for the upcoming service.

When King delivered his eulogy for the murdered children late that month, he attempted to fathom this grotesque act. He explained again how the girls' "unmerited suffering" would be "redemptive." The children were not only the "martyred heroines of a holy crusade for freedom and human dignity," King insisted, but also stirred the conscience of "every minister of the gospel who has remained silent behind the safe security of stained-glass windows."[14] The bombing condemned apathetic or fearful black Southerners who had stayed on the sidelines during the freedom struggle. Comprehending the death of the four girls meant understanding the entire system that had produced those who had murdered them and renewing the commitment to make the American dream real for those who had never experienced it.

In the mid-1960s, while student activists pressed for the realization of King's dream, the white Mississippi establishment resisted its fulfillment. In 1964, SNCC organized a group of about eight hundred white and black student volunteers from all over the country to participate in "Freedom Summer." They came to Mississippi intending to register black voters, run "freedom schools," and generally undermine the intractable white establishment of the Magnolia State. When they could, the activists worked in cooperation with a small but determined number of black churches to make local contacts and hold meetings.

In June, a member of a Methodist church located near the town of Philadelphia, Mississippi, arranged for three civil rights workers—Michael Schwerner, Andrew Goodman, and James Chaney—to speak to his congregation
about Freedom Summer. The congregation also agreed to host a freedom
school. The Ku Klux Klan, acting on information from helpful local white officials, fought back immediately. A group of Klansmen assaulted members of
the congregation and later burned down the church building. Klansmen ab-
ducted and murdered the three SNCC workers, burying them in an earthen
dam in a remote area of the county. The victims were discovered weeks later,
when national public pressure compelled an FBI investigation.

Black Mississippians learned firsthand that white state and federal authorities often ignored or downplayed the violence directed against them.
Even churches that had closed their doors to civil rights meetings had been
bombed, showing the mistake of assuming that avoiding civil rights involvement would provide protection from white supremacist attacks. In midsum-
mer of 1964, for example, three black churches burned in Pike and Amite
counties in Mississippi, despite the fact that the parishioners in these congregations had not been politically active. Many churches closed themselves off,
and only a few residents risked putting themselves on the front lines.

During and after Freedom Summer, numerous violent attacks on ministers
and churches in McComb, Mississippi, led to the city's reputation as the
"bombing capital of the world." On September 7, 1964, in McComb, Klansmen bombed the homes of a black minister and school principal, neither of
whom had been noted for their involvement in civil rights protests. That
same month, arsonists torched another Baptist congregation in town after
the church transgressed sacred Southern mores by loaning its mimeograph
machine to voter registration activists. "God damn, how much blood do
they want," a SNCC worker asked upon surveying the ruins of that wrecked
church.[15]

Despite increased violence, or perhaps because of it, Freedom Summer
and the religiously inspired spirit of numerous black activists in Mississippi
revived the struggling movement, as local youth shamed established religious
leaders into involvement. Even if ministers were recalcitrant, deacons and
parishioners could be educated and motivated. Activist Amzie Moore chided
one black minister for preaching holiness and claiming that God could do
anything while not really believing that God could keep the white man
off him. "I used to tell them that [the] white man was their God," Moore
remembered.[16] If God was all-powerful and on their side, then He could
provide for them even in the face of violent resistance, Moore told black
church members. A growing number of parishioners agreed with Moore and

publicly attacked the timidity of their religious leaders. Emboldened by their faith, they found the courage to stand up against a white supremacist system that had oppressed them.

Grassroots organization depended on black Southerners whose deep religious faith emboldened them to action. In the mid-1960s, Rev. J. J. Russell of Holmes County, Mississippi, opened his church to movement meetings, despite threats of white attacks. For his own protection, Russell turned off his car lights when driving and used special signals to indicate his arrival home. In 1964, local whites burned one of his churches and shot the windows out of other congregations in the county. Despite the harassment, Russell never carried a gun. Instead, he trusted in his personal Bible as his spiritual weapon. Several times, when pulled over by police, he was taken to the courthouse, where he brandished his Bible and challenged the authorities with his scriptural knowledge. After that, he found that the local police stopped arresting him.

SNCC activists depended on "local people" such as Russell to put their bodies on the line and challenge the deeply rooted system of racial injustice in Mississippi. Unita Blackwell, a poor woman from Mayersville, Mississippi, was teaching Sunday school in 1964 when SNCC activists called on her. Student organizers asked her about registering to vote, and she volunteered to come to the courthouse. Some of the deacons in her church, fearing the consequences of her action, tried to convince her to stay away from the students. Blackwell persevered, however, and quoted the Bible, where she found that "all men were created equal and I didn't understand that how come that this was my constitutional right and I couldn't have that. I got mad and I was determined that I wasn't gonna take no more."[17] Like many other activists, Blackwell used the language of evangelicalism and infused Christianity into the tenets of the U.S. Constitution.

Mississippi's activists articulated a liberation theology forged not by formal study but by a deep sense of Christian freedom. No one better exemplified the Christian civil rights struggle than Fannie Lou Hamer. As an ill-educated rural sharecropper, she hardly had spoken in public prior to 1962, but in later years she routinely addressed thousands, including her nationally televised address during the Democratic National Convention of 1964. Only God could have given her the strength to do that, she said. She deployed her biblical knowledge in public rebukes of the timid, insisting that God would honor those who took a stand and registered to vote. Christ would side with the sharecroppers in Mississippi during their struggle. Answering the inevitable charges that civil rights workers were agitators and communists, she retorted, "If Christ were here today, he would be branded a radical, a militant, and would probably be branded as 'red.'" Christ was a "revolutionary person, out there where it was happening. That's what God is all about, and that's where I get my strength." Summing up her life's work, she explained, "We can't separate Christ from freedom, and freedom from Christ."[18] This also summarized the philosophy of generations of churchpeople before her, including Richard Allen, Sojourner Truth, Henry McNeal Turner, Mahalia Jackson, as well as the leaders of the contemporary civil rights movement.

Extraordinarily brave individuals such as Hamer kept their faith in nonviolence and the realization of the beloved community, but daily doses of harassment and violence wore down many activists. The Birmingham bombing, the murder of the SNCC workers in 1964, and the beatings and killings that accompanied all phases of the movement took their toll. SNCC members pondered painful questions. Could the sacrifice be justified? Was it moral to ask student activists or local black residents to risk their lives, jobs, homes, and churches in pursuit of equality? For many in the movement, the beatings in 1965 of former Baptist seminary student John Lewis and scores of others who attempted to march across the Edmund Pettis Bridge in Selma, Alabama, marked the end for the philosophy of nonviolence. The philosophy had been effective, but costly. And those costs made many deeply question the religious impulse that lay behind the movement's nonviolent emphases. Starting about 1965, a new generation of leaders emerged who rejected the philosophy of nonviolent civil disobedience and, in some cases, black Christianity itself. Some activists toted guns along with their Bibles. As one black Mississippian told a SNCC worker, "I believe in the Bible, the Lord, and my 30-30."[19]

Anne Moody's story in *Coming of Age in Mississippi* (1968) suggests the kinds of inner turmoil many black Southern Christians felt during this tumultuous time. Moody grew up a working-class churchgoing girl in a small Mississippi town. While attending a black college in Jackson, Mississippi, in the early 1960s, she joined the civil rights movement. Like many of her generation, the movement became her church and her religion, and she deified its heroes. She participated in "pray-ins" in Jackson, organized by integrated student groups that tried to attend white churches to dramatize segregation in God's house. Like Richard Allen and the black Methodists in Philadelphia experienced in the 1790s, white church officials who were determined to prevent their prayers dragged them away.

At civil rights meetings, Moody joined in freedom songs. But she began to wonder about their efficacy. Older black congregants at meetings sang freedom songs passionately, much as slaves had in the antebellum era. But when she looked at the expressions on their faces, she got cold chills. These older congregants, she was convinced, had given up struggling for a better life on earth. They were yearning for heaven, where their troubles would finally be over. Many younger people, by contrast, believed in their power to revolutionize a system that had defeated their elders. They sang freedom songs with a faith that they could overcome oppression and injustice.

Moody knew about a merciful God but had seen that philosophy turned against black Southerners. They had been humble Christians, yet had suffered for their faith and patience, while those who committed violence against them escaped any retribution. After the Birmingham bombing, she queried God about race and injustice: "Are you going to forgive their killers? You not gonna answer me, God, hmm?" For Moody, nonviolence had become too passive. It seemed to accept the violence of white supremacists and urged protestors simply to endure them. "If you don't believe that," she wrote to God, "then I know you must be white, too. And if I ever find out that you are white, then I'm through with you. And if I find out you are black, I'll try my best to kill you when I get to heaven."[20] Disillusioned by her experience, Moody left the movement. SNCC itself began to disintegrate after about 1965, a victim of deep divisions within it concerning the efficacy of nonviolence and the possibility of realizing the American dream in what many came to perceive as an American nightmare. The practice of Christian nonviolence imposed heavy costs on many who were least able to pay it.

While not all black Christians lost their faith in the revolutionary nature of Christ, many perceived the unbearable whiteness of American Christianity as too great to overcome. In 1969, nine years after the original drafting of SNCC's manifesto, former SNCC member James Forman ascended the pulpit of New York City's famous Riverside Church, a premier liberal Protestant congregation, and issued his "Black Manifesto." Calling for 500 million dollars in reparations for black people—or, as Forman put it with sarcastic venom, "$15 per nigger"—the manifesto demanded the same patience and understanding from whites that they historically had demanded of blacks. Overcoming a passive Christianity and forcibly demanding their rights even from the pulpits of the wealthiest churches would emancipate black people. Many of them had accepted Christianity and not questioned its complicity in creating America's racial order, but black power theology could show them how the racist hypocrisy of the white Christian church had worked as part of a system that abused African Americans.

Whereas Howard Thurman's generation would have preferred to deracialize Christ, to remove his whiteness but not replace it with blackness, the theological generation of the 1960s perceived imparting blackness (whether physically or metaphorically) on God or Jesus as a necessary instrument of liberation. In 1967, civil rights activist and close King associate Vincent Harding argued, in the liberal Protestant mouthpiece magazine *Christian Century*, that black theology had grown from a "deep ambivalence" to the images of Christ blacks encountered all around them. In his attempt to interpret black theology for a largely white, liberal Protestant audience, Harding insisted that the public expression of black anger was much healthier than the silent seething that could explode into anger or violence. "Millions of black children had the picture of this pseudo-Nazarene burned into their memory," Harding said of the ubiquitous images of the blond-haired and fair-skinned Jesus. Books, paintings, and films all portrayed a white Christ who shamed those who did not look like him. This was a Christ who "condemned us for our blackness, for our flat noses, for our kinky hair, for our power, our strange power of expressing emotion in singing and shouting and dancing. He was sedate, so genteel, so white. And as soon as we were able, many of us tried to be like him." The black awakening of the 1960s meant that African American Christians could now repudiate rather than meekly accept these images. In place of the "redemptive suffering" preached by SNCC, black power could be the "redemptive anger" to bring down judgment on a white Christianity based on white supremacist power.[21]

The black theology of the civil rights era originated in Northern seminaries, often from the voices of Southern-born men and women who knew segregation firsthand. James Cone, the best known exponent of black theology, grew up in Arkansas as the son of an African Methodist Episcopal minister. He understood that black churches historically preached a spirituality that was focused primarily on preserving souls within a social order designed to destroy them. Cone's works of the 1960s and early 1970s, including *Black Theology and Black Power* (1969), inspired a generation of thinkers, artists, writers, and others who redefined the white Christ. God's revelation on earth, he said, always had come in symbols that represented the cries of the oppressed. Cone reasoned: "When we can see a people who are being controlled by an ideology of whiteness, then we know what reconciliation must mean. The coming of Christ . . . means denying the white devil in us."[22]

During the 1960s and 1970s, many black churches throughout the country adopted an imagery of Christ that celebrated their African heritage. While Cone and others argued that God is black, Albert Cleage, founder of the Black Church of the Madonna in Detroit (with its famous image of a black Mary) suggested that the Holy Spirit was as well, because this Spirit allowed for identification with the "rage of suffering oppressed people everywhere." The Holy Spirit, harnessed on behalf of social justice, had moved world events, such as the Montgomery bus boycott, by empowering individuals to act courageously in the face of oppression. Jesus was a "Black Messiah sent by God to lead men in a revolutionary struggle for liberation," Cleage preached.[23] Cleage seized on the powerful rhetoric of Malcolm X and Black Muslims who taught that white oppression destroyed black people. While black theologians preached of the beauty of blackness, Cleage exclaimed, violence and oppression continued unabated, and black children still encountered unequal opportunities. He called for capturing the Pentecostal power of the Spirit in the service of liberation. Every form of black religious expression, he believed, including music, dance, preaching, and art, should dramatize the black movement to freedom.

During the civil rights years, black Christianity motivated many to challenge oppression directly, to claim their freedom, and to value their African American heritage. In all those ways, the freedom struggle revolutionized America. The civil rights movement opened up opportunities for many African Americans to change their residencies, workplaces, shopping habits, and church homes. No longer legally and extralegally confined by a segregated society, African Americans could make the kinds of personal choices that had historically been afforded only to whites.

Or at least they could in theory. In reality, of course, the civil rights movement of the 1950s and 1960s certainly did not produce a postracial utopia. Difficult, seemingly intractable issues of persistent, structural economic inequality plague American society today, and a substantial percentage of African Americans still live in a de facto segregated world. In the early twenty-first century, the black church encompasses an array of choices for black worshippers. Many African Americans continue to attend historically black religious institutions and remain loyal to their denominational homes. Yet many have either dropped out of church altogether or joined other religions or social groupings. As a result, many historically strong black churches have struggled to attract a younger generation and maintain congregations sizable enough to pay the bills.

Other black religious leaders have rejected black Christianity in ways akin to figures of the interwar years such as Noble Drew Ali, Elijah Muhammad, and other black skeptics and advocates of alternative religions. Black Christianity remains challenged by a variety of religious competitors, such as the Nation of Islam. From its birth in the 1920s and 1930s, it found success in attracting young men, including many prisoners such as Malcolm Little, later Malcolm X. Black Islam flourished in the 1960s. Its message appealed to celebrity athletes such as Muhammad Ali and Kareem Abdul-Jabbar. In 1994, under the leadership of Louis Farrakhan, the Nation of Islam sponsored a "Million Man March" in Washington, D.C. There, Farrakhan preached his message of black economic empowerment, separate black institutions, and race pride. At the same time, the Nation of Islam experienced a number of splits and internal conflicts, which has limited its influence.

While the Black Muslims and other groups present competing alternatives to black Christianity, many churchpeople and ministers from the era of the civil rights movement have continued to carry the torch of the struggle, believing that the power of nonviolence can address persistent issues of racial inequality. This civil rights faith, for example, may be seen in the career of Jesse Jackson, a native of South Carolina who joined the SCLC as a young minister in the mid-1960s. When Martin Luther King's campaign for justice came to Chicago in 1965, the civil rights leader appointed the young Jackson to head Operation Breadbasket, which focused on issues of unemployment, poverty, and poor education in the areas of Chicago where black migrants had settled over the past generation. His work, first in Operation Breadbasket and then, in 1971, in civil and human rights groups (such as People United to Serve Humanity, or PUSH), extended the work of the SCLC. During these years, Jackson pressured the city government of Chicago to extend employment opportunities and better social services to black residents. Through his base in the black churches and his work in everyday economic issues, Jackson played a role much like Adam Clayton Powell Jr. had in Harlem during the 1930s and 1940s. In 1984, Jackson mounted a campaign for the nomination of the Democratic Party to the presidency. He delivered a memorable address before the 1984 Democratic National Convention calling for a "rainbow coalition" of ordinary Americans of all colors to unite on behalf of economic justice for all—to "keep hope alive," in Jackson's best-known phrase.

The civil rights movement opened opportunities for the growing black middle class, many of whom responded to a version of the black "prosperity gospel." Its exponents assured listeners that God wanted to bless them financially as well as spiritually. The best known minister of this movement, Thomas Dexter (T. D.) Jakes, gained tremendous popularity with his novel *Woman, Thou Art Loosed* (2004), later turned into a series of films. Using his multifaceted talents as a charismatic preacher and savvy entrepreneur, Jakes grew his megachurch—Potter's House in Dallas, Texas—from a group of fifty families in 1996 to a membership of 30,000 by 2008. He preached a message of empowerment to black women who historically had been the backbone of the church.

Perhaps most significantly for black church history, Jakes's church is non-denominational. Like many successful white religious entrepreneurs, Jakes found his recipe for success by stepping outside of the conventional church world, appealing to white as well as black audiences. In this way, he traced the steps of many other successful American religious entrepreneurs who have skillfully deployed the latest communication technologies to spread their message, including mass print in the nineteenth century, radio in the 1920s, and television in the post–World War II era. Today, figures such as Jakes have developed websites, Facebook "fan" pages, Twitter followerships, and the other accoutrements of religious businesses based on charismatic personalities. The civil rights movement and the growth of megachurches opened up the religious marketplace in ways unprecedented in African American religious history.

Numerous African American televangelists, prosperity gospel advocates, and defenders of conservative "family values" rhetoric have followed in Jakes's footsteps in delivering conservative views on human sexuality. In recent years, some black churches have become avid defenders of "traditional" marriage—that is, the nuclear family model of one man and one woman. They have made known their staunch opposition to gay marriage, in spite of the obvious connection of gay marriage to the history of civil rights. National polling data, for example, suggest that black churchgoers tend on average to be more opposed to gay marriage than white church members. On this issue and other matters defined as morals or values issues, white religious conservatives have made effective common cause with numerous black Protestant churches that normally differ with them politically but agree with them on standards of morality that they perceive as deriving from their biblical faith.

African American churches exist today in a country that is religiously pluralist in a way that no founding father could have imagined, a product of a major change in immigration laws in 1965. Since that time, the American religious landscape has incorporated Muslims, Buddhists, Hindus, Sikhs, and practitioners of African-based religions coming from the Caribbean such as Haitian Vodun and Cuban Santería. African American congregations have developed a history in America that sets them apart from the religious expressions pursued by African immigrants. Black Americans' relationship with Africa as a place and as a symbol has been complex, and that has extended into contemporary religious relations.

By the 1990s, congregations largely composed of recent African immigrants were springing up throughout urban America. The boroughs of New York City boasted well over a hundred such congregations. Missionaries and native African preachers recruited many African immigrants into "mainline" Protestant denominations or Catholic parishes. In many cases, Africans have developed their own branches of these churches. Even more significant was the growth of independent African and Pentecostal churches. Over the last generation, Pentecostalism has become the fastest growing Christian movement worldwide, primarily because of its appeal in Latin America and Africa. Pentecostalism has sprouted hundreds of religious organizations worldwide, with dozens in the United States alone. As with other religious traditions that emphasize the call of the spirit over any formal qualifications, Pentecostalism remains an open field for religious entrepreneurs and innovators who infuse it with their own fresh touches of doctrine, practice, or simply personal charisma.

The immigration of African believers has not only introduced a whole new set of personalities and institutions to African American Pentecostalism but also created tensions between Africans and black Americans. In the New York area, African congregations often attract relatively well-educated and prosperous congregants. African parents who came here in search of a better life see their churches as a way to pass on their values to their children. In many cases, African immigrants find urban African American culture alien, and they have no point of identification with the historic black churches in America. Like other immigrant groups, many Africans are interested in the gospel of success and in preserving their own cultural values. Their churches serve as ethnic havens in which cultural customs, such as naming ceremonies for children, can be observed. African immigrant churches thus serve as places of ethnic bonding but remain usually separate and distinct from the historic African American churches.

The same might be said for Ethiopian immigrants, tens of thousands of whom arrived as refugees from famine, civil war, and political dictatorship between the 1970s and the 1990s. Most Ethiopians historically practiced Eastern Orthodoxy, the form of Catholicism that centuries ago had split off from Roman Catholicism and established a rival Catholic center in the Byzantine world. Ethiopia also was home to a small, secretive black Jewish community, as well as a minority of Muslims. Historically, Ethiopia was a kind of mythic home for many black Americans. Sunday school lessons in black churches dwelled on figures such as the Queen of Sheba in the Bible. In the twentieth century, urban black Northern churches took on names that reflected the mythos of Ethiopianism, such as the Abyssinian Baptist Church or the Solomon Temple of God. For many African Americans, "Ethiopia" was symbolic of Africa and of aspirations for pan-Africanism among people throughout the African diaspora. But Ethiopia was not part of the slave trade to the New World, and Ethiopians generally considered themselves a different people from sub-Saharan Africans, including the West and Central

Africans who comprised the ancestors of the majority of black Americans. Thus, Ethiopian churches in America maintain an ethnic distinctiveness, adding to the pluralization of African American religion.

Large-scale immigration from Brazil, Central America, and the Caribbean has further pluralized African American religious expression in the United States. To take just one example, the boroughs of Brooklyn and Queens in New York City are home to well over 500,000 Haitians, people who in the United States are de facto classified as black. In Florida, close to a million Cubans, many having at least some African ancestry, live in the Miami area, and another 150,000 have made new homes in New York. Scores of other West Indian immigrants have settled throughout the country.

The recent influx of black Catholics from the West Indies has changed the religious demography of African Americans. The prevalence of Haitian immigrants alone has significantly increased (to over 10 percent) the percentage of Americans of African descent who are Catholics. Historically, Catholics constituted a very small percentage of the African American population, and most of those lived in Maryland, Kentucky, and Louisiana, the historic centers of early Catholic settlement in America. In more recent years, black Catholics have grown in numbers and percentages. Part of this comes from the systems of Catholic parochial schools, which have attracted African American parents seeking to educate their children outside declining and failing urban public school systems. But the most important demographic factor in the Catholicization of black Americans clearly has been the impact of the immigration of black Catholics from the Caribbean islands, Brazil, and parts of Latin America.

Black Catholics in America have been part of the "re-Africanizing" of black congregations in historically white-dominated institutions. In recent years, and following the innovations in liturgical practice introduced by the reforms of Vatican II in the 1960s, groups such as the National Black Catholic Conference have advocated increased inclusion of historic African American worship styles in Catholic parishes, the appointment of black priests to predominantly black parishes, and the promotion of black Catholics to higher levels in the Church hierarchy. In a predominantly white world where African Americans rarely can express themselves fully, one black Catholic recently asked, "Why must we become white to be permitted to worship alongside our fellow European American Catholics? After all, we have had a stake in Catholicism from the very beginning, with the Ethiopian eunuch of Acts 8:26, who led Africa's generous acceptance of the Jewish Jesus as its savior."[24] Meanwhile, historic black Catholic orders, such as the Sisters of the Holy Family in New Orleans, established in 1842, quietly

Photo 6.1.   Portrait of female initiates into the Sisters of the Holy Family, the first order for black nuns in the United States, established originally in New Orleans. Courtesy of the Library of Congress.

continue to preserve black American Catholic traditions and educational institutions.

Caribbean Catholics also have introduced other Catholic and African traditions, such as Vodun from Haiti and Santería from Cuba. The huge population percentage of blacks, as opposed to Europeans, on the islands, and the relatively constant infusions of Africans during the slave trade, insured a steady transmission and stronger presence of African traditions. In Haiti, home of the only successful revolution that resulted in the abolition of a colonial slave regime, African religions influenced the creation of Vodun, a formalized system of appeasing spirits that drew from the Orisha religions of West and Central Africa along with a hierarchy of saints drawn from Catholicism. In Haiti, people joke that 85 percent of the inhabitants are Catholics, 15 percent are Protestants, and 100 percent pay homage to the Vodun spirits.

Other Caribbean-born religious practitioners have combined Catholic and African traditions. The best-known practitioner of an eccentric form of Vodun in America, a woman commonly known as Mama Lola (or sometimes as Alourdes, her given name), combines diverse practices of Haitian magical religion and healing alongside Catholicism and other African ritualized forms. From a basement in her home in Flatbush, New York, she has created a haven for fellow Haitians and other seekers, full of objects employed in her healing rituals. These objects include everything from whiskey bottles to candles, blinking Christmas lights, stuffed animals, perfume bottles, and fish skeletons draped from a heating element. More successful or middle-class Haitians often leave behind what they perceive as backward religions. But for many Haitians and other Caribbean immigrants, who are a cornerstone of the working class in American neighborhoods where they have settled, figures such as Mama Lola provide them with a connection to their homelands, to the spirits, and to physical healing and psychological therapy.

Mama Lola invokes the *loas* (sometimes spelled *lowas*), spirits who can guide individual decisions, mend social rifts, empower troubled individuals, or bedevil one's enemies. Like the spirits of African religious ancestry, the loas might also possess individuals, speak to them in dreams, and compel ritual dancing to embody and "act out" the message of the spirit. Mama Lola and scores of other religious practitioners like her have been part of the re-Africanizing of African American religion. In a new age of cultural pluralism, traditions derived from Africa are no longer automatically scorned as below respectability, and Afro-Caribbean immigrants value them as the transmitters of a religious heritage.

New Orleans, which maintained a close connection to Haiti because of their mutual origins as French colonies and the influx of Haitian refugees to New Orleans in the late eighteenth century, has served as home to the various traditions formally known as *Vodou* or Vodun, more informally called "voodoo" or "hoodoo." The latter terms refer to the ad hoc, less systematized forms of Vodun that took root in North America, such as conjure. In the twentieth century, those traditions have been commercialized, with stores selling potions of "High John the Conqueror," a plant root that conjure men commonly prescribed as a sexual aphrodisiac. Characters such as Marie Laveau, a highly successful, if partly mythical, voodoo practitioner in nineteenth-century New Orleans, spawned a legion of imitators and gave the Crescent City a reputation as a haven for African-based religious practices. But even in New Orleans, there was little in the way of the more elaborate and formalized practices of Vodun or Candomble, the African-based religious systems of Haiti and Brazil.

Another black Caribbean import, Santería, has shaped the religious practices of a sizable group of black immigrants in contemporary America. Santería is a fusion of traditional Yoruba Orisha rites and Cuban Catholicism. Historically practiced among people of African descent in Cuba,

Santería was led by priests, the "fathers of Orisha"; at the top of the priestly hierarchy was the *babalawo*, or "father who knows the secrets," who communicated with the supreme God Ifa. Santería was established formally in the United States in 1974, with the incorporation of its first church near Miami. It achieved further recognized status in the Supreme Court case of *Church of Lukumi Babalu Aye v. City of Hialeah* (1993). The case arose when a local ordinance in a Florida town specifically forbade animal sacrifice for any reason beyond the preparation of food. There was no larger compelling state interest to justify the local ordinance, the Court ruled. Instead, the law specifically prohibited a practice central to Santería, clearly violating constitutional protections of religious freedom. For the first time in American history, the state recognized an African-based religion to be a legitimate religious expression.

African immigrant and black Caribbean religions have not only diversified African American religion but also re-Africanized African American Christianity in a way comparable to the large-scale infusions of African peoples in the late eighteenth century. These immigrant African religions are diverse, but many of them share common characteristics. They cultivate spirit possessions, healings, exorcisms, and ritually hypnotic music. These were the kinds of practices that the black Protestant hierarchy unsuccessfully had attempted to suppress in the nineteenth century. Through the recent influx of African immigrants, African expressions have once again exercised a vital influence on black American religion.

From the civil rights years, into the period of black theology and cultural expression, and through the recent period of immigration, the religions of the African diaspora have flourished in a pluralist American society. The civil rights movement had prepared the way for this pluralism by demanding the rights of black Americans as full citizens, and that insistence arose in large measure from the long legacy of black Christian culture, from the slave spirituals to the hopeful sounds of gospel to the freedom songs of the 1960s. It arose, too, from the history of black Christian activism, from antebellum abolitionists to the black church's role during Reconstruction to the vitality of religious life in Northern cities during the Great Migration. As Sam Cooke sang, it was a long time coming, but black Christianity had taught generations of African Americans that change was going to come.

⌒

Righteous Anger and Visionary Dreams

Contemporary Black Religion, Politics, and Culture

During the 2008 election campaign, a United Church of Christ minister named Jeremiah Wright became a political liability for presidential contender Barack Obama, who was then locked in a hard-fought Democratic primary battle with Sen. Hillary Clinton. Obama had attended Wright's Trinity United Church of Christ in Chicago since he moved there in 1985. Suddenly, televised replays of one of Wright's sermons from 2003 filled the airwaves and the Internet. In the sermon, which condemned America's historic practice of racism, Wright claimed incredulously that the government "wants us to sing God bless America? No, no, no. Not God bless America; God damn America! That's in the Bible, for killing innocent people. God damn America for treating her citizen as less than human. God damn America as long as she keeps trying to act like she is God and she is supreme!"[1]

Those familiar with the tradition of black religious anger, including David Walker's *Appeal*, Henry McNeal Turner's "God Is a Negro," Howard Thurman's *Jesus and the Disinherited*, and even some of Martin Luther King's more searing indictments of America's dishonorable history of racial repression, found little of surprise in the sermon. As a military veteran and a longtime pastor of a church in a historically white denomination, Wright's career hardly seemed radical. Wright was not a Black Panther, nor a Black Muslim. He was a minister in the United Church of Christ, a denomination descended from Puritan New England, who preached messages akin to countless others passed down through the black Christian tradition.

Once Wright's message, particularly the line "God damn America," became a national sensation, Barack Obama had to address it. His campaign theme of "hope" seemed drowned out by Wright's condemnatory sermon. Obama himself is of mixed-race parentage. His father, a Kenyan, was nominally a Muslim by birth but in practice an atheist. His mother, a white woman originally from Kansas, was an academic anthropologist and religious "seeker" whose personal and intellectual journeys took her from Kansas to Africa, Indonesia, and Hawaii. Thus, while counted as "black" in the American racial system, Obama had little personal experience with the "black church." When the future president moved to Chicago, where he served as a community organizer, he gradually developed ties to historically black institutions. Later, he took his children to be christened in Wright's congregation.

The dialogue between Jeremiah Wright and Barack Obama expressed two major themes of black Christianity throughout its history: righteous anger, and visionary dreams of a beloved community. Wright's angry sermon came straight from the legacy of black American preaching about the ills of American racism. Obama's response arose from another black American religious tradition: the hope that America would live up to its promise of equal opportunity and equality. Obama's newfound connection with the black American experience inspired him. In his memoir *Dreams from My Father* (1995), he wrote of his compelling experience in a black Protestant congregation in Chicago. He saw people shouting and rising from their seats to cry out and express their divine hope that they would emerge victorious just like biblical figures from the Old Testament. The stories he heard there, he wrote, were the product of the blood, sweat, and tears of the African American experience, and the church where he witnessed these emotional encounters "seemed once more a vessel carrying the story of a people into future generations and into a larger world."[2]

Obama's religious experience in Chicago churches allowed him to understand those with whom he worked as a community organizer. It was there, he said in a 2004 interview, that his initial rational view of religion deepened into something more heartfelt. His adult "conversion" paralleled that of King's vision at his kitchen table in 1956, when he felt the voice of God speak directly to him as he struggled with his newfound leadership role in the nascent civil rights movement. Obama also had an "intellectual" interest in religious faith but found a much more personal experience relating to God in his Chicago church, one felt in the body as much as in the mind. As he spent time with churchpeople, he learned how black churches and religious faith had given people courage to prevail through the storm of slavery and the night of segregation and poverty. Black Christianity taught him what it meant to *be* black in America.[3]

Jeremiah Wright and Barack Obama articulated two major themes of the black American religious experience—the righteous jeremiad and the gospel of hope. Citing the long history of racial oppression in this country, Wright concluded that God would damn America. But Obama reached a different conclusion. In his inaugural address in January 2009, he told the nation that because of their experience during slavery and segregation, black Americans were positioned to help others understand that the "old hatreds shall some-day pass; that the lines of tribe shall soon dissolve; that as the world grows smaller, our common humanity shall reveal itself."[4]

The expression of a gospel of hope and righteous anger emerged also in the respective careers and hit records of gospel star Kirk Franklin and rap artists such as Kanye West and KRS-One. Born in 1970 into a black Baptist family, Franklin had a troubled youth. In the 1990s, he found his way back to his religious faith and formed the gospel group the Family, which has dominated the gospel music charts since its inception. Franklin's 1995 *Why We Sing* was the first gospel album to sell more than a million copies. The album furthered the innovations of the original gospel music composers such as Thomas Dorsey. Franklin added more elaborate and harmonically complex arrangements, funky rhythmic settings, and guest stars singing on the records. Lyrically, his themes reprised the familiar thread of black gospel: Jesus provides hope and can get you through life's troubles. "Someone asked the question / Why do we sing?" Franklin begins. His answer: "I sing because I'm happy / I sing because I'm free."

While black gospel has retained its solid niche market, it also has faced a new set of musical challengers. Black Christian musicians have tried to hone in on popular styles to communicate their message. This was the case in the past as well—in fact, the original term for gospel was "gospel blues," indicating the way early gospel pioneers incorporated the musical "sound" of blues to attract audiences. The same goes for "Christian rock" and "Christian rap." These forms generally are ignored or scorned by listeners outside very particular audiences. Urban working-class blacks who once had been the base of gospel music have directed angry critiques *at* black Christianity. Rap, or hip-hop, once called the "CNN of the black community," originated among poor and working-class neighborhoods in New York in the 1970s. It quickly developed as an immensely powerful subculture. In the 1990s, hip-hop rocketed to international success. Black gospel remains largely an American phenomenon, with a domestic audience, while rap has gone global.

Rappers have explored religious themes, but outside the conventional norms of the black Christian tradition. Some rappers have taken up themes that would sound familiar to black skeptics of Christianity, including Noble Drew Ali, Elijah Muhammad, Malcolm X, and many others. Lawrence Parker, a native of Brooklyn who took the stage name KRS-One, went in search of his own version of religious meaning in "A Higher Level." He angrily rejected Christianity, summing up in his lyrics a long line of black nationalist thought about how blacks had accepted the "oppressor's religion" and a God that justified slavery as right, and asking where the God was that "looks like me," one that could be trusted. Ice Cube's lyric "the Devil made you slave and he gave you a Bible" reinforced this view—that Christianity enriched preachers, white and black, and historically had sustained white power.

Many rap lyrics speak of a profound yearning for, but disconnection from, the historic African American spiritual themes of redemption from suffering in this world. Kanye West's "Jesus Walks" (2004) best exemplifies this feeling, reprising some of the conflicts between bodily desires and spiritual quests—the same internal struggles that informed the lyrics of blues music earlier in the century:

> God show me the way because the devil
>   trying to break me down (Jesus walks)
> The only thing that that I pray is that my feet don't
>   fail me now (Jesus walks)
> And I don't think there's nothing I can do now to
>   right my wrongs (Jesus walks with me)
> I want to talk to God but I'm afraid because we
>   ain't spoke in so long[5]

As seen in figures as diverse as T. D. Jakes, Mama Lola, Barack Obama, Kirk Franklin, Jesse Jackson, and Kanye West, the spiritual struggles of black Americans continue to be expressed in diverse, creative, and sometimes contradictory ways. Throughout the history of black Christianity, black believers and skeptics have debated the usefulness of Christianity for oppressed African peoples in the United States. Spiritual practices derived from Africa survived, often in underground forms. More recently, they have emerged in public form, especially in African immigrant churches and in Afro-Caribbean practices. Meanwhile, black Protestant leaders historically have urged a restrained religious practice focused on "uplift." Black secular and gospel blues singers competed for the allegiance of souls and fans, as did black preachers and conjurers, and as do gospel musicians and rappers. "Integrationists" and "nationalists" have debated each other through much of this history, from Frederick Douglass's public arguments with Henry Highland Garnet in the 1840s, to the internal battles within the African Methodist Episcopal Church between Daniel Alexander Payne and Henry McNeal Turner, to the heated discussions about the efficacy of nonviolence between Martin Luther King Jr. and his numerous critics.

In more recent years, scholars have battled over whether the black church is dead, while ordinary black churchpeople have confronted difficult questions of persistent poverty and violence in black urban communities. Political leaders such as Jesse Jackson and Al Sharpton have emerged from the church and the civil rights movement to become nationally known spokesmen. They have carried on the tradition of the political black minister that emerged originally in the nineteenth century and shaped the country during the civil rights years of the 1960s. Meanwhile, black men and women have fought out their gender battles within the church, with black churchwomen frequently pointing out that there scarcely could be a black church at all without their numerically predominant presence. Moreover, as believers take sides on controversial social issues (abortion, gay marriage, gay people in the pew and in the pulpit), black churches are divided along ideological lines, much as are churches in white denominations.

African American religious expression has undergone massive transformations throughout American history. Perhaps most significant were the middle passage for the gods, when the brutal forces of the slave trade destroyed African religious systems, and the rise of Afro-evangelicalism in the eighteenth and nineteenth centuries, when Christianity fundamentally shaped religious expression for African Americans. Following the Civil War, another revolution occurred: the rise of independent black churches and denominations throughout the country. A more recent set of transformations for black Christianity took place through the era of the Great Migration and the civil rights movement of the twentieth century.

Throughout its history, black American Christianity has served as a forum African Americans have used to secure their place in a country that historically has denied them citizenship and equality. Black Christianity has survived through the storm and through the night of American history, and it remains a vital element of American religious life today. The church is not (and never has been) the Alpha and Omega of all things, but it is far from dead. Listen to the sounds emanating from black congregations on a Sunday morning, and the entire complex, diverse, and tenacious history of African American Christianity will come alive.

Primary Source Documents

Virginia Laws on Baptism and Slavery

Beginning in the 1660s, as slavery initially took off in the Chesapeake Bay region, colonial assemblies started to craft laws that defined the status of slaves. Since some slaves had been baptized and claimed freedom on that basis, the assemblies made it legally clear that baptism would not lead slaves to freedom. By doing so, masters asserted that baptism would not provide black people with an escape from slavery. The idea that "heathens" could be enslaved, while Christians could not, would no longer suffice, for black Christians would remain enslaved. Some legislators actually hoped to help Christian proselytization, since masters would not have to fear that slaves could claim freedom after their baptism.

Virginia Law, September 1667

Whereas some doubts have risen whether children that are slaves by birth, and by the charity and piety of their owners made partakers of the blessed sacrament of baptism, should by virtue of their baptism be made free, it is enacted and declared by this Grand Assembly, and the authority thereof, that the conferring of baptism does not alter the condition of the person as to his bondage or freedom; that diverse masters, freed from this doubt may more carefully endeavor the propagation of Christianity by permitting children, through slaves, or those of greater growth if capable, to be admitted to that sacrament.

Virginia, 1682

Act I. It is enacted that all servants . . . which shall be imported into this country either by sea or by land, whether Negroes, Moors [Muslim North Africans], mulattoes or Indians who and whose parentage and native countries are not Christian at the time of their first purchase by some Christian . . . and all Indians, which shall be sold by our neighboring Indians, or any other trafficing with us for slaves, are hereby adjudged, deemed and taken to be slaves to all intents and purposes any law, usage, or custom to the contrary notwithstanding.

Source: Black Laws of Virginia (New York: Negro Universities Press, 1969), available at http://www.pbs.org/wgbh/aia/part1/1h315t.html.

⌒

Francis Le Jau Reflects on Proselytization of the Slaves in South Carolina, Early Eighteenth Century

Francis Le Jau served as a missionary for the Society for the Propagation of the Gospel in Foreign Parts (SPG) in early eighteenth-century South Carolina. His reports on his attempts to preach the gospel among the slaves illuminate the roots of the resistance of both planters and enslaved Africans to Christian proselytization. Le Jau emphasized that converts could live in good order and that Christianity could render them obedient workers. His reports also suggest that early African American Christians took the opportunity to create their own interpretations of biblical passages and Christian doctrine. These apocalyptic and messianic visions from the biblical passages frequently discomfited Le Jau as well as local planters.

March 22, 1709

I thought to have baptized some more Negro Slaves this Advent they are well Instructed and I hear no complaint concerning them. Their Masters Seem very much Averse to my Design, Some of them will not give them Leave to come to Church to learn how to Pray to God and to Serve him, I cannot find any reason for this New Opposition but the Old pretext that Baptism makes the Slaves proud and Undutifull: I endeavour to convince them of the Contrary from the Example of those I have baptized, and Chiefly those who are Admitted to our holy Comunion who behave themselves very well.

To remove all pretence from the Adult Slaves I shall baptize of their being free upon that Account, I have thought fit to require first their consent to this following declaration *You declare in the Presence of God and before this congregation that you do not "ask for the holy baptism out of any design to free yourself from the Duty and Obedience you owe to your Master while you live, but merely for the good of your Soul and to partake of the Graces and Blessings promised to the Members of the Church of Jesus Christ."*

February 1, 1710

The best Scholar of all the Negroes in my Parish and a very sober and honest Liver, thro' his Learning was like to Create some Confusion among all the Negroes in this Country; he had a Book wherein he read some description of the several judgmts. That Chastise Men because of their Sins in these latter days, that description made an Impression upon his Spirit, and he told his Master abruptly there wou'd be a dismal time and the Moon wou'd be turned into Blood, and there wou'd be dearth of darkness and went away. . . . Some Negroe overheard a part, and it was publickly blazed abroad that an Angel came and spake to the Man, he had seen a hand that gave him a Book, he had heard Voices, seen fires &c. . . . I have often observed and lately hear that it had been better if persons of a Melancholy Constitution or those that run into the Search after Curious matter had never seen a Book.

December 11, 1712

Many Masters can't be persuaded that Negroes and Indians are otherwise than Beasts . . . and use them like such. I endeavour to let them know better things . . . but not all to my great Sorrow, on the Contrary what I do out of Charity is not well received. I wou'd think my self guilty of their own sins if I shou'd wink at things evidently evil.

Source: Le Jau to the Secretary, St. James, Goose Creek, South Carolina, March 22, 1709; February 1, 1710; and December 11, 1712, all in SPG Manuscripts, Library of Congress Transcriptions, A5. With the permission of the Trustees of the Lambeth Palace Library. Also reproduced in Frank Klingberg, ed., *The Carolina Chronicle of Dr. Francis Le Jau, 1706–1717* (Berkeley: University of California Press, 1956), 55, 70, 125.

⌐

Christianized Slaves Beg for Freedom to Anglican Bishop, 1723

This recently rediscovered letter from a group of unknown slaves demonstrates that some slaves continued to equate Christianity and a free status, while slave owners resisted that connection. These slaves had been brought up in the Anglican Church, felt themselves to be true Christians, and bitterly complained about the ill treatment provided them by their masters. They sent this letter to a new bishop appointed to oversee Anglican affairs in the colonies. The letter later got misfiled and ended up in an archive in the Caribbean, where it lay unread and forgotten until its recent recovery. The letter makes clear how some slaves during these early years understood that Christian belief gave them access to the levers of power.

August the forth 1723

To the Right ~~Righ~~ Raverrand father in god my Lord arch Bishop of Lonnd this coms to sattesfie your honour that there is this Land of verJennia a Sort of people that is Calld molatters which are Baptised and brouaht up in the way of the Christian faith ~~and the~~ and followes the wayes and Rulles of the Church of England and sum of them has white fathers and sum white mothers and there is in this Land ~~a L~~ a Law or act which keeps and makes them and there seed Slaves forever. . . .

And most honoured sir a mongst the Rest of your Charitabell acts and deed wee ~~humbly~~ your humbell and ~~pou~~ poore partishinners doo begg Sir your aid and assistance in this one thing which Lise as I doo understand ~~of~~ in your LordShips brest which is that ~~yr honour~~ will by the help of our Suf~~fervering~~ [i.e., sovereign] Lord King George and the Rest of the Rullers will Releese us out of this Cruell Bondegg and this wee beg for Jesus Christs his ~~of~~ Sake who has commaded us to seeke first the kingdom of ~~god~~ god and all things shall be addid ~~un~~ un to us. . . .

and here it is to bee notd that one brother is Slave to another and one Sister to an othe which is quite out of the way and as for mee [cancellation] my self I am my brothers Slave but my name is Secrett. . . . and here it is to bee noted againe that weee are commandded to keep holey the Sabbath day and wee doo hardly know when it comes for our [cancellation] task mastrs are has hard with us as the Egypttions was with the Chilldann of Issarall god be marcifll unto us

Here follows our ~~hard service~~ Sevarity and Sorrowfull Sarvice we are hard used up on Every account ~~wee f~~ in the first place wee are in Ignorance of our Salvation and in the next place wee are kept out of the Church ~~and~~ and matrimony is denied us

and to be plain they doo Look no more up on us then if wee ware dogs which I hope when these Strange Lines comes to your Lord Ships hands will be Looket in to

and here wee beg for Jesus Christs his Sake that as your honour do hope for the marcy of god att the day of death and the Redemtion of our Savour Christ that when this comes to your Lord Ships hands your honour will Take Sum pitty of us who is your humble butt Sorrowfull portitinors and Sir wee your humble perticners do humbly beg the favour of your Lord Ship that your honour will grant and Settell one thing upon us which is that our ᴄʜ childarn may be broatt up in the way of the Christtian faith and our desire is that they may be Larnd the Lords prayer the creed and the ten commandements and that they may appear e Every Lord's day att Church before the Ǝ Curatt to bee Exammond for our desire is that godliness Shoulld abbound amongs us and wee desire that our Children be putt to Scool and and Larnd to Reed through the Bybell. . . .

wee dare nott Subscribe any mans name to this for feare of our masters ᵻf for if they knew that wee have Sent home to your honour wee Should goo neare to Swing upon the gallass tree

Source: Thomas Ingersoll, "'Releese Us Out of This Cruell Bondegg': An Appeal from Virginia in 1723," *William and Mary Quarterly*, 3rd ser., 54 (October 1994): 777–82. With the permission of the Trustees of Lambeth Palace Library.

⌒

Catholic Influences on the
Stono Rebellion in South Carolina, 1739

This account of the Stono Rebellion demonstrates how Spanish Catholicism in Florida lured slaves from the English colonies. Slaves from the Kongo, who had long had exposure to Christianity via Portuguese missionaries, led the rebellion, and the Spanish in Florida recognized the opportunity provided by discontented slaves in South Carolina who could be used to their advantage in the struggle for control of the southeastern seaboard.

Sometime since there was a Proclamation published at Augustine, in which the King of Spain (then at Peace with Great Britain) promised Protection and Freedom to all Negroes Slaves that would resort thither. Certain Negroes belonging to Captain Davis escaped to Augustine, and were received there. They were demanded by General Oglethorpe who sent Lieutenant Demere to Augustine, and the Governour assured the General of his sincere Friendship, but at the same time showed his Orders from the Court of Spain, by which he was to receive all Run away Negroes. Of this other Negroes having notice, as it is believed, from the Spanish Emissaries, four or five who were Cattel-Hunters, and knew the Woods, some of whom belonged to Captain Macpherson, ran away with His Horses, wounded his Son and killed another Man. These marched f [sic] for Georgia, and were pursued, but the Rangers being then newly reduced the Countrey people could not overtake them, though they were discovered by the Saltzburghers, as they passed by Ebenezer. They reached Augustine, one only being killed and another wounded by the Indians in their flight. They were received there with great honours, one of them had a Commission given to him, and a Coat faced with Velvet. Amongst the Negroe Slaves there are a people brought from the Kingdom of Angola in Africa, many of these speak Portugueze (which Language is as near Spanish as Scotch is to English,) by reason that the Portugueze have considerable Settlement, and the Jesuits have a Mission and School in that Kingdom and many Thousands of the Negroes there profess the Roman Catholic Religion. Several Spaniards upon diverse Pretences have for some time past been strolling about Carolina, two of them, who will give no account of themselves have been taken up and committed to Jayl in Georgia. The good reception of the Negroes at Augustine was spread about, Several attempted to escape to the Spaniards, & were taken, one of them was hanged at Charles Town.

Source: Allen Chandler, ed., *The Colonial Records of the State of Georgia*, vol. 22 (Atlanta: Chas. P. Byrd Press, 1913), 232–36.

⌢

Autobiography of Omar Ibn Said, Muslim Slave Captured and Brought to North Carolina

Omar Ibn Said's autobiographical excerpts, written originally in Arabic and in 1831 translated for the American audience, are a rare firsthand account from a Muslim slave. Though he later converted to Christianity, he still continued his Muslim religious practices well into the antebellum era. Said's narrative gives us a glimpse into the important influence of Islam as one of several religious traditions that slaves brought to North America. Far from being heathens or pagans, as Englishmen often assumed, Africans carried with them a rich variety of religious beliefs and practices, which heavily influenced how they came to practice religion as slaves in North America.

Before I came to the Christian country, my religion was the religion of "Mohammed, the Apostle of God—may God have mercy upon him and give him peace." I walked to the mosque before day-break, washed my face and head and hands and feet. I prayed at noon, prayed in the afternoon, prayed at sunset, prayed in the evening. I gave alms every year, gold, silver, seeds, cattle, sheep, goats, rice, wheat, and barley. I gave tithes of all the above-named things. I went every year to the holy war against the infidels. I went on pilgrimage to Mecca, as all did who were able.—My father had six sons and five daughters, and my mother had three sons and one daughter. When

I left my country I was thirty-seven years old; I have been in the country of the Christians twenty-four years.—Written A.D. 1831. . . .

Formerly I, Omar, loved to read the book of the Koran the famous. General Jim Owen and his wife used to read the gospel, and they read it to me very much,—the gospel of God, our Lord, our Creator, our King, He that orders all our circumstances, health and wealth, willingly, not constrainedly, according to his power.—Open thou my heart to the gospel, to the way of uprightness.—Thanks to the Lord of all worlds, thanks in abundance. He is plenteous in mercy and abundant in goodness. . . .

When I was a Mohammedan I prayed thus: "Thanks be to God, Lord of all worlds, the merciful the gracious, Lord of the day of Judgment, thee we serve, on thee we call for help. Direct us in the right way, the way of those on whom thou hast had mercy, with whom thou hast not been angry and who walk not in error. Amen."—But now I pray "Our Father", etc., in the words of our Lord Jesus the Messiah.

I reside in this our country by reason of great necessity. Wicked men took me by violence and sold me to the Christians. We sailed a month and a half on the great sea to the place called Charleston in the Christian land. I fell into the hands of a small, weak and wicked man, who feared not God at all nor did he read [the gospel] at all nor pray.

I was afraid to remain with a man so depraved and who committed so many crimes and I ran away. After a month our Lord God brought me forward to the hand of a good man, who fears God, and loves to do good.

Source: "Autobiography of Omar ibn Said, Slave in North Carolina, 1831," ed. John Franklin Jameson, *American Historical Review* 30 (July 1925): 787–95; available at http://docsouth.unc.edu/nc/omarsaid/menu.html.

⌒

Samuel Davies on the Great Awakening in Virginia, 1757

In this excerpt, the Presbyterian New Light itinerant minister Samuel Davies recounts some early experiences proselytizing among Virginia slaves in the mid-1750s. His narrative provides one of the earliest accounts of slave Christianization during the Great Awakening. His account, read by many early evangelicals, gives a glimpse of how African American converts responded enthusiastically to the warmth and fervor of evangelical worship as it developed during the Awakening. Davies also makes a plea that teaching slaves the "pacific religion" of Jesus would help secure the colony during the uncertain political conflict between the English and the French for control of North America.

For some time after this, the *poor Slaves*, whenever they could get an hour's leisure from their masters, would hurry away to my house; and received the Charity with all the genuine indications of passionate gratitude, which un-polished nature could give; and which affectation and grimace would mimic in vain. The books were all *very acceptable*; but none more so than the *Psalms* and *Hymns*, which enabled them to gratify their peculiar taste for *Psalmody*. Sundry of them have lodged all night in my kitchen; and, sometimes, when I have awaked about two or three a-clock in the morning, a torrent of sacred harmony poured into my chamber, and carried my mind away to Heaven. . . .

The *good effects* of this pious Charity are already apparent. It convinces the *Heathen*, that however vicious, and careless about the Religion they profess, the generality of the white People are; yet, there are some who really look upon it as a matter of the utmost importance, and universal concern, and are actuated with a disinterested zeal to promote it—It has excited some of their *Masters* to emulation. . . . This CHARITY may also be of singular service in a POLITICAL VIEW; for now, when the *French and Indians* are invading our country, and perpetrating the most shocking barbarities and depredations upon our frontiers; we have not been without alarming ap-prehensions of Insurrection and Massacre; from the *numerous Slaves* among ourselves, whom they might seduce to their interest by the delusive promises of Liberty. And while they do not feel the restrains of Conscience and Chris-tianity, our apprehensions are but too well grounded. I have done my utmost, without hinting my design to them, to prevent so dismal a calamity; and for this purpose, I have endeavoured to convince them, that there are many of the *English*, as well as myself, who are really solicitous for their welfare, which has given me no small popularity among them; and especially to bring them under the restraints of the pacific religion of Jesus, which has so friendly an influence upon society, and teaches a proper conduct for every station in life. *Source:* Samuel Davies, *Letters from the Rev. Samuel Davies* (London, 1757), 15–17, reprinted in Thomas Kidd, ed., *The Great Awakening: A History in Documents* (Boston: Bedford Books, 2007), 117–19.

~

Richard Allen on His Conversion and Removal from a White Methodist Church in Philadelphia

Along with Absalom Jones, Richard Allen was one of the founders of the first inde-pendent black denomination in America, the African Methodist Episcopal (AME) Church. Here, he recounts the humiliating experience of being segregated at the altar of his Philadelphia Methodist Church, and their subsequent self-removal that led to the formation of the AME Church. A devoted Methodist who worked closely with Francis Asbury, the organizing genius of the American incarnation of Methodism, Allen and his comrades carried on a long struggle to establish and maintain a separate black church in the face of white attempts to assert control over it.

I had it often impressed upon my mind that I should one day enjoy my freedom; for slavery is a bitter pill, notwithstanding we had a good master. But when we would think that our day's work was never done, we often thought that after our master's death we were liable to be sold to the highest bidder, as he was much in debt; and thus my troubles were increased, and I was often brought to weep between the porch and the altar. But I have had reason to bless my dear Lord that a door was opened unexpectedly for me to buy my time and enjoy my liberty. When I left my master's house I knew not what to do, not being used to hard work, what business I should follow to pay my master and get my living. I went to cutting of cord wood. The first day my hands were so blistered and sore, that it was with difficulty I could open or shut them. I kneeled down upon my knees and prayed that the Lord would open some way for me to get my living. In a few days, my hands recovered and became accustomed to cutting of wood and other hardships; so I soon became able to cut my cord and a half and two cords a day. . . . I used ofttimes to pray, sitting, standing or lying; and while my hands were employed to earn my bread, my heart was devoted to my dear Redeemer. Sometimes I would awake from my sleep, preaching and praying. I was after this employed in driving of wagon in time of the Continental war, in drawing salt from Rehoboth, Sussex County, in Delaware. I had my regular stops and preaching places on the road. I enjoyed many happy seasons in meditation and prayer while in this employ. December 1784, General Conference sat in Baltimore, the first General Conference ever held in America. . . . This was the beginning of the Episcopal Church amongst the Methodists. Many of the ministers were set apart in holy orders at this conference, and were said to be entitled to the gown; and I have thought religion has been declining in the church ever since. There was a pamphlet published by some person, which stated, that when the Methodists were no people, then they were a people; and now they have become a people they were no people; which had often serious weight upon my mind.

In 1785 the Rev. Richard Whatcoat was appointed on Baltimore circuit. He was, I believe, a man of God. I found great strength in travelling with him a father in Israel. In his advice he was fatherly and friendly. He was of a mild and serene disposition. My lot was cast in Baltimore, in a small meeting-house called Methodist Alley. . . . Rev. Bishop Asbury sent for me to meet him at Henry Gaff's. I did so. He told me he wished me to travel with him. He told me that in the slave countries, Carolina and other places, I must not intermix with the slaves, and I would frequently have to sleep in his carriage, and he would allow me my victuals and clothes. I told him I would not travel with him on these conditions. He asked me my reason. I told him if I was taken sick, who was to support me? and that I thought people ought to lay up something while they were able, to support themselves in time of sickness or old age. He said that was as much as he got, his victuals and clothes. I told him he would be taken care of, let his afflictions be as they were, or let him be taken sick where he would, he would be taken care of; but I doubted whether it would be the case with myself. He smiled, and told me he would give me from then until he returned from the eastward to make up my mind, which would be about three months. But I made up my mind that I would not accept of his proposals. . . .

A number of us usually attended St. George's church in Fourth street; and hence the colored people began to get numerous in attending the church, they moved us from the seats we usually sat on, and placed us around the wall, and on Sabbath morning we went to church and the sexton stood at the door, and told us to go in the gallery. He told us to go, and we would see where to sit. We expected to take the seats over the ones we formerly occupied below, not knowing any better.

Meeting had begun, and they were nearly done singing, and just as we got to the seats, the elder said, "Let us pray." We had not been long upon our knees before I heard considerable scuffling and low talking. I raised my head up and saw one of the trustees, H-M-, having hold of the Rev. Absalom Jones, pulling him up off of his knees, and saying, "You must get up—you must not kneel here." Mr. Jones replied, "Wait until prayer is over." Mr. H-M- said "No, you must get up now, or I will call for aid and force you away." Mr. Jones said, "Wait until prayer is over, and I will get up and trouble you no more." With that he beckoned to one of the other trustees, Mr. L- S- to come to his assistance. He came, and went to William White to pull him up. By this time prayer was over, and we all went out of the church in a body, and they were no more plagued with us in the church.

Source: From the Life Experience and Gospel Labors of the Rt. Rev. Richard Allen (Philadelphia: F. Ford and M. A. Ripley, 1880), available at http://docsouth. unc.edu/neh/allen/menu.html.

⌣

Jarena Lee Narrates Her Desire to Preach the Gospel

Jarena Lee was one of a number of black female evangelists, mostly among the black Methodist denominations, who felt the call to preach. Denied the opportunity to establish themselves as ordained ministers in pulpits, they crisscrossed the North in the early and mid-nineteenth century, establishing a significant legacy of black female religious oratory. Their preaching aroused controversy. Established denominations, dominated by men, increasingly disallowed female preaching in the early nineteenth century, even though it had been quite common during the early years of the Great Awakening in the mid-eighteenth century. Disallowed or not, Lee carried on, preaching even to whites, many of whom believed that black people had no souls, as she recounts here.

I now began to think seriously of breaking up housekeeping, and forsaking all to preach the everlasting Gospel. I felt a strong desire to return to the place of my nativity, at Cape May, after an absence of about fourteen years. To this place, where the heaviest cross was to be met with, the Lord sent me, as Saul of Tarsus was sent to Jerusalem, to preach the same gospel which he had neglected and despised before his conversion. I went by water, and on my passage was much distressed by sea sickness, so much so that I expected to have died, but such was not the will of the Lord respecting me. After I had disembarked, I proceeded on as opportunities offered toward where my mother lived. When within ten miles of that place, I appointed an evening meeting. There were a goodly number came out to hear. The Lord was pleased to give me light and liberty among the people. After meeting, there came an elderly lady to me and said, she believed the Lord had sent me among them: she then appointed me another meeting there two weeks from that night. The next day I hastened forward to the place of my mother who was happy to see me, and the happiness was mutual between us. With her I left my poor sickly boy while I departed to do my Master's will. In this neighborhood I had an uncle, who was a Methodist and who gladly threw open his door for meetings to be held there. At the first meeting which I held at my uncle's house, there was, with others who had come from curiosity to hear the woman preacher, an old man, who was a Deist, and who said he did not believe the coloured people had any souls—he was sure they had none. He took a seat very near where I was standing, and boldly tried to look me out of countenance. But as I labored on in the best manner I was able, looking to God all the while, though it seemed to me I had but little liberty, yet there went an arrow from the bent bow of the gospel, and fastened in his till then obdurate heart. After I had done speaking, he went out, and called the people around him, said that my preaching might seem a small thing, yet be believed I had the worth of souls at heart. This language was different from what it was a little time before, as he now seemed to admit that coloured people had souls, as it was to these I was chiefly speaking; and unless they had souls, whose good I had in view, his remark must have been without meaning. He now came into the house, and in the most friendly manner shook hands with me, saying, he hoped God had spared him to some good purpose. This man was a great slave holder, and had been very cruel, thinking nothing of knocking down a slave with a fence stake, or whatever might come to hand. From this time it was said of him that he became greatly altered in his ways for the better. At that time he was about seventy years old, his head as white as snow; but whether he became a converted man or not, I never heard.

The week following, I had an invitation to hold a meeting at the Court House of the County, when I spoke from the 53d chap. of Isaiah, 3d verse. It was a solemn time, and the Lord attended the word I had life and liberty, though there were people there of various denominations. Here again I saw the aged slaveholder, who notwithstanding his age, walked about three miles to hear me. This day I spoke twice, and walked six miles to the place appointed. There was a magistrate present, who showed his friendship, by saying in a friendly manner, that he had heard of me: he handed me a hymn book, pointing to a hymn which he had selected. When the meeting was over, he invited me to preach in a schoolhouse in his neighborhood, about three miles distant from where I then was. During this meeting one backslider was reclaimed. This day I walked six miles, and preached twice to large congregations, both in the morning and evening. The Lord was with me, glory be to his holy name. I next went six miles and held a meeting in a coloured friend's house, at eleven o'clock in the morning, and preached to a well behaved congregation of both coloured and white. After service I again walked back, which was in all twelve miles in the same day. This was on Sabbath, or as I sometimes call it, seventh day; for after my conversion I preferred the plain language of the Friends. On the fourth day, after this, in compliance with an invitation received by note, from the same magistrate who had heard me at the above place I preached to a large congregation, where we had a precious time: much weeping was heard among the people. The same gentleman, now at the close of the meeting, gave out another appointment at the same place, that day week. Here again I had liberty, there was a move among the people. Ten years from that time, in the neighborhood of Cape May, I held a prayer meeting in a school house, which was then the regular place of preaching for the Episcopal Methodists, after service, there came a white lady, of great distinction, a member of the Methodist Society, and told me that at the same school house ten years before, under my preaching the Lord first awakened her. She rejoiced much to see me, and invited me home with her, where I staid till the next day. This was bread cast upon the water, seen after many days.

Source: *Religious Experience and Journal of Mrs. Jarena Lee, Giving an Account of Her Call to Preach the Gospel* (Philadelphia, 1849), available at http://www. umilta.net/jarena.html.

⌒

David Walker's *Appeal*

David Walker's Appeal to the Colored Citizens of the World *was a fiery polemic against slavery. Originally published in 1829, the* Appeal *came from the pen of a free colored man who died mysteriously shortly after its publication. Two years later, many blamed Walker for fomenting Nat Turner's rebellion in Virginia. Walker's* Appeal *shows the deep influence of Christian thought on black abolitionism. The close proximity of the publication of the appeal and Turner's 1831 revolt also helped to unify the white South, which immediately took action. White Southern authorities shut down many quasi-independent black churches, barred abolitionist mailings, and made it virtually impossible to manumit slaves.*

All persons who are acquainted with history, and particularly the Bible, who are not blinded by the God of this world, and are not actuated solely by avarice—who are able to lay aside prejudice long enough to view candidly and impartially, things as they were, are, and probably will be—who are willing to admit that God made man to serve Him alone, and that man should have no other Lord or Lords but Himself—that God Almighty is the sole proprietor or master of the WHOLE human family, and will not on any consideration admit of a colleague, being unwilling to divide his glory with another—and who can dispense with prejudice long enough to admit that we are men, notwithstanding our improment noses and woolly heads, and believe that we feel for our fathers, mothers, wives and children, as well as the whites do for theirs.—I say, all who are permitted to see and believe these things, can easily recognize the judgments of God among the Spaniards. Though others may lay the cause of the fierceness with which they cut each other's throats, to some other circumstance, yet they who believe that God is a God of justice, will believe that SLAVERY is the principal cause. . . .

Are we MEN!!—I ask you, O my brethren! are we MEN? Did our Creator make us to be slaves to dust and ashes like ourselves? Are they not dying worms as well as we? Have they not to make their appearance before the tribunal of Heaven, to answer for the deeds done in the body, as well as we? Have we any other Master but Jesus Christ alone? Is he not their Master as well as ours?—What right then, have we to obey and call any other Master, but Himself? How we could be so submissive to a gang of men, whom we cannot tell whether they are as good as ourselves or not, I never could conceive. However, this is shut up with the Lord, and we cannot precisely tell—but I declare, we judge men by their works.

Source: *Walker's Appeal, in Four Articles; Together with a Preamble, to the Coloured Citizens of the World, but in Particular, and Very Expressly, to Those of the United States of America, Written in Boston, State of Massachusetts, September 28, 1829,* available at http://docsouth.unc.edu/nc/walker/walker.html.

⌒

Nat Turner's *Confessions*

In late August 1831, Nat Turner led the most significant slave revolt of the antebellum era, in Southampton County, Virginia. He and his group of rebels slaughtered dozens of whites before a posse captured him. Prior to his execution, Turner related his life story to lawyer Thomas Gray. While there is some controversy as to how much Gray embellished Turner's words in hopes of scoring a best seller, it is clear that Turner saw himself as a religious messianist, as he explains here. Turner's account was, for white Virginians, a chilling conclusion to an incident that spelled the end of an internal debate within the state as to the future of slavery in the Commonwealth.

I was thirty-one years of age the second of October last, and born the property of Benjamin Turner, of this county. In my childhood a circumstance occurred which made an indelible impression on my mind, and laid the groundwork of that enthusiasm which has terminated so fatally to many, both white and black, and for which I am about to atone at the gallows. It is here necessary to relate this circumstance. Trifling as it may seem, it was the commencement of that belief which has grown with time; and even now, sir, in his dungeon, helpless and forsaken as I am, I cannot divest myself of. Being at play with other children, when three or four years old, I was telling them something, which my mother, overhearing, said it had happened before I was born. I stuck to my story, however, and related some things which went, in her opinion, to confirm it. Others being called on, were greatly astonished, knowing that these things had happened, and caused them to say, in my hearing, I surely would be a prophet, as the Lord had shown me things that had happened before my birth. And my mother and grandmother strengthened me in this my first impression, saying, in my presence, I was intended for some great purpose, which they had always thought from certain marks on my head and breast. . . .

My grandmother, who was very religious, and to whom I was much attached . . . my master, who belonged to the church, and other religious persons who visited the house, and whom I often saw at prayers, noticing the singularity of my manners, I suppose, and my uncommon intelligence for a child, remarked I had too much sense to be raised, and, if I was, I would never be of any service to any one as a slave. To a mind like mine, restless, inquisitive, and observant of everything that was passing, it is easy to suppose that religion was the subject to which it would be directed; and, although this subject principally occupied my thoughts, there was nothing that I saw or heard of to which my attention was not directed. The manner in which I learned to read and write, not only had great influence on my own mind, as I acquired it with the most perfect ease,—so much so, that I have no recollection whatever of learning the alphabet; but, to the astonishment of the family, one day, when a book was shown me, to keep me from crying, I began spelling the names of different objects. This was a source of wonder to all in the neighborhood, particularly the blacks—and this learning was constantly improved at all opportunities. When I got large enough to go to work, while employed I was reflecting on many things that would present themselves to my imagination; and whenever an opportunity occurred of looking at a book, when the school-children were getting their lessons, I would find many things that the fertility of my own imagination had depicted to me before. All my time, not devoted to my master's service, was spent either in prayer, or in making experiments in casting different things in moulds made of earth, in attempting to make paper, gunpowder, and many other experiments, that, although I could not perfect, yet convinced me of its practicability if I had the means. . . .

I now withdrew myself as much as my situation would permit from the intercourse of my fellow-servants, for the avowed purpose of serving the Spirit more fully; and it appeared to me, and reminded me of the things it had already shown me, and that it would then reveal to me the knowledge of the elements, the revolution of the planets, the operation of tides, and changes of the seasons. After this revelation in the year 1825, and the knowledge of the elements being made known to me, I sought more than ever to obtain true holiness before the great day of judgment should appear, and then I began to receive the true knowledge of faith. And from the first steps of righteousness until the last, was I made perfect; and the Holy Ghost was with me, and said, "Behold me as I stand in the heavens." And I looked and saw the forms of men in different attitudes; and there were lights in the sky, to which the children of darkness gave other names what they really were; for they were the lights of the Saviour's hands, stretched forth from east to west, even as they were extended on the cross on Calvary for the redemption of sinners. And I wondered greatly at these miracles, and prayed to be informed of a certainty of the meaning thereof; and shortly afterwards, while laboring in the field, I discovered drops of blood on the corn, as though it were dew from heaven; and I communicated it to many, both white and black, in the neighborhood—and I then found on the leaves in the woods hieroglyphic characters and numbers, with the forces of men in different attitudes, portrayed in blood, and representing the figures I had seen before in the heavens. And now the Holy Ghost had revealed itself to me, and made plain the miracles it had shown me; for as the blood of Christ had been shed on this earth, and had ascended to heaven for the salvation of sinners, and was now returning to earth again in the form of dew,—and as the leaves on the trees bore the impression of the figures I had seen in the heavens,—it was plain to me that the Saviour was about to lay down the yoke he had borne for the sins of men, and the great day of judgment was at hand. . . .

About this time I told these things to a white man [Etheldred T. Brantley], on whom it had a wonderful effect; and he ceased from his wickedness, and was attacked immediately with a cutaneous eruption, and blood oozed from the pores of his skin, and after praying and fasting nine days he was healed. And the Spirit appeared to me again, and said, as the Saviour had been baptized, so should we be also; and when the white people would not let us be baptized by the church, we went down into the water together, in the sight of many who reviled us, and were baptized by the Spirit. After this I rejoiced greatly, and gave thanks to God. And on the 12th of May, 1828, I heard a loud noise in the heavens, and the Spirit instantly appeared to me and said the Serpent was loosened, and Christ had laid down the yoke he had borne for the sins of men, and that I should take it on and fight against the Serpent, for the time was fast approaching when the first should be last and the last should be first. *Ques.* Do you not find yourself mistaken now? *Ans.* "Was not Christ crucified." And by signs in the heavens that it would make known to me when I should commence the great work, and until the first sign appeared I should conceal it from the knowledge of men; and on the appearance of the sign (the eclipse of the sun, last February), I should arise and prepare myself, and slay my enemies with their own weapons. And immediately on the sign appearing in the heavens, the seal was removed from my lips, and I communicated the great work laid out for me to do, to four in whom I had the greatest confidence. . . . It was intended by us to have begun the work of death on the 4th of July last. Many were the plans formed and rejected by us, and it affected my mind to such a degree that I fell sick, and the time passed without our coming to any determination how to commence—still forming new schemes and rejecting them, when the sign appeared again, which determined me not to wait longer.

Source: Thomas R. Gray, *Confessions of Nat Turner* (Richmond, 1882), available at http://docsouth.unc.edu/turner/turner.html.

Lyrics from Slave Spirituals

The slave spirituals represent one of the richest legacies of black religious expression in American history. Discovered during the Civil War by whites, the songs express the deep spiritual longings of slaves. This was the music most often heard in the "brush harbors" (or "hush harbors") where slaves conducted their own services. White recorders of these songs found it almost impossible to transcribe them in traditional Western notation or to describe the physical movement that accompanied the singing of the spirituals. The African heritage of the music of the spirituals was a startling revelation to nineteenth-century whites, who often described the spirituals as "strange," "haunting," "plaintive," or "weird." Below are the lyrics to three traditional songs.

Steal Away to Jesus

Steal away, steal away, steal away to Jesus!
Steal away, steal away home.
I ain't got long to stay here.
Steal away, steal away, steal away to Jesus!
Steal away, steal away home.
I ain't got long to stay here.
My Lord, He calls me, He calls me by the thunder,
The trumpet sounds within-a my soul,
I ain't got long to stay here.
Steal away, steal away, steal away to Jesus!
Steal away, steal away home,
I ain't got long to stay here.
Steal away, steal away, steal away to Jesus!
Steal away, steal away home.
I ain't got long to stay here.
Green trees a-bending, po' sinner stand a-trembling,
The trumpet sounds within-a my soul,
I ain't got long to stay here,
Oh, Lord, I ain't got long to stay here.

I Know Moon-Rise

I know moon-rise, I know star rise,
Lay dis body down.
I walk in de moonlight, I walk in de starlight,
To lay dis body down.
I'll walk in de graveyard, I'll walk through de graveyard,
To lay dis body down.
I'll lie in de grave and stretch out my arms;
Lay dis body down.
I go to de judgment in de evenin' of de day,
When I lay dis body down;
And my soul and your soul will meet in de day
When I lay dis body down.

Ride In, Kind Saviour

Ride in, kind Saviour!
No man can hinder me.
O, Jesus is a mighty man!
No man can hinder me.
We're marching through Virginny fields.
No man can hinder me.
O, Satan is a busy man,
No man can hinder me.
And he has his sword and shield,
No man can hinder me,
O, old Secesh done come and gone!
No man can hinder me.

Source: Negrospirituals.com database, http://www.negrospirituals.com/
search.htm.

⌒

Cordelia Anderson Jackson, Wash Wilson, and William Adams Describe Slave Religious Meetings and Slave Conjure in the Antebellum South

In the 1930s, interviewers representing the federal government's Works Progress Administration recorded and transcribed questions and answers with hundreds of ex-slaves. One of the questions they were required to ask involved the religious practices of slaves. The answers provided by these elderly interviewees show some of the variety of slave religious expression, as well as the influence of folk beliefs and practices that came to be called "conjure."

Cordelia Jackson

White folks tells stories 'bout 'ligion. Dey tells stories 'bout it kaise dey's 'fraid of it. I stays independent of what white folks tells me when I shouts. De Spirit moves me every day, dat's how I stays in. White folks don't feel sech as I does; so dey stays out. Can't serve God all de time; allus something getting in de way. Dey tries me and den I suddenly draps back to serving de Holy God. Never does it make no difference how I's tossed about, Jesus, He comes and save me everytime.

Wash Wilson

When de niggers go round singin' "Steal Away to Jesus," dat mean dere gwine [going to] be a 'ligious meetin' dat night. Dat de sig'fication of a meetin'. De masters 'fore and after freedom didn't like dem 'ligious meetin's, so us natcherly slips off at night, down in de bottoms or somewheres. Sometimes us sing and pray all night.

William Adams

'Member de Lawd, in some of His ways, can be mysterious. De Bible says so. There am some things de Lawd wants all folks to know, some things jus' de chosen few to know, and some things no one should know. Now, jus' 'cause yous don't know 'bout some of de Lawd's laws, 'taint superstition if some other person understands and believes in sich. . . .

De old folks in dem days knows more about de signs dat de Lawd uses to reveal His laws den de folks of today. It am also true of de cullud folks in Africa, dey native land. Some of de folks laughs at their beliefs and says it am superstition, but it am knowin' how de Lawd reveals His laws.

Source: Library of Congress, *Born in Slavery: Slave Narratives from the Federal Writers' Project, 1936–1938*, available at http://memory.loc.gov/ammem/ snhtml/, and *Religious Practice of Enslaved African Americans*, available at http://nationalhumanitiescenter.org/pds/maai/community/text3/religion-slaveswpa.pdf.

⌢

Peter Randolph on the Slaves' Brush Harbor Meetings

In this narrative, escaped slave Peter Randolph remembers the nature of slave religious meetings in the backwoods. He recounts how "brush harbors" (often called "hush harbors," since they were secretive places) were constructed, how slaves learned to hide their private religious ceremonies from their masters, and how slaves found a warm communion with each other through these religious rituals. Randolph's account was one of numerous narratives published by ex-slaves and runaway slaves in the antebellum era, and they drew a considerable readership from white Northerners who increasingly feared the "slave power conspiracy" that they believed controlled the South.

Not being allowed to hold meetings on the plantation, the slaves assemble in the swamps, out of reach of the patrols. They have an understanding among themselves as to the time and place of getting together. This is often done by the first one arriving breaking boughs from the trees, and bending them in the direction of the selected spot. Arrangements are then made for conducting the exercises. They first ask each other how they feel, the state of their minds, &c. The male members then select a certain space, in separate groups, for their division of the meeting. Preaching in order, by the brethren; then praying and singing all round, until they generally feel quite happy. The speaker usually commences by calling himself unworthy, and talks very slowly, until, feeling the spirit, he grows excited, and in a short time, there fall to the ground twenty or thirty men and women under its influence. Enlightened people call it excitement; but I wish the same was felt by every-body, so far as they are sincere.

The slave forgets all his sufferings, except to remind others of the trials during the past week, exclaiming: "Thank God, I shall not live here always!" Then they pass from one to another, shaking hands, and bidding each other farewell, promising, should they meet no more on earth, to strive and meet in heaven, where all is joy, happiness and liberty. As they separate, they sing a parting hymn of praise.

Sometimes the slaves meet in an old log-cabin, when they find it neces-sary to keep a watch. If discovered, they escape, if possible; but those who are caught often get whipped. Some are willing to be punished thus for Jesus' sake. Most of the songs used in worship are composed by the slaves them-selves, and describe their own sufferings.

Source: Peter Randolph, Sketches of Slave Life (self-published, 1855), 31–32, available at http://docsouth.unc.edu/neh/randol55/randol55.html.

⌣

Frederick Douglass on Slaveholding Religion

In this excerpt from his famous autobiography, the preeminent black abolitionist leader of the nineteenth century, himself an escaped slave from Maryland, rails *against the proslavery interpretation of the Bible that characterized white religion in the antebellum South. Frederick Douglass's personal narrative was republished, revised, and updated several times through the course of the nineteenth century and generally is considered the single most important firsthand narrative of an ex-slave ever published. Douglass was famous for being able to imitate perfectly the hypocritical pieties of Southern slaveholding preachers and often brought audiences to tears of laughter through his skill at mockery.*

What I have said respecting and against religion, I mean strictly to apply to the *slaveholding religion* of this land, and with no possible reference to Christianity proper; for, between the Christianity of this land, and the Christianity of Christ, I recognize the widest, possible difference—so wide, that to receive the one as good, pure, and holy, is of necessity to reject the other as bad, corrupt, and wicked. To be the friend of the one, is of necessity to be the enemy of the other. I love the pure, peaceable, and impartial Christianity of Christ: I therefore hate the corrupt, slaveholding, women-whipping, cradle-plundering, partial and hypocritical Christianity of this land. Indeed, I can see no reason, but the most deceitful one, for calling the religion of this land Christianity. I look upon it as the climax of all misnomers, the boldest of all frauds, and the grossest of all libels. Never was there a clearer case of "stealing the livery of the court of heaven to serve the devil in." I am filled with unutterable loathing when I contemplate the religious pomp and show, together with the horrible inconsistencies, which every where surround me. We have men-stealers for ministers, women-whippers for missionaries, and cradle-plunderers for church members. The man who wields the blood-clotted cow skin during the week fills the pulpit on Sunday, and claims to be a minister of the meek and lowly Jesus. The man who robs me of my earnings at the end of each week meets me as a class-leader on Sunday morning, to show me the way of life, and the path of salvation. He who sells my sister, for purposes of prostitution, stands forth as the pious advocate of purity. He who proclaims it a religious duty to read the Bible denies me the right of learning to read the name of the God who made me. He who is the religious advocate of marriage robs whole millions of its sacred influence, and leaves them to the ravages of wholesale pollution. The warm defender of the sacredness of the family relation is the same that scatters whole families,—sundering husbands and wives, parents and children, sisters and brothers, leaving the hut vacant, and the hearth desolate. We see the thief preaching against theft, and the adulterer against adultery. We have men sold to build churches, women sold to support the gospel, and babes sold to purchase Bibles for the *poor heathen! all for the glory of God and the good of souls!* The slave auctioneer's bell and the church-going bell chime in with each other, and the bitter cries of the heart-broken slave are drowned in the religious shouts of his pious master. Revivals of religion and revivals in the slave-trade go hand in hand together. The slave prison and the church stand near each other. The clanking of fetters and the rattling of chains in the prison, and the pious psalm and solemn prayer in the church, may be heard at the same time. The dealers in the bodies and souls of men erect their stand in the presence of the pulpit, and they mutually help each other. The dealer gives his blood-stained gold to support the pulpit, and the pulpit, in return, covers his infernal business with the garb of Christianity. Here we have religion and robbery the allies of each other— devils dressed in angels' robes, and hell presenting the semblance of paradise. *Source: Narrative of the Life of Frederick Douglass* (Boston: Anti-Slavery Office, 1845), 118–20, available at http://docsouth.unc.edu/douglass/douglass. html.

⌣

Slave Spirituals in a
Black Union Army Regiment during the Civil War

Thomas Wentworth Higginson served as the commander of the First South Carolina Volunteers, the first black Civil War regiment authorized by the federal government. During that time, he recorded these impressions of the religious music that the men under his command loved. Higginson's account, originally published in Atlantic Monthly *magazine (a favorite intellectual periodical of the Northern middle class of that era) and later collected in a classic work called* Army Life in a Black Regiment, *brought the slave spirituals to a wider white audience. This audience was fascinated to learn everything they could about freedpeople who were just then becoming citizens of the United States.*

Some of the songs had played an historic part during the war. For singing the next, for instance, the negroes had been put in jail in Georgetown, S.C., at the outbreak of the Rebellion. "We 'll soon be free," was too dangerous an assertion; and though the chant was an old one, it was no doubt sung with redoubled emphasis during the new events. "De Lord will call us home," was evidently thought to be a symbolical verse; for, as a little drummer-boy explained to me, showing all his white teeth as he sat in the moonlight by the door of my tent, "Dey tink *de Lord* mean for say *de Yankees.*"

XXXIV. WE'LL SOON BE FREE.
"We'll soon be free,
We'll soon be free,

We'll soon be free,
When de Lord will call us home.
My brudder, how long,
My brudder, how long,
My brudder, how long,
'Fore we done sufferin' here?
It won't be long (*Thrice.*)
'Fore de Lord will call us home.
We'll walk de miry road (*Thrice.*)
Where pleasure never dies. . . .
We'll soon be free (*Thrice.*)
When Jesus sets me free.
We'll fight for liberty (*Thrice.*)
When de Lord will call us home."

The suspicion in this case was unfounded, but they had another song to which the Rebellion had actually given rise. This was composed by nobody knew whom—though it was the most recent, doubtless, of all these "spirituals,"—and had been sung in secret to avoid detection. It is certainly plaintive enough. The peck of corn and pint of salt were slavery's rations.

XXXV. MANY THOUSAND GO.
"No more peck o' corn for me,
No more, no more,—
No more peck o' corn for me,
Many tousand go.
"No more driver's lash for me, (*Twice.*)
No more, &c.
"No more pint o' salt for me, (*Twice.*)
No more, &c.
"No more hundred lash for me, (*Twice.*)
No more, &c.
"No more mistress' call for me,
No more, No more,—
No more mistress' call for me,
Many tousand go."

Source: Thomas Wentworth Higginson, "Negro Spirituals," *Atlantic Monthly*, June 1867, available at http://xroads.virginia.edu/~hyper/twh/higg.html.

〜

Planning for Reconstruction

On January 12, 1865, during William Tecumseh Sherman's "March to the Sea" and occupation of Savannah, Georgia, a group of local black men, led by black Baptist minister Garrison Frazier, met with the Union general and his aides. The Union officials solicited the views and advice of the freedpeople as to the best policy for freedom and Reconstruction. At the meeting, Frazier spoke eloquently of the meaning of slavery, freedom, and the Civil War. Frazier's words were instrumental in persuading Sherman to set aside lands in the low country of the Savannah region and the Sea Islands for use by the approximately 15,000 ex-slaves who were, in effect, made war refugees when their masters fled.

MINUTES OF AN INTERVIEW BETWEEN THE COLORED MINISTERS AND CHURCH OFFICERS AT SAVANNAH WITH THE SECRETARY OF WAR AND MAJOR-GEN. SHERMAN.

HEADQUARTERS OF MAJ.-GEN. SHERMAN, CITY OF SAVANNAH, GA., Jan., 12, 1865–8 P.M.

Garrison Frazier being chosen by the persons present to express their common sentiments upon the matters of inquiry, makes answers to inquiries as follows: . . .

Garrison Frazier being chosen by the persons present to express their common sentiments upon the matters of inquiry, makes answers to inquiries as follows: . . .

Second–State what you understand by Slavery and the freedom that was to be given by the President's proclamation.

Answer–Slavery is, receiving by *irresistible power* the work of another man, and not by his *consent*. The freedom, as I understand it, promised by the proclamation, is taking us from under the yoke of bondage, and placing us where we could reap the fruit of our own labor, take care of ourselves and assist the Government in maintaining our freedom.

Third: State in what manner you think you can take care of yourselves, and how can you best assist the Government in maintaining your freedom.

Answer: The way we can best take care of ourselves is to have land, and turn it and till it by our own labor–that is, by the labor of the women and children and old men; and we can soon maintain ourselves and have something to spare. And to assist the Government, the young men should enlist in the service of the Government, and serve in such manner as they may be wanted. (The Rebels told us that they piled them up and made batteries of them, and sold them to Cuba; but we don't believe that.) We want to be placed on land until we are able to buy it and make it our own.

Fourth: State in what manner you would rather live–whether scattered among the whites or in colonies by yourselves.

Answer: I would prefer to live by ourselves, for there is a prejudice against us in the South that will take years to get over; but I do not know that I can answer for my brethren. [Mr. Lynch says he thinks they should not be separated, but live together. All the other persons present, being questioned one by one, answer that they agree with Brother Frazier.] . . .

Twelfth: State what is the feeling of the colored people in regard to Gen. Sherman; and how far do they regard his sentiments and actions as friendly to their rights and interests, or otherwise?

Answer: We looked upon Gen. Sherman prior to his arrival as a man in the Providence of God specially set apart to accomplish this work, and we unanimously feel inexpressible gratitude to him, looking upon him as a man that should be honored for the faithful performance of his duty. Some of us called upon him immediately upon his arrival, and it is probable he would not meet the Secretary with more courtesy than he met us. His conduct and deportment toward us characterized him as a friend and a gentleman. We have confidence in Gen. Sherman, and think that what concerns us could not be under better hands.

Source: "Negroes of Savannah," *New York Daily Tribune*, February 13, 1865, reprinted at http://www.history.umd.edu/Freedmen/savmtg.htm.

⌒

Description of a Ring Shout from Daniel Payne, 1868

In 1852, Daniel Alexander Payne was named the successor to Richard Allen as the head bishop of the African Methodist Episcopal Church. A man who prided himself on education and decorum, he deplored the kinds of folk religious practices he saw in black churches before and after the Civil War. Here, he records his encounter with a group of black parishioners performing a "ring shout," which Payne believed to be uncivilized. Payne's campaign for what he perceived to be "civilized religion" encountered resistance in local congregations. His efforts preceded many such cultural struggles within African American churches that would occur through the twentieth century, including during the early years of gospel music. Payne's account also suggests how class divisions within African American Christianity would come to define black religious culture after the Civil War.

I have mentioned the "Praying and Singing Bands" elsewhere. The strange delusion that many ignorant but well-meaning people labor under leads me to speak particularly of them. About this time I attended a "bush meeting," where I went to please the pastor whose circuit I was visiting. After the sermon they formed a ring, and with coats off sung, clapped their hands and stamped their feet in a most ridiculous and heathenish way. I requested the pastor to go and stop their dancing. At his request they stopped their dancing and clapping of hands, but remained singing and rocking their bodies to and fro.

This they did for about fifteen minutes. I then went, and taking their leader by the arm requested him to desist and to sit down and sing in a rational manner. I told him also that it was a heathenish way to worship and disgraceful to themselves, the race, and the Christian name. In that instance they broke up their ring; but would not sit down, and walked sullenly away. After the sermon in the afternoon, having another opportunity of speaking alone to this young leader of the singing and clapping ring, he said: "Sinners won't get converted unless there is a ring." Said I: "You might sing till you fell down dead, and you would fail to convert a single sinner, because nothing but the Spirit of God and the word of God can convert sinners." He replied: "The Spirit of God works upon people in different ways. At camp-meeting there must be a ring here, a ring there, a ring over yonder, or sinners will not get converted." This was his idea, and it is also that of many others. These "Bands" I have had to encounter in many places, and, as I have stated in regard to my early labors in Baltimore, I have been strongly censured because of my efforts to change the mode of worship or modify the extravagances indulged in by the people. In some cases all that I could do was to teach and preach the right, fit, and proper way of serving God. To the most thoughtful and intelligent I usually succeeded in making the "Band" disgusting; but by the ignorant masses, as in the case mentioned, it was regarded as the essence of religion. So much so was this the case that, like this man, they believed no conversion could occur without their agency, nor outside of their own ring could any be a genuine one. . . .

We need a host of Christian reformers like St. Paul, who will not only speak against these evils, but who will also resist them, even if excommunication be necessary. The time is at hand when the ministry of the A. M. E. Church must drive out this heathenish mode of worship or drive out all the intelligence, refinement, and practical Christians who may be in her bosom. *Source:* Daniel Payne, *Recollections of Seventy Years* (Nashville, TN: A.M.E. Union, 1888), available at http://docsouth.unc.edu/church/payne70/menu. html.

⌒

Henry McNeal Turner
Expresses an Early Vision of Black Theology

Henry McNeal Turner was born a free man of color in South Carolina and became one of the most important leaders of the AME Church. He was also the progenitor of what later came to be called "black theology," the idea that God identified with oppressed African Americans, as well as a proponent of emigration to Africa. In this early statement of black theology, Turner recognized that, while as a spiritual matter God had no color, for most Americans God was implicitly white. By envisioning the divine as a white man, many Americans gave divine meaning to whiteness, and by extension condemned blackness. Turner made this connection explicit, and proclaimed that "God is a Negro." Later in the twentieth century, proponents of black theology such as James Cone revived Turner's ideas from this era.

We have as much right biblically and otherwise to believe that God is a Negro, as you buckra, or white, people have to believe that God is a fine looking, symmetrical and ornamented white man. For the bulk of you, and all the fool Negroes of the country, believe that God is white-skinned, blue-eyed, straight-haired, projecting-nosed compressed-lipped and finely-robed white gentleman sitting upon a throne somewhere in the heavens.

Every race of people since time began who have attempted to describe their God by words, or by paintings, or by carvings, or by any other form or figure have conveyed the idea that the God who made them and shaped their destinies was symbolized in themselves, and why should not the Negro believe that he resembles God as much as other people? We do not believe that there is any hope for a race of people who do not believe that they look like God.

Demented though we be, whenever we reach the conclusion that God or even that Jesus Christ, while in the flesh, was a white man, we shall hang our gospel trumpet upon the willow and cease to preach.

We had rather be an atheist and believe in no God or a pantheist and believe that all nature is God, than to believe in the personality of a God and not believe that He is Negro. Blackness is much older than whiteness, for black was here before white. . . . We do not believe in the eternity of matter, but we do believe that chaos floated in infinite darkness or blackness, millions, billions, quintillions and eons of years before God said, "Let there be light," and that during that time God had no material light Himself and was shrouded in darkness, so far as *human* comprehension is able to grasp the situation.

Yet we are no stickler as to God's color, anyway, but if He has any we should prefer to believe that it is nearer symbolized in the blue sky above us and the blue water of the seas and oceans; but we certainly protest against God being a white man or against God being white at *all*; abstract as this theme must forever remain while we are in the flesh. This is one of the reasons we favor African emigration, or Negro nationalization, wherever we can find a domain, for as long as we remain among whites, the Negro will believe that the devil is black and that he (the Negro) favors the devil, and that God is white and he (the Negro) bears no resemblance to Him, and the effect of such a sentiment is contemptuous and degrading, and one-half of the Negro race will be trying to get white and the other half will spend their days trying to be white men's scullions in order to please the whites; and the time they should be giving to the study of such things will dignify and make our race great will be devoted to studying about how unfortunate they are in not being white.

We conclude these remarks by repeating for the information of the *Observer* what it adjudged us demented for—*God is a Negro.*
Source: Henry McNeal Turner, *Voice of Missions*, February 1898; reprinted in *Respect Black: The Writings and Speeches of Henry McNeal Turner*, ed. Edwin Redkey (New York: Arno Press, 1971), 176–77.

⌒

Du Bois on the Negro Church

The great black intellectual W. E. B. Du Bois was, among many other things, a sensitive observer who wrote some of the most influential passages about the meaning of black religious expression. Du Bois was a bitter critic of the church, which he perceived as doing little to improve the lives of people. But Du Bois also appreciated the cultural legacy of slave religion as it was transmitted to black churches after the Civil War. Here, in a passage from his classic work Souls of Black Folk, *he reflects on the meaning of rural Southern black Christianity and the role of the black church in African American life.*

Those who have not thus witnessed the frenzy of a Negro revival in the untouched backwoods of the South can but dimly realize the religious feeling of the slave; as described, such scenes appear grotesque and funny, but as seen they are awful. Three things characterized this religion of the slave, —the Preacher, the Music, and the Frenzy. The Preacher is the most unique personality developed by the Negro on American soil. A leader, a politician, an orator, a "boss," an intriguer, an idealist,—all these he is, and ever, too, the centre of a group of men, now twenty, now a thousand in number. The combination of a certain adroitness with deep-seated earnestness, of tact with consummate ability, gave him his preeminence, and helps him maintain it. The type, of course, varies according to time and place, from the West Indies in the sixteenth century to New England in the nineteenth, and from the Mississippi bottoms to cities like New Orleans or New York.

The Music of Negro religion is that plaintive rhythmic melody, with its touching minor cadences, which, despite caricature and defilement, still remains the most original and beautiful expression of human life and longing yet born on American soil. Sprung from the African forests, where its counterpart can still be heard, it was adapted, changed, and intensified by the tragic soul-life of the slave, until, under the stress of law and whip, it became the one true expression of a people's sorrow, despair, and hope. Finally the Frenzy of "Shouting," when the Spirit of the Lord passed by, and, seizing the devotee, made him mad with supernatural joy, was the last essential of Negro religion and the one more devoutly believed in than all the rest. It varied in expression from the silent rapt countenance or the low murmur and moan to the mad abandon of physical fervor, —the stamping, shrieking, and shouting, the rushing to and fro and wild waving of arms, the weeping and laughing, the vision and the trance. All this is nothing new in the world, but old as religion, as Delphi and Endor. And so firm a hold did it have on the Negro, that many generations firmly believed that without this visible manifestation of the God there could be no true communion with the Invisible. . . .

Moreover, the religious growth of millions of men, even though they be slaves, cannot be without potent influence upon their contemporaries. The Methodists and Baptists of America owe much of their condition to the silent but potent influence of their millions of Negro converts. Especially is this noticeable in the South, where theology and religious philosophy are on this account a long way behind the North, and where the religion of the poor whites is a plain copy of Negro thought and methods. The mass of "gospel" hymns which has swept through American churches and well-nigh ruined our sense of song consists largely of debased imitations of Negro melodies made by ears that caught the jingle but not the music, the body but not the soul, of the Jubilee songs. It is thus clear that the study of Negro religion is not only a vital part of the history of the Negro in America, but no uninteresting part of American history.

The Negro church of to-day is the social centre of Negro life in the United States, and the most characteristic expression of African character. Take a typical church in a small Virginia town: it is the "First Baptist"—a roomy brick edifice seating five hundred or more persons, tastefully finished in Georgia pine, with a carpet, a small organ, and stained-glass windows. Underneath is a large assembly room with benches. This building is the central club-house of a community of a thousand or more Negroes. Various orga-nizations meet here,—the church proper, the Sunday-school, two or three insurance societies, women's societies, secret societies, and mass meetings of various kinds. Entertainments, suppers, and lectures are held beside the five or six regular weekly religious services. Considerable sums of money are col-lected and expended here, employment is found for the idle, strangers are in-troduced, news is disseminated and charity distributed. At the same time this social, intellectual, and economic centre is a religious centre of great power. Depravity, Sin, Redemption, Heaven, Hell, and Damnation are preached twice a Sunday after the crops are laid by; and few indeed of the community have the hardihood to withstand conversion. Back of this more formal reli-gion, the Church often stands as a real conserver of morals, a strengthener of family life, and the final authority on what is Good and Right.

Thus one can see in the Negro church to-day, reproduced in microcosm, all the great world from which the Negro is cut off by color-prejudice and social condition. In the great city churches the same tendency is notice-able and in many respects emphasized. A great church like the Bethel of Philadelphia has over eleven hundred members, an edifice seating fifteen hundred persons and valued at one hundred thousand dollars, an annual budget of five thousand dollars, and a government consisting of a pastor with several assisting local preachers, an executive and legislative board, financial boards and tax collectors; general church meetings for making laws; sub-divided groups led by class leaders, a company of militia, and twenty-four auxiliary societies. The activity of a church like this is immense and far-reaching, and the bishops who preside over these organizations throughout the land are among the most powerful Negro rulers in the world.

Such churches are really governments of men, and consequently a little investigation reveals the curious fact that, in the South, at least, practically every American Negro is a church member. Some, to be sure, are not regu-larly enrolled, and a few do not habitually attend services; but, practically, a proscribed people must have a social centre, and that centre for this people is the Negro church. The census of 1890 showed nearly twenty-four thousand Negro churches in the country, with a total enrolled membership of over two and a half millions, or ten actual church members to every twenty-eight persons, and in some Southern States one in every two persons. Besides these there is the large number who, while not enrolled as members, attend and take part in many of the activities of the church. There is an organized Negro church for every sixty black families in the nation, and in some States for every forty families, owning, on an average, a thousand dollars' worth of property each, or nearly twenty-six million dollars in all.

Source: W. E. B. Du Bois, *Souls of Black Folk* (Chicago: A. C. McClurg & Co., 1903), chap. 10, available at http://www.gutenberg.org/etext/408.

~

Mahalia Jackson Describes Her Career in Gospel Singing

Mahalia Jackson was a native of New Orleans, who in 1927 moved to Chicago as part of the Great Migration. In the 1930s, she teamed up with Thomas Dorsey to create the sound of what came to be called black gospel music. She generally is considered the greatest gospel singer of the twentieth century. Here, she reflects on her early life and musical influence, emphasizing especially the impact of the music of the Holiness and Pentecostal churches in her own musical formation. Like the Pentecostals, Jackson brought a heavy downbeat and "blue notes" into her singing. This style shocked many more staid churchgoers but soon became the genesis of the most popular form of religious music from black America. It came to have wide influence in the sound of American music generally.

I know now that a great influence in my life was the Sanctified or Holiness Churches we had in the South. I was always a Baptist, but there was a Sanctified Church right next door to our house in New Orleans.

Those people had no choir and no organ. They used the drum, the cymbal, the tambourine, and the steel triangle. Everybody in there sang and they clapped and stomped their feet and sang with their whole bodies. They had a beat, a powerful beat, a rhythm we held on to from slavery days, and their music was so strong and expressive it used to bring the tears to my eyes.

I believe the blues and jazz and even the rock and roll stuff got their beat from the Sanctified Church. We Baptists sang sweet, and we had the long and short meter on beautiful songs . . . but when those Holiness people tore into "I'm So Glad Jesus Lifted Me Up!" they came out with real jubilation. . . .

Many of the young colored people lost their way during Depression times in Chicago. The times were so hard that it broke their spirits. And although I didn't realize it at the time, I know now that the Lord must have had his arms around me in those days and he protected me. God moves in mysterious ways . . . in a mysterious way, the Depression became responsible for my whole career in gospel singing. . . .

A lot of folks don't know that gospel songs have not been handed down like spirituals. Most gospel songs have been composed and written by Negro musicians like Professor [Thomas] Dorsey.

Before he got saved by the Lord and went into the church, Professor Dorsey was a piano player for Ma Rainey, one of the first of the blues singers. . . . When he began to write gospel music he still had a happy beat in his songs. They're sung by thousands of people like myself who believe religion is a joy. . . .

The more gospel singing took hold in Chicago and around the country, the more some of the colored ministers objected to it. They were cold to it. They didn't like the hand-clapping and the stomping and they said we were bringing jazz into the church and it wasn't dignified. Once at church one of the preachers got up on the pulpit and spoke out against me.

I got right up, too. I told him I was born to sing gospel music. Nobody had to teach me. I was serving God. . . .

In those days the big colored churches didn't want me and they didn't let me in. I had to make it my business to pack the little basement-hall congregations and store-front churches and get their respect that way. When they began to see the crowds I drew, the big churches began to sit up and take notice because even inside the church there are people who are greedy for money.

Source: Mahalia Jackson, with Evan McLeod Wylie, *Movin' On Up* (New York: Hawthorn Books, 1966).

⁓

Miles Mark Fisher, Organized Religion, and the Cults

Black Baptist minister and scholar Miles Mark Fisher was an early student of what in the 1930s were called "black cults"—new black religious movements that existed outside mainstream black Christianity. Here, in an article for the National Association for the Advancement of Colored People's journal Crisis, *Fisher urges that these new religious movements be included and counted in the religious census of 1936. The 1936 census was the last time the government made a concerted effort to count religious bodies. Fisher realized that the methods used by the enumerators would probably completely miss the entire strata of smaller storefront churches and newly emerging black religious organizations that were drawing the attention of discontented churchgoers as well as academic sociologists during this era.*

I nominate the religious movements which are led by Bishop Grace, Elder Michaux, Father Divine et al. for inclusion in the *Census of Religious Bodies: 1936.* Kindred holiness and Pentecostal groups with 1248 churches and a membership of 70,500 persons are included in the 1926 Religious Census. These represent 8 of the 54 denominations which enroll Negroes—the Church of the Living God, Christian Workers for Fellowship, organized in

1889; The Church of Christ (Holiness) U.S.A., 1894; the Church of God in Christ, 1895; the Church of God and Saints of Christ, 1896; the Pentecostal Assemblies of the World, 1908; the Churches of God, Holiness, 1914; the Apostolic Overcoming Holy Church of God, 1916; and the Church of the Living God, "The Pillar and Ground of Truth," 1925.

Of the 54 denominations, 24 "were exclusively Negro," and there were "30 which were primarily white." Yet denominations like the Church of God and Saints of Christ and the Pentecostal Assemblies of the World belong neither to the "exclusively Negro" or to the "primarily white" religious bodies. The Census itself states that the Church of God and Saints of Christ was begun by "William S. Crowdy, a Negro man," its first bishop, and that "one white man who was associated with him was subsequently raised to the same office." . . . It would seem, therefore, that some holiness and Pentecostal churches have protested against the "exclusively Negro" and the "primarily white" denominations and have organized, shall I say, "Christian churches"?

The Religious Census of the United States could not possibly mention individuals like Elder James Morris Webb, who helped to revive racialism within the Negro churches when he published *The Black Man the Father of Civilization Proven by Biblical History.* . . . Elder Webb's *Lecture: Jesus Was Born out of the Black Tribe*, which was published in Chicago, was widely received because Negro churches delighted to hear "that the blood of the Negro coursed through the veins of Jesus and Solomon."

The "exclusively Negro" churches have been multiplying. The United Holy Church of America, founded at Durham, North Carolina, in 1894, must be added to the number. This church has reached points as far removed as the Bermuda Islands and California. Then there are the House of Jacob, Holiness and Sanctified Church, which was founded by the late Supreme Chief and Bishop, G. W. Israel, and Bishop W. D. Barbour's Triumph Church of the New Age at Pittsburgh. . . .

Islam is spreading in the United States from its Chicago headquarters. Both the beliefs of Mohammed and of Jesus were drawn upon by Timothy Drew who founded the religious race-conscious, philanthropic Moorish Science Temple at Chicago in 1925. The Moors, as the disciples of this cult are called, are still prominent in Chicago and Baltimore. . . .

It is not accidental that church attendance, particularly on Sunday nights, has decreased while cult attendance has increased, that cult meetings become crowded on Sundays after the churches have about dismissed and that the cults hold meetings during the week at times when the churches have no worship service. As a matter of fact, the holiness and Pentecostal groups are modeled after the Baptist and Methodist churches, are often led by ex-Baptists and ex-Methodists and enroll many members who formerly belonged to the popular denominations.

Source: Miles Mark Fisher, "Organized Religion and the Cults," Crisis 44, no. 1 (January 1937): 8.

⌣

A Service in Elder Lucy Smith's Church, Chicago, 1930s

Lucy Smith was one of a generation of pioneering black female religious singers, ministers, and entrepreneurs. A native of the South, she migrated to Chicago in the 1910s. Soon thereafter, she started dispensing faith healing to needy fellow migrants. In 1916, she created the All Nations Pentecostal Church, a black Pentecostal congregation that broadcast services throughout the nation and provided much-needed social services to needy people, black and white, in Chicago during the Great Depression. In the following document, a student of Smith's movement reports on a service he attended in the 1930s.

Everyone was seated except the choir. The organist left the console and stepped out in front of the choir in the role of director; a man stepped to the piano in front of the pulpit; around him were gathered several musicians who made up the band. The instruments were cymbal, French horn, cornet, tambourine, two guitars, and a drum. At a sign from the director the choir started singing to the accompaniment of the band. The song was one of the ordinary Billy Sunday revival type. But it was sung differently. The music was syncopated, with an ever-increasing tempo that seemed to whip singers and players into a frenzy. Suddenly, in the midst of the singing, the choir members began to clap their hands. The "Saints" in front joined them, and, in a moment about seventy people were clapping their hands all at the same time according to the rhythmic beat of the music. The band accelerated the tempo until the singing and clapping of hands became almost hysterical in their intensity and speed. The music beat with a savage throbbing insistence upon one's consciousness. . . .

After this preparation the pastor rose and spoke. There is an easy informality about her language and manner. No attempt was made to be oratorical. . . . One feels as he listens to her numerous references to her successes as a healer that mistakes in grammar are of no consequence to this woman who feels that God is using her to restore sight or to cure cancer. Her attitude is not that of the bragger, but simply of a person who believes absolutely in her own ability.

Source: Herbert M. Smith, "Three Negro Preachers in Chicago; A Study in Religious Leadership" (Master's thesis, University of Chicago, 1935).

⌣

Howard Thurman Explores the Need for
Black Liberation from a White-Defined Christianity

Howard Thurman was a black minister and humanist theologian in the mid-twentieth century. Here, in a passage from his famous book Jesus and the Disinherited, *he reflects on the religious implications of segregation. Thurman's work deeply influenced a younger generation of ministers and theologians, including Martin Luther King Jr. Thurman's writings and teachings helped to revive the "social gospel" that had been important in early twentieth-century America but had fallen somewhat into disrepute during the interwar years.*

Given segregation as a factor determining relations, the resources of the environment are made into instruments to enforce the artificial position. Most of the accepted social behavior patterns assume segregation to be normal—if normal, then correct; if correct, then moral; if moral, then religious. Religion is thus made a defender and guarantor of the presumptions. God, for all practical purposes, is imaged as an elderly, benign white man, seated on a white throne, with bright, white light emanating from his counterthrone, with bright, white light emanating from his countenance. Angels are blond and brunets suspended in the air around his throne to be his messengers and execute his purposes. Satan is viewed as being red with the glow of fire. But the imps, the messengers of the devil, are black. . . . The implications of such a view are simply fantastic in the intensity of their tragedy. Doomed on earth to a fixed and unremitting status of inferiority, of which segregation is symbolic, and at the same time cut off from the hope that the Creator intended it otherwise, those who are thus victimized are stripped of all social protection. . . . Under such circumstances, there is but a step from being despised to despising oneself.

Source: Howard Thurman, *Jesus and the Disinherited* (Boston: Beacon Press, 1949), 43–44.

⌒

Christian Nonviolence: Its Philosophy and Its Costs

Many leaders of the civil rights movement followed a philosophy of nonviolent civil disobedience, which they drew from a combination of Christian and Gandhian teaching. Nonviolence proved enormously effective as a tactic in dramatizing the brutality of Southern segregation, particularly when caught on television cameras and reported at length in major newspapers. But the philosophy of nonviolence had its limitations, as those in the movement fully recognized. Nonviolence had its costs, including the physical and psychological trauma visited on protesters who repeatedly were mistreated, arrested, jailed, beaten, and sometimes killed. The following selections, taken from an oral history of civil rights activists, reflect on the origins, practice, and discipline of Christian nonviolent civil disobedience.

John Lewis

They believed in the philosophy and discipline of nonviolence, and it was not just a tactic, as a technique to be used, but I think for some of the people it became a philosophy. It became a way of life, a way of doing things, a way of living. When we would go down to sit-in, I think, you had to be prepared not to just go there to sit and be denied service. . . . It was like going to church, I guess. You would put on your church-going clothes, Sunday clothes, and we took books and papers and did our homework at the lunch counter, just quiet and trying to be as dignified as possible.

I recall I drew up some rules. It was my responsibility to draw up some dos and don'ts on the sit-in movement. I may have some copies of them around and some place if I can find them. . . . It was some simple rules, and the whole idea, matter of fact, came from the Montgomery Bus Boycott. This was telling people what to do. Don't talk back. Sit straight up. Don't laugh out. Don't curse. And at the end of the rules, it said something like, "Remember the teachings of Jesus, Gandhi, Martin Luther King. God bless you all."

James Farmer

And we were singing the songs, the freedom songs, which they hated. "You gotta stop that singing." You know, "O-o-h, freedom, o-o-o-o-h, free-*dom*, before I'd be a slave, I'd be buried in my grave and go home to my Lord and be free." . . . "Stop that singing!" The other prisoners upstairs began joining in on the singing. . . . They were in for murder, rape, theft, what have you. We developed a communications system by sending a message up a wire. They'd pull it up . . . an old electric wire that wasn't in use. "Stop that singing!" We refused to stop and kept on singing, and they then stopped bringing in the knickknacks.

Connie Curry

See, we used to have argument after argument of whether or not nonviolence was a technique or a way of life, and that was probably one of the biggest debates in the early days of SNCC [Student Nonviolent Coordinating Committee]. Because I maintained, as did other people, that nonviolence as a way of life was good as an ideal, but it was something that was absolutely alien to all of our backgrounds and the way that we were raised. . . . That's why being beaten and thrown into jail and trying to love everybody, while they did it to you . . . was bound to mess you up. So I really do think that the toll that was taken in those early days was just tremendous, much more so than for the people who came after who knew what the stakes were.

Also, for those early sit-inners and SNCC people . . . really believed that they were going to win. It was the whole thing of "We Shall Overcome." They really sorta thought there was an end in sight, and when they would sing "God is on our side," I would never sing that verse. . . . I don't think that anybody ever envisioned the long years of struggle and violence and everything—anguish. I don't think they were really aware of it. And as it emerged I think it was just a terrible, terrible toll.

Andrew Marrisett

Dr. King, of course, was *the* influence at the mass meetings. And our job was to every time we saw a guy that was really, really enraged and we thought we could at least talk to right then, we would try to get him to the mass meeting and get him involved. We would sit beside him or close around him, a group of us, and get him involved in the spirit, and we would sing the songs and do the chants and freedom-now things, and then we'd hear Dr. King speak, and that would quiet down the angriest lion, because he just had that thing about him, that halo that he would shine.

Source: Howell Raines, My Soul Is Rested: The Story of the Civil Rights Movement in the Deep South (New York: Penguin, 1977), 99, 107, 126, 149.

⌒

Student Nonviolent Coordinating Committee, Statement of Purpose

In April 1960, the Student Nonviolent Coordinating Committee formed in North Carolina to support student sit-ins in Greensboro. For the next several years, SNCC energized the civil rights movement, forcing significant change on the national agenda through its daring acts of protests such as the Freedom Rides and Mississippi Freedom Summer in 1964. Its original statement of purpose, written primarily by the Reverend James Lawson, is one of the great manifestos of religious idealism in American history. In the late 1960s, many SNCC members rejected their founding statement as hopelessly idealistic about how power actually operated in American society.

We affirm the philosophical or religious ideal of nonviolence as the foundation of our purpose, the presupposition of our faith, and the manner of our action. Nonviolence as it grows from Judaic-Christian traditions seeks a social order of justice permeated by love. Integration of human endeavor represents the crucial first step towards such a society.

Through nonviolence, courage displaces fear; love transforms hate. Acceptance dissipates prejudice; hope ends despair. Peace dominates war; faith reconciles doubt. Mutual regard cancels enmity. Justice for all overthrows injustice. The redemptive community supersedes systems of gross social immorality.

Love is the central motif of nonviolence. Love is the force by which God binds man to Himself and man to man. Such love goes to the extreme; it remains loving and forgiving even in the midst of hostility. It matches the capacity of evil to inflict suffering with an even more enduring capacity to absorb evil, all the while persisting in love.

By appealing to conscience and standing on the moral nature of human existence, nonviolence nurtures the atmosphere in which reconciliation and justice become actual possibilities.

Source: "Statement of Purpose," drafted for the Student Nonviolent Coordinating Committee by Rev. James Lawson, May 14, 1960, available at http://www2.iath.virginia.edu/sixties/HTML_docs/Sixties.html.

⌢

Vincent Harding, Black Power, and the American Christ

In the late 1960s, as the earlier, more optimistic mood of the civil rights movement gave way to urban protest and violence, black theologians such as Vincent Harding and James Cone took up themes first advanced by nineteenth-century black churchmen such as Henry McNeal Turner. In this piece, Harding, a close associate of Martin Luther King, reflects on the psychic impact of the images of a white Jesus that dominated American Christianity. Like Turner, Harding recognized that the white imagery of American Christianity imparted a sense of divinity to whiteness itself.

The mood among many social-action-oriented Christians today suggests that it is only a line thin as a razor blade that divides sentimental yearning over the civil rights activities of the past from present bitter recrimination against "Black Power." As is so often the case with reminiscences, the nostalgia may grow more out of a sense of frustration and powerlessness than out of any true appreciation of the meaning of the past. This at least is the impression one gets from those seemingly endless gatherings of old "true believers" which usually produce both the nostalgia and the recriminations. Generally the cast of characters at such meetings consists of well-dressed, well-fed Negroes and whites whose accents almost blend into a single voice as they recall the days "when we were all together, fighting for the same cause." The stories evoke again the heady atmosphere, mixed of smugness and self-sacrifice, that surrounded us in those heroic times when nonviolence was our watchword and integration our heavenly city. One can almost hear the strains of "our song" as men and women remember how they solemnly swayed in the aisles or around the charred remains of a church or in the dirty southern jails. Those were the days when Martin Luther King was the true prophet and when we were certain that the civil rights movement was God's message to the churches—and part of our smugness grew out of the fact that *we* knew it while all the rest of God's frozen people were asleep. . . .

The trouble with these meetings is that they are indeed becoming ritual, cultic acts of memory that blind us to creative possibilities. Because that "veil" may be a wall, not primarily for separating but for writing on—both sides of it. Or it may be a great sheet "let down from heaven"; or a curtain before the next act can begin. Most of us appear totally incapable of realizing that there may be more light in blackness than we have yet begun to glimpse. . . .

Perhaps the first and central discovery is also the most obvious: there is a strong and causative link between Black Power and American Christianity. Indeed one may say with confidence that whatever its other sources, the ideology of blackness surely grows out of the deep ambivalence of American Negroes to the Christ we have encountered here. . . .

If the American Christ and his followers have indeed helped to mold the Black Power movement, then might it not be that the God whom many of us insist on keeping alive is not only alive but just? May he not be attempting to break through to us with at least as much urgency as we once sensed at the height of the good old "We Shall Overcome" days? Perhaps he is writing on the wall, saying that we Christians, black and white, must choose between death with the American Christ and life with the Suffering Servant of God. Who dares deny that God may have chosen once again the black sufferers for a new assault on the hard shell of indifference and fear that encases so many Americans?

If these things are difficult to believe perhaps we need to look more closely both at the American Christ and the black movement he has helped to create. From the outset, almost everywhere we blacks have met him in this land, this Christ was painted white and pink, blond and blue-eyed—and not only in white churches but in black churches as well. Millions of black children had the picture of this pseudo-Nazarene burned into their memory. The books, the windows, and paintings, the filmstrips all affirmed the same message—a message of shame. This Christ shamed us by his pigmentation, so obviously not our own. He condemned us for our blackness, for our flat noses, for our kinky hair, for our power, our strange power of expressing emotion in singing and shouting and dancing. He was sedate, so genteel, so white. And as soon as we were able, many of us tried to be like him.

Source: Vincent Harding, "Black Power and the American Christ," Christian Century, January 4, 1967.

⌒

Jesse Jackson's 1984 Democratic National Convention Address

The black Baptist minister Jesse Jackson came out of the civil rights movement of the 1960s. A close associate of Martin Luther King, he attempted to implement King's vision in electoral politics as well as in organizations such as Operation Hope. In 1984, Jackson mounted a serious campaign for the presidential nomination of the Democratic Party. Although he fell short of securing the nomination, Jackson's campaign inspired grassroots enthusiasm among African American voters. His speech before the 1984 convention introduced the term "rainbow coalition" into national politics, which quickly became Jackson's trademark for advocating on behalf of a cross-racial coalition of poor and working-class people. Jackson's run also paved the way for future candidates, including Barack Obama, who secured the Democratic nomination in 2008.

Throughout this campaign, I've tried to offer leadership to the Democratic Party and the nation. If, in my high moments, I have done some good, offered some service, shed some light, healed some wounds, rekindled some hope, or stirred someone from apathy and indifference, or in any way along the way helped somebody, then this campaign has not been in vain.

For friends who loved and cared for me, and for a God who spared me, and for a family who understood, I am eternally grateful.

If, in my low moments, in word, deed or attitude, through some error of temper, taste, or tone, I have caused anyone discomfort, created pain, or revived someone's fears, that was not my truest self. If there were occasions when my grape turned into a raisin and my joy bell lost its resonance, please forgive me. Charge it to my head and not to my heart. My head—so limited in its finitude; my heart, which is boundless in its love for the human family.

I am not a perfect servant. I am a public servant doing my best against the odds. As I develop and serve, be patient: God is not finished with me yet.

This campaign has taught me much; that leaders must be tough enough to fight, tender enough to cry, human enough to make mistakes, humble enough to admit them, strong enough to absorb the pain, and resilient enough to bounce back and keep on moving. . . .

We must forgive each other, redeem each other, regroup, and move on. Our flag is red, white and blue, but our nation is a rainbow—red, yellow, brown, black and white—and we're all precious in God's sight.

America is not like a blanket—one piece of unbroken cloth, the same color, the same texture, the same size. America is more like a quilt: many patches, many pieces, many colors, many sizes, all woven and held together by a common thread. The white, the Hispanic, the black, the Arab, the Jew, the woman, the native American, the small farmer, the businessperson, the environmentalist, the peace activist, the young, the old, the lesbian, the gay, and the disabled make up the American quilt. . . .

From Fannie Lou Hamer in Atlantic City in 1964 to the Rainbow Coalition in San Francisco today; from the Atlantic to the Pacific, we have experienced pain but progress, as we ended American apartheid laws. We got public accommodations. We secured voting rights. We obtained open housing, as young people got the right to vote. . . . The team that got us here must be expanded, not abandoned.

Twenty years ago, tears welled up in our eyes as the bodies of Schwerner, Goodman, and Chaney were dredged from the depths of a river in Mississippi. Twenty years later, our communities, black and Jewish, are in anguish, anger, and pain. Feelings have been hurt on both sides. There is a crisis in communications. Confusion is in the air. But we cannot afford to lose our way. We may agree to agree; or agree to disagree on issues; we must bring back civility to these tensions.

We are co-partners in a long and rich religious history—the Judeo-Christian traditions. Many blacks and Jews have a shared passion for social justice at home and peace abroad. We must seek a revival of the spirit, inspired by a new vision and new possibilities. We must return to higher ground. We are bound by Moses and Jesus, but also connected with Islam and Mohammed. These three great religions, Judaism, Christianity, and Islam, were all born in the revered and holy city of Jerusalem.

We are bound by Dr. Martin Luther King Jr. and Rabbi Abraham Heschel, crying out from their graves for us to reach common ground. We are bound by shared blood and shared sacrifices. We are much too intelligent, much too bound by our Judeo-Christian heritage, much too victimized by racism, sexism, militarism, and anti-Semitism, much too threatened as historical scapegoats to go on divided one from another. We must turn from finger pointing to clasped hands. We must share our burdens and our joys with each other once again. We must turn to each other and not on each other and choose higher ground.

Source: http://www.americanrhetoric.com/speeches/jessejackson1984dnc. htm.

⌇

Jeremiah Wright Damns America
and Barack Obama Responds to His Former Pastor

During the 2008 presidential election, candidate Barack Obama faced a major crisis when sermons from his former pastor Jeremiah Wright of the Trinity United Church of Christ in Chicago were replayed on the airwaves and Internet. Wright's refrain of "God damn America," a sentiment common in black pulpit critiques of American racism, compelled candidate Obama to respond. Given in March 2008, Obama's speech addressed the issue of race (and religion) with great insight and historical understanding.

Jeremiah Wright

And the United States of America government, when it came to treating her citizens of Indian descent fairly, she failed. She put them on reservations. When it came to treating her citizens of Japanese descent fairly, she failed. She put them in internment prison camps. When it came to treating citizens of African descent fairly, America failed. She put them in chains. The government put them in slave quarters, put them on auction blocks, put them in cotton fields, put them in inferior schools, put them in substandard housing, put them in scientific experiments, put them in the lowest paying jobs, put them outside the equal protection of the law, kept them out of their racist bastions of higher education and locked them into positions of hopelessness and helplessness. The government gives them the drugs, builds bigger prisons, passes a three-strike law, and then wants us to sing God bless America? No, no, no. Not God bless America; God damn America! That's in the Bible, for killing innocent people. God damn America for treating her

citizen as less than human. God damn America as long as she keeps trying to act like she is God and she is supreme!
Source: http://www.pbs.org/moyers/journal/04252008/transcript1.html.

Barack Obama

I have already condemned, in unequivocal terms, the statements of Rev. Wright that have caused such controversy. For some, nagging questions remain.

Did I know him to be an occasionally fierce critic of American domestic and foreign policy? Of course. Did I ever hear him make remarks that could be considered controversial while I sat in church? Yes. Did I strongly disagree with many of his political views? Absolutely—just as I'm sure many of you have heard remarks from your pastors, priests or rabbis with which you strongly disagreed.

But the remarks that have caused this recent firestorm weren't simply controversial. They weren't simply a religious leader's effort to speak out against perceived injustice.

Instead, they expressed a profoundly distorted view of this country—a view that sees white racism as endemic, and that elevates what is wrong with America above all that we know is right with America. . . .

As such, Rev. Wright's comments were not only wrong but divisive, divisive at a time when we need unity; racially charged at a time when we need to come together to solve a set of monumental problems—two wars, a terrorist threat, a falling economy, a chronic health care crisis and potentially devastating climate change; problems that are neither black or white or Latino or Asian, but rather problems that confront us all. . . .

But the truth is, that isn't all that I know of the man. The man I met more than 20 years ago is a man who helped introduce me to my Christian faith, a man who spoke to me about our obligations to love one another; to care for the sick and lift up the poor. . . .

In my first book, *Dreams from My Father*, I described the experience of my first service at Trinity:

> People began to shout, to rise from their seats and clap and cry out, a forceful wind carrying the reverend's voice up into the rafters. . . . And in that single note—hope!—I heard something else; at the foot of that cross, inside the thousands of churches across the city, I imagined the stories of ordinary black people merging with the stories of David and Goliath, Moses and Pharaoh, the Christians in the lion's den, Ezekiel's field of dry bones.

Those stories—of survival, and freedom, and hope—became our story, my story; the blood that had spilled was our blood, the tears our tears; until this black church, on this bright day, seemed once more a vessel carrying the story of a people into future generations and into a larger world. . . .

That has been my experience at Trinity. Like other predominantly black churches across the country, Trinity embodies the black community in its entirety—the doctor and the welfare mom, the model student and the former gang-banger.

Like other black churches, Trinity's services are full of raucous laughter and sometimes bawdy humor. They are full of dancing, clapping, screaming and shouting that may seem jarring to the untrained ear.

The church contains in full the kindness and cruelty, the fierce intelligence and the shocking ignorance, the struggles and successes, the love and yes, the bitterness and bias that make up the black experience in America.

And this helps explain, perhaps, my relationship with Rev. Wright. As imperfect as he may be, he has been like family to me. He strengthened my faith, officiated my wedding, and baptized my children.

Source: http://edition.cnn.com/2008/POLITICS/03/18/obama.transcript/.

⌢

Rap and Religion: "Jesus Walks" by Kanye West

From its origins on the streets of the New York metropolitan area in the 1970s, rap music has grown to be a global phenomenon. In the first decade of the twenty-first century, Kanye West became one of the genre's foremost artists. In these lyrics from his song "Jesus Walks," from 2003, West explores the meaning of race and religious longings in his life. His sense of disconnection from (and yet yearning toward) the black Christian tradition expressed the feelings of a generation of black urban youths, who often grew up outside of, or suspicious of, the black churches that were nonetheless still central to their communities.

Yo, We at war
We at war with terrorism, racism, and most of all
   we at war with ourselves
(Jesus Walks)
God show me the way because the Devil trying to
   break me down
(Jesus Walks with me) with me, with me, with me
   [fades]

You know what the Midwest is?
Young & Restless
Where restless (Niggas) might snatch your necklace
And next these (Niggas) might jack your Lexus
Somebody tell these (Niggas) who Kanye West is
I walk through the valley of the shadow of death is
Top floor the view alone will leave you breathless
    Uhhhh!
Try to catch it Uhhhh! It's kinda hard hard
Getting choked by the detectives yeah yeah now
    check the method
They be asking us questions, harass and arrest us
Saying "we eat pieces of shit like you for breakfast"
Huh? Yall eat pieces of shit? What's the basis?
We ain't going nowhere but got suits and cases
A trunk full of coke rental car from Avis
My momma used to say only Jesus can save us
Well momma I know I act a fool
But I'll be gone 'til November I got packs to move I
    Hope

[Hook x2]
(Jesus Walks)
God show me the way because the Devil trying to
    break me down (Jesus Walks with me)
The only thing that that I pray is that my feet don't
    fail me now (Jesus Walks)
And I don't think there is nothing I can do now to
    right my wrongs (Jesus Walks with me)
I want to talk to God but I'm afraid because we ain't spoke in so long
To the hustlers, killers, murderers, drug dealers
    even the strippers (Jesus walks with them)
To the victims of Welfare for we living in hell here
    hell yeah (Jesus walks with them)
Now hear ye hear ye want to see Thee more clearly
I know he hear me when my feet get weary
Cause we're the almost nearly extinct
We rappers are role models we rap we don't think
I ain't here to argue about his facial features, But
    here to convert atheists into believers
I'm just trying to say the way school need teachers
The way Kathie Lee needed Regis that's the way I
    need Jesus. . . .

Then I hope this take away from my sins
And bring the day that I'm dreaming about
Next time I'm in the club everybody screaming out
    (Jesus Walks)
God show me the way because the devil trying to
    break me down (Jesus Walks)
The only thing that that I pray is that my feet don't
    fail me now (Jesus Walks)
And I don't think there's nothing I can do now to
    right my wrongs (Jesus walks with me . . .) [fades]
I want to talk to God but I'm afraid because we
    ain't spoke in so long

Source: Kanye West, "Jesus Walks." Written by Miri Ben Ari, Leon Curtis Lundy, Che Smith, and Kanye West. Performed by Kanye West. Publishers/ Administrators: Solomon Ink, c/o Universal Music-MGB Songs, 2100 Colorado Ave., Santa Monica, CA 90404; and Universal Music-MGB Songs, 15031 Collections Center Dr., Chicago, IL 60693. Used by permission.

~

Notes

Introduction

1. *North Star*, February 16, 1849.

2. W. E. B. Du Bois, *Souls of Black Folk* (Chicago: A. C. McClurg & Co., 1903), chap. 10, available from the Gutenberg Project at http://www.gutenberg.org/files/408/408-h/408-h.htm or http://xroads.virginia.edu/~HYPER/DUBOIS/ch10.html.

3. Eddie Glaude, "The Black Church Is Dead," *Huffington Post*, February 24, 2010, http://www.huffingtonpost.com/eddie-glaude-jr-phd/the-black-church-is-dead_b_473815.html.

4. Curtis Evans, *The Burden of Black Religion* (New York: Oxford University Press, 2008), 280.

5. "The Black Church Is Dead, Long Live the Black Church," *Religion Dispatches*, http://www.religiondispatches.org/archive/atheologies/2331/updated_with_response:_the_black_church_is_dead—long_live_the_black_church, March 9, 2010.

Chapter 1: Middle Passage for the Gods

1. Quoted in Albert Raboteau, *Slave Religion: The Invisible Institution in the Antebellum South* (New York: Oxford University Press, 1978), 100.

2. See Rebecca Goetz, "From Potential Christians to Hereditary Heathens: Religion and Race in the Early Chesapeake, 1590–1740" (Ph.D. diss., Harvard University, 2006), 142–45.

3. Quoted in Sylvia Frey and Betty Wood, *Come Shouting to Zion: African American Protestantism in the American South and British Caribbean to 1830* (Chapel Hill: University of North Carolina Press, 1998), 47.

4. Quoted in Mechal Sobel, *Trabelin' On: The Slave Journey to an Afro-Baptist Faith* (Princeton, NJ: Princeton University Press, 1997), 60.

5. Quoted in Winthrop Jordan, *White over Black: American Attitudes toward the Negro, 1550–1812* (Chapel Hill: University of North Carolina Press, 1968), 199–200.

6. Francis Le Jau, *The Carolina Chronicle of Dr. Francis Le Jau, 1706–1717*, ed. Frank Klingberg (Berkeley: University of California Press, 1956), 125.

7. Ibid., 70.

8. Report from William Bull, found at http://www.pbs.org/wgbh/aia/part1/1h311t.html.

Chapter 2: The Birth of Afro-Christianity

1. John Marrant, *Narrative of John Marrant*, quoted in Thomas Kidd, ed., *The Great Awakening: A Brief History with Documents* (Boston: Bedford Books, 2007), 86–88.

2. Quoted in Sylvia Frey and Betty Wood, *Come Shouting to Zion: African American Protestantism in the American South and British Caribbean to 1830* (Chapel Hill: University of North Carolina Press, 1998), 93–94.

3. Quoted in Raboteau, *Slave Religion*, 146.

4. Samuel Davies, "On Virginia's Christian Slaves," quoted in Kidd, *Great Awakening*, 118–19.

5. Quoted in Jeffrey Robert Young, *Domesticating Slavery: The Master Class in South Carolina and Georgia, 1670–1837* (Chapel Hill: University of North Carolina Press, 1999), 143.

6. Ball, quoted in Ira Berlin, *Generations of Captivity* (Cambridge, MA: Belknap Press of Harvard University Press, 2003), 207.

7. Richard Allen, *The Life, Experience and Gospel Labours of the Rt. Rev. Richard Allen* (Philadelphia, 1833), available at http://docsouth.unc.edu/neh/allen/menu.html.

8. Quoted in James Campbell, *Songs of Zion: The African Methodist Episcopal Church in the United States and South Africa* (New York: Oxford University Press, 1994), 51.

9. *Walker's Appeal, in Four Articles; Together with a Preamble, to the Coloured Citizens of the World, but in Particular, and Very Expressly, to Those of the United States of America, Written in Boston, State of Massachusetts, September 28, 1829*, available at http://docsouth.unc.edu/nc/walker/walker.html.

10. Jarena Lee, *The Life and Religious Experience of Jarena Lee*, reprinted in William L. Andrews, *Sisters of the Spirit: Three Black Women's Autobiographies of the Nineteenth Century* (Bloomington: Indiana University Press, 1986), 36.

11. Nat Turner, "Confession," in Kenneth Greenberg, *Confessions of Nat Turner and Related Documents* (Boston: Bedford Books, 1996), 46, 64–65, 72.

12. Report, possibly written by Thomas R. Gray, in the *Constitutional Whig*, September 17, 1831, reprinted in Greenberg, *Confessions of Nat Turner*, 80–81.

Chapter 3: Through the Night

1. Harriet Jacobs, *Incidents in the Life of a Slave Girl*, originally published in 1861, available at http://xroads.virginia.edu/~HYPER/JACOBS/hj-site-index.htm.

2. Quoted in Berlin, *Generations of Captivity*, 194.

3. Quoted in Christine Heyrman, *Southern Cross: The Origins of the Bible Belt* (Chapel Hill: University of North Carolina Press, 1997), 198.

4. *Autobiography of Omar ibn Said, Slave in North Carolina, 1831*, available at http://docsouth.unc.edu/nc/omarsaid/menu.html; Raboteau, *Slave Religion*, 46–47.

5. Charles Colcock Jones, *The Religious Instruction of the Negroes in the United States* (Savannah: Thomas Purse, 1842), 125–26.

6. Du Bois, *Souls of Black Folk*, chap. 10.

7. Anderson Edwards, "Two Ways of Preaching the Gospel," in *Lay My Burden Down: A Folk History of Slavery*, ed. B. A. Botkin (1945; Athens: University of Georgia Press, 1989), 26.

8. Cordelia Jackson, *South Carolina Narratives*, vol. 14 of *The American Slave: A Composite Autobiography*, ed. George Rawick (Westport, CT: Greenwood Press, 1972–1979), part 3, p. 5. Also available at http://memory.loc.gov/ammem/snhtml/.

9. James Watkins, *Narrative of the Life of James Watkins* (Bolton, England: Kenyon & Abbatt, 1852), 18–21, available at http://docsouth.unc.edu/neh/watkin52/menu.html.

10. Maria Stewart, "Productions," in Richard Newman et al., eds., *Pamphlets of Protest: An Anthology of Early African American Protest Literature, 1790–1865* (New York: Routledge, 2000), 125.

11. Frederick Douglass, "The Southern Style of Preaching to Slaves," address delivered on January 1, 1842, in John W. Blassingame and John R. McKivigan, eds., *The Frederick Douglass Papers: Speeches, Debates, and Interviews*, vol. 1, *1841–1846* (New Haven, CT: Yale University Press, 2001), 17.

12. Ibid.

13. Henry Highland Garnet, "Address to the Slaves of the United States" (1848), in Newman et al., *Pamphlets of Protest*, 161.

14. Ibid., 164.

15. "Proceedings of the National Convention of Colored People" (1847), in Newman et al., *Pamphlets of Protest*, 177.

16. Martin Delany, "Political Destiny of the Colored Race on the North American Continent" (1854), in Newman et al., *Pamphlets of Protest*, 227, 239.

Chapter 4: Day of Jubilee

1. Arthur Waddell, in *American Baptist*, September 3, 1867.

2. Thomas Wentworth Higginson, "The Negro Spiritual," *Atlantic Monthly*, June 1867, available at http://xroads.virginia.edu/~hyper/twh/higg.html.

3. Quotations taken from Paul Harvey, *Freedom's Coming: Religious Cultures and the Shaping of the South from the Civil War through the Civil Rights Era* (Chapel Hill: University of North Carolina Press, 2005), 37.

4. Richard Boyd, speech to the General Missionary Baptist Convention of Texas (1894), *Minutes*, p. 25, American Baptist Historical Society Archives, Mercer University, quoted in Paul Harvey, "Richard Henry Boyd: Black Business and Religion in the Jim Crow South," in Nina Mjagkij, ed., *Portraits of African American Life since 1865* (Wilmington, DE: Scholarly Resources, 2003), 51–68.

5. Quoted in Bobby Donaldson, "Standing on a Volcano: The Leadership of William Jefferson White," in Glenn Eskew and Edward J. Cashin, eds., *Paternalism in a Southern City: Race, Religion, and Gender in Augusta, Georgia* (Athens: University of Georgia Press, 2001), 161.

6. Henry McNeal Turner, *Respect Black: The Writings and Speeches of Henry McNeal Turner*, ed. Edwin Redkey (New York: Arno Press, 1971), 72.

7. *Voice of Missions*, February 1898, reprinted in Turner, *Respect Black*, 176–77.

8. Quoted in Art Rosenbaum, *Shout Because You're Free: The African American Ring Shout Tradition in Coastal Georgia* (Athens: University of Georgia Press, 1998), 28–30, 41.

9. Daniel Alexander Payne, *Recollections of Seventy Years* (Nashville, TN: A.M.E. Union, 1888), 255–56, 285–86.

10. Quoted in Harvey, *Freedom's Coming*, 115–16.

Chapter 5: Jesus on the Main Line

1. Quoted in Harvey, *Freedom's Coming*, 71.

2. James Oglethorpe Patterson, *History and Formative Years of the Church of God in Christ* (Memphis: Church of God in Christ Publishing House, 1969), 19.

3. Quoted in Harvey, *Freedom's Coming*, 144–45.

4. *W. E. B. Du Bois Speaks: Speeches and Addresses, 1920–1963*, ed. Philip Foner (New York: Pathfinder Press, 1970), 110.

5. Mahalia Jackson, with Evan McLeod Wylie, *Movin' On Up* (New York: Hawthorn Books, 1966), 32–33.

6. Quoted in Nick Salvatore, *Singing in a Strange Land: C. L. Franklin, the Black Church, and the Transformation of America* (New York: Little, Brown, 2005), 32.

7. Lyrics transcribed in Horace Clarence Boyer, *The Golden Age of Gospel* (Urbana: University of Illinois Press, 1995), 61.

8. Jackson, *Movin' On Up*, 63.

9. Jerma Jackson, *Singing in My Soul: Black Gospel Music in a Secular Age* (Chapel Hill: University of North Carolina Press, 1993).

10. Son House, *Preachin the Blues* (CD, Catfish Records, 2000).

11. Quoted in Guthrie P. Ramsey, *Race Music: Black Cultures from Bebop to Hip-Hop* (Berkeley: University of California Press, 2003), 52.

12. *Bible Way News Voice*, November–December 1947, in Dupree Collection, Schomburg Center for Research in Black Culture, New York Public Library, box 1, folder 7.

Chapter 6: Freedom's Main Line

1. Howard Thurman, *Jesus and the Disinherited* (1949; reprint, Boston: Beacon Press, 1996), 43.

2. Ibid.

3. Martin Luther King Jr., *Stride toward Freedom: The Montgomery Story* (New York: Harper, 1958), 134–35.

4. Martin Luther King Jr., *Strength to Love* (New York: Harper & Row, 1963), 106–7.

5. Martin Luther King Jr., "An Experiment in Love," from *A Testament of Hope: The Essential Writings and Speeches of Martin Luther King, Jr.* (San Francisco: HarperCollins, 1986), 16.

6. Martin Luther King Jr., "MIA Mass Meeting at Holt Street Baptist Church," December 5, 1955, in *The Papers of Martin Luther King, Jr.*, vol. 3, *Birth of a New Age, December 1955–December 1956*, ed. Clayborne Carson et al. (Berkeley: University of California Press, 1997), 73.

7. Quoted in Frederick Harris, *Something Within: Religion and African American Political Activism* (New York: Oxford University Press, 1999), 78.

8. Quoted in Charles Payne, *I've Got the Light of Freedom: The Organizing Tradition and the Mississippi Freedom Struggle* (Berkeley: University of California Press, 1994), 231.

9. SNCC, "Statement of Purpose," available at the Sixties Project, http://www2.iath.virginia.edu/sixties/HTML_docs/Sixties.html.

10. Quoted in Harvey, *Freedom's Coming*, 192.

11. "Ain't Scared of Your Jails," episode 3 of *Eyes on the Prize* (video, Blackside Productions, 1987).

12. Bernice Johnson Reagon interview in *The Eyes on the Prize Civil Rights Reader: Documents, Speeches, and Firsthand Accounts from the Black Freedom Struggle*, ed. Clayborne Carson et al. (New York: Penguin, 1991), 143–45.

13. More information and background on Curtis Mayfield and "People Get Ready" may be found at http://www.npr.org/news/specials/march40th/people.html.

14. Martin Luther King Jr., "Eulogy for the Martyred Children," in *A Testament of Hope*, 221–23.

15. Mendy Samstein, "The Murder of a Community," *Student Voice*, September 23, 1964.

16. Payne, *I've Got the Light of Freedom*, 196.

17. Payne, *I've Got the Light of Freedom*, 80; Vicki Crawford, "Beyond the Human Self: Grassroots Activists in the Mississippi Civil Rights Movement," in Vicki L. Crawford et al., eds., *Women in the Civil Rights: Trailblazers and Torchbearers, 1941–1965* (Bloomington: Indiana University Press, 1993), 21–22.

18. Fannie Lou Hamer, "Sick and Tired of Being Sick and Tired," *Katallagete* (Fall 1968), 26.

19. "Lee County Report, December 1962," in Larry Rubin Papers, box 1, folder 8, Wisconsin Historical Society, Madison.

20. Anne Moody, *Coming of Age in Mississippi* (New York: Dell, 1968), 271, 285, 336.

21. Vincent Harding, "Black Power and the American Christ," *Christian Century*, January 4, 1967.

22. Quoted in Colin Kidd, *The Forging of Races: Race and Scripture in the Protestant Atlantic World, 1600–2000* (Cambridge: Cambridge University Press, 2006), 260.

23. Albert Cleage, "Let's Not Waste the Holy Spirit," in *Columbia Documentary History of Religion in America since 1945*, eds. Paul Harvey and Philip Goff (New York: Columbia University Press, 2005), 394.

24. Bishop Perry, "Black Catholic Worship: Some Reflections," http://www.americancatholicpress.org/Bishop_%20Perry_Black_Catholic_Worship.html.

Epilogue

1. Transcribed at http://www.pbs.org/moyers/journal/04252008/transcript1.html.

2. Barack Obama, *Dreams from My Father: A Story of Race and Inheritance* (New York: Random House, 1995), quoted by Obama in a March 18, 2008, speech, transcribed at http://edition.cnn.com/2008/POLITICS/03/18/obama.transcript/.

3. Barack Obama, "Obama on Faith," interview by Cathleen Falsani, March 27, 2004, http://cathleenfalsani.wordpress.com/obama-on-faith-the-exclusive-interview/.

4. Barack Obama, Inaugural Address, January 21, 2009, available at http://www.whitehouse.gov/blog/inaugural-address/.

5. Kanye West, "Jesus Walks," on *The College Dropout* (CD, Roc-a-Fella and Def Jam Records, 2004). Words and Music by Kanye West, Curtis Lundy, Che Smith and Miri Ben Ari

Glossary of Key Terms

Abolitionism An antebellum American radical reform movement, heavily influenced by the perfectionist tendencies within American evangelicalism, demanding an immediate and uncompensated end to slavery.

African Methodist Episcopal (AME) Church First independent black denomination in the United States, formed by Richard Allen and other black Philadelphians originally in the late 1780s. The AME Church was officially incorporated as a denomination in 1816 and soon became one of the most influential expressions of black Christianity in the United States.

Anglican Member of the Church of England, a hybrid faith of Protestant beliefs and Roman Catholic worship style.

Baptist Follower of a religious movement—later a variety of denominations—originating in seventeenth-century England, that emphasized the necessity of baptism by total water immersion and total autonomy of each congregation. Coming to America in the seventeenth century, Baptists spread quickly in both the North and South and grew to be one of the major evangelical traditions of the United States.

Black gospel music A form of music originated in the early twentieth century by Thomas Dorsey and others, featuring an incorporation of blues sounds and syncopated rhythms with sacred lyrics focusing especially on the figure of Jesus.

Black Muslim Adherent of an African American version of Islam, originated in America by Noble Drew Ali and given prominence by Elijah

Muhammad and his protégé Malcolm X in the 1960s. Black Muslims preach black self-determination and opposition to white Christianity.

Black theology An intellectual movement that identified God with African Americans (and, by implication, with all poor and oppressed people). Dating from the nineteenth century and Henry McNeal Turner but blossoming in the 1960s and 1970s with such writers as James Cone, black theology served as a critique of the white supremacist assumptions of American Christianity.

Brush harbor A secluded informal structure, often built with tree branches, set in places away from masters so that slaves could meet to worship in private.

Church of God in Christ (COGIC) The largest organization of black Pentecostals in the United States, headquartered in Memphis, Tennessee.

Conjure An African American folk tradition with origins in African practices, invoking the supernatural powers of items such as roots and herbs in healing, harming, and protecting individuals. Widespread in the slave community, conjure lived on into the twentieth century and entered the broader streams of American folk culture (also *conjuring* or *conjuration*).

Evangelicalism A religious movement reflecting the surge of spiritual life after the Great Awakening. Emphasizing religious experience, particularly one's conversion or "new birth," evangelicalism came to dominate Protestant culture in the nineteenth century.

Great Awakening A massive evangelical revival that occurred along the entire English-speaking Atlantic seaboard in the late 1730s and 1740s, and again in America in the Second Great Awakening from about 1800 to 1830.

Holiness tradition Body of theological thought and practice, originating from Methodism in the mid-eighteenth century, that emphasized the purification of the soul and quest for sanctification that defines the Christian believer's pilgrimage following conversion.

Methodism A reform movement within the Anglican Church, initiated by Charles and John Wesley in the 1740s, that later went on to become the dominant American denomination of the nineteenth century because of its emphasis on free will and divine grace and its successful system of itinerating preachers combined with a close church organization overseen by bishops and an elaborate structural hierarchy.

Nation of Islam Official organization of the Black Muslims, made most famous by Malcolm X.

Orisha religion General term used to describe West and Central Africa–based religions that emphasized paying obeisance to lesser deities who influenced human affairs, and stressed healing practices through concocting bags of special natural materials thought to have supernatural power and by rectifying social conflicts.

Pentecostalism Twentieth-century theological and denominational movement emphasizing the "third blessing" of the Holy Spirit, as evidenced by speaking in tongues, as the final culmination of the Christian journey. The black minister William Seymour, who led the Azusa Street revivals in Los Angeles in 1906, helped to spread early Pentecostalism.

Ring shout A West African religious tradition, often followed by slaves in the American South, wherein members would rotate counterclockwise while singing, chanting, and dancing.

Santería Cuban-based Afro-Caribbean religion mixing Catholicism with worship of African deities and ancestors.

Social gospel Theological and social movement dating from the late nineteenth and early twentieth centuries that emphasized the role of individual believers and churches in reforming and perfecting this world in preparation for the final coming of God's Kingdom.

Southern Christian Leadership Conference (SCLC) Civil rights organization formed out of the Montgomery bus boycott of 1955–1956. The SCLC became internationally known for its leaders, including Martin Luther King Jr. and Ralph Abernathy, and its instrumental role in organizing a campaign of nonviolent civil disobedience in Southern cities such as Birmingham during the American civil rights struggle.

Spirituals Black religious folk songs, of uncertain or collective authorship, originating during the period of the rise of evangelicalism among African American slaves, including classics such as "Steal Away to Jesus," "Swing Low, Sweet Chariot," and "Roll, Jordan, Roll."

Student Nonviolent Coordinating Committee (SNCC) Civil rights organization formed at a meeting of youth volunteers for the Southern Christian Leadership Conference in 1960. SNCC soon became one of the best known and most fearless of civil rights activist groups in the early 1960s. Its initial emphasis on Christian love, justice, and nonviolence gradually gave way to a more pronounced tilt toward black power, before the group disbanded in the later 1960s.

Vodun Afro-Caribbean religious system centered in Haiti based on notions of drumming and chanting to invoke spirit possession by gods and on practices of healing produced by those possessions. In North America, a less formal version of these beliefs was passed down as "voodoo."

~

Bibliographic Essay

General Secondary Sources and Anthologies

The field of black church history written in the style of modern historical narratives more or less started with Carter G. Woodson's *The History of the Negro Church* (Washington, DC: Associated Publishers, 1921); it was the first modern study of the history of black Christianity in America. In midcentury, E. Franklin Frazier's *The Negro Church in America* and then, one generation later, C. Eric Lincoln's *The Black Church since Frazier* both surveyed and critiqued the "black church," with Frazier bitterly criticizing the bourgeois pretensions of black churchgoers. These two works may be consulted together in a single volume published by Shocken Books in 1974.

In the late 1960s, black liberation theologians examined the story of the relationship between black religion and black politics and struggles for freedom during slavery and freedom. The best volume from that era is Gayraud Wilmore's *Black Religion and Black Radicalism: An Interpretation of the Religious History of the Afro-American People* (reprint, Maryknoll, NY: Orbis, 1998). Students wanting a general overview of African American Christian history may start with C. Eric Lincoln and Lawrence Mamiya, *The Black Church in the African American Experience* (Durham, NC: Duke University Press, 1990), an important modern historical and sociological study that provides a huge amount of data on black churches in modern America. For a more general popular history, focusing especially on individual life stories from various periods of African American Christian history, consult Juan Williams and Quinton Dixie, *This Far by Faith: Stories from the African-American Religious*

Experience (New York: William Morrow, 2003), a survey of African American religious history designed to accompany a PBS television series of the same title.

For more recent analytical texts that survey and critique scholarly studies of black Christianity, see Curtis Evans, *The Burden of Black Religion* (New York: Oxford University Press, 2007), and Allen Callahan, *The Talking Book: African Americans and the Bible* (New Haven, CT: Yale University Press, 2006). Evans provides a highly perceptive analysis of how and why "too heavy a burden" historically has been placed on black churches, while Callahan's work is an influential theological study of the uses African Americans have made of the Bible during slavery and freedom.

A lengthy and extremely valuable anthology of articles and book excerpts from all periods of African American religious history may be found in Cornel West and Eddie Glaude, eds., *African American Religious Thought: An Anthology* (Louisville, KY: Westminster John Knox Press, 2003). Another useful compilation of articles and book excerpts is Larry Murphy, *Down by the Riverside: Readings in African American Religion* (New York: New York University Press, 2000). Frederick Harris's *Something Within: Religion in African American Political Activism* (New York: Oxford University Press, 2001) is a good place to start for a survey of the relationship of African American religion and politics since the Civil War. Michael Gomez's *Black Crescent: The Experience and Legacy of African Muslims in the Americas* (New York: Cambridge University Press, 2005) is the most extensive and encyclopedic study of African American Islam throughout the Americas during slavery and freedom, with fruitful comparisons to the history of black Christianity.

Published Primary Source Anthologies

The most essential and comprehensive anthology of primary sources in black religious history is Milton Sernett, ed., *African American Religious History: A Documentary Witness*, 2nd ed. (Durham, NC: Duke University Press, 1999). *Social Protest Thought in the African Methodist Episcopal Church, 1862–1939*, edited by Stephen Angell and Anthony B. Pinn (Knoxville: University of Tennessee Press, 2000), is an invaluable compilation of writings from publications of the African Methodist Episcopal Church. In *African Muslims in Antebellum America: A Sourcebook* (New York: Routledge, 1997), Allan Austin traces the stories of some seventy-five Muslims taken from sub-Saharan Africa and enslaved in North America from the 1730s to the 1860s. A wonderful source for black folk religion, conjure, and folklore, full of reprinted primary sources from the nineteenth-century journal the *Southern Workman*, may be found in Donald J. Waters, ed., *Strange Ways and Sweet Dreams: Afro-American Folklore from the Hampton Institute* (Boston: G. K. Hall & Co., 1983).

For the autobiographies of black female evangelists of the nineteenth century, a handy beginning point is William Andrews, *Sisters of the Spirit: Three Black Women's Autobiographies of the Nineteenth Century* (Bloomington: Indiana University Press, 1986). A more complete anthology of black women's religious oratory may be found in Bettye Collier-Thomas, *Daughters of Thunder: Black Women Preachers and Their Sermons, 1850–1979* (San Francisco: Jossey-Bass, 1997).

The most complete compilation of source material from the civil rights era, including hundreds of pages of transcripts taken from recordings not previously available in print, is Davis W. Houck and David Dixon, eds., *Rhetoric, Religion, and the Civil Rights Movement, 1954–1965* (Waco, TX: Baylor University Press, 2008). For an anthology focusing on the writings of Martin Luther King, students should consult James Melvin Washington, *A Testament of Hope: The Essential Writings and Speeches of Dr. Martin Luther King, Jr.* (New York: HarperOne, 1990).

Secondary Sources by Chapter

Chapter 1: Middle Passage for the Gods

For the early history of enslaved Muslims, see Sylviane Diouf, *Servants of Allah: African Muslims Enslaved in the Americas* (New York: New York University Press, 1998). An excellent recent work exploring cultural connections between a specific region of Africa and the destination point in the Americas for humans transported from that region is Jason R. Young's *Rituals of Resistance: African Atlantic Religion in the Kongo and the Lowcountry South in the Era of Slavery* (Baton Rouge: Louisiana State University Press, 2007).

Chapter 2: The Birth of Afro-Christianity

Albert Raboteau's *Slave Religion: The "Invisible Institution" in the Antebellum South* (New York: Oxford University Press, 1978) is a classic that remains the best place for students to gain an overview of the origins, rise, and development of African American Christianity from the middle passage to the Civil War. A highly engaging older interpretive study is Mechal Sobel, *Trabelin' On: The Slave Journey to an Afro-Baptist Faith* (reprint, Princeton, NJ: Princeton University Press, 1987); Sobel also provides extensively researched details on the history of independent black churches in the antebellum era. Sylvia Frey and Betty Wood's *Come Shouting to Zion: African American*

Protestantism in the American South and the Caribbean to 1830 (Chapel Hill: University of North Carolina Press, 1998) is a most informative recent comparative study of the rise of black Protestantism in the eighteenth and early nineteenth centuries, while Joanna Brooks's *American Lazarus: Religion and the Rise of African-American and Native American Literature* (New York: Oxford University Press, 2003) is the single most important study of early black Christian authors.

Chapter 3: Through the Night

James Campbell's *Songs of Zion: The African Methodist Episcopal Church in the United States and South Africa* (New York: Oxford University Press, 1994) is a sweeping study of the AME Church from its origins in America to its spread to South Africa. For an intensive and moving study of Charles Colcock Jones and his slaves in the Georgia low country, see Erskine Clarke, *Dwelling Place: A Plantation Epic* (New Haven, CT: Yale University Press, 2005). Charles Joyner studies one lowcountry slave community in *Down by the Riverside: A South Carolina Slave Community* (Urbana: University of Illinois Press, 1986). In *Slave Missions and the Black Church in the Antebellum South* (Columbia: University of South Carolina Press, 1999), Janet Cornelius provides a close study of the relationship between white missionaries and black slaves in the late antebellum era. For conjure, folk traditions, and "black magic," consult Yvonne Chireau, *Black Magic: Religion and the African American Conjuring Tradition* (Berkeley: University of California Press, 2003).

Chapter 4: Day of Jubilee

William Montgomery's *Under Their Own Vine and Fig Tree: The African American Church in the South, 1865–1900* (Baton Rouge: Louisiana State University Press, 1993) takes the reader on a thorough and informative study of black churches after the Civil War, while Reginald Hildebrand's *Day of Jubilee: Methodist Preachers and the Crisis of Emancipation* (Durham, NC: Duke University Press, 1995) analyzes the influences of Methodist preachers on theological understandings of the Civil War, emancipation, and Reconstruction.

For an excellent biographical study of the postwar organizer of the AME Church in the South, see Stephen Angell, *Henry McNeal Turner and African American Religion in the South* (Knoxville: University of Tennessee Press, 1992). A fine intellectual history of black thought, focusing on the writing of black history by African American authors, may be found in Laurie Maffly-Kipp, *Setting Down the Sacred Past: African American Race Histories, 1780–1910* (Cambridge, MA: Harvard University Press, 2010).

Chapter 5: Jesus on the Main Line

The "cultural turn" in black religious studies is exemplified in John Giggie, *After Redemption: Jim Crow and the Transformation of African American Religion in the Delta, 1875–1915* (New York: Oxford University Press, 2008), as well as in Michael Harris, *The Rise of the Gospel Blues: The Music of Thomas Andrew Dorsey in the Urban Church* (New York: Oxford University Press, 1994). Students of black religion and the Great Migration should begin with Milton Sernett, *Bound for the Promised Land: African American Religion and the Great Migration* (Durham, NC: Duke University Press, 1997), and then continue with a biographical study of the Chicago-based black female Pentecostal pioneer Lucy Smith, as covered in Wallace Best, *Passionately Human, No Less Divine: Religion and Culture in Black Chicago, 1915–1952* (Princeton, NJ: Princeton University Press, 2007).

Two seminal studies of women's central roles in black denominations are Evelyn Brooks Higginbotham's *Righteous Discontent: The Woman's Movement in the Black Baptist Church, 1880–1920* (Cambridge, MA: Harvard University Press, 1992) and Anthea Butler's *Women in the Church of God in Christ: Making a Sanctified World* (Chapel Hill: University of North Carolina Press, 2007).

The essential source for understanding the religious influences behind the writings of America's greatest black intellectual, W. E. B. Du Bois, is Edward J. Blum, *W. E. B. Du Bois, American Prophet* (Philadelphia: University of Pennsylvania Press, 2007). Students interested in the fascinating figure of Father Divine should consult Jill Watts, *God, Harlem U.S.A.: The Father Divine Story* (Berkeley: University of California Press, 1995).

An earlier classic that introduced ethnographic methods into the study of black urban religions is Arthur Huff Fauset's *Black Gods of the Metropolis: Negro Religious Cults of the Urban North* (reprint, Philadelphia: University of Pennsylvania Press, 1970). A similar approach to black Spiritual churches in New Orleans may be found in Claude Jacobs and Andrew J. Kaslow, *Spiritual Churches of New Orleans: Origins, Beliefs, and Rituals of an African American Religion* (Knoxville: University of Tennessee Press, 2001). For an analytical survey of the kinds of work done on the study of black religion in the twentieth century, focusing especially on its assumptions and limitations, see Barbara Dianne Savage, *Your Spirits Walk Beside Us: The Politics of Black Religion* (Cambridge, MA: Harvard University Press, 2008).

Chapter 6: Freedom's Main Line and Epilogue

Taylor Branch's *Parting the Waters: America in the King Years, 1954–1963* (New York: Harper & Row, 1988) is a magisterial popular history of the impact of Martin Luther King Jr. and the civil rights movement on America from the Montgomery bus boycott to the Birmingham protests. David Chappell's *Stone of Hope: Prophetic Religion and the Death of Jim Crow* (Chapel Hill: University of North Carolina Press, 2004) is notable for explaining how a black "prophetic religion," rooted in a fundamental sense of human sin and evil, empowered the civil rights movement; Chappell's work should be read alongside Paul Harvey's *Freedom's Coming: Religious Cultures and the Shaping of the South from the Civil War through the Civil Rights Era* (Chapel Hill: University of North Carolina Press, 2005).

For women and the civil rights tradition, the seminal work is Bettye Collier-Thomas, *Jesus, Jobs, and Justice: African American Women and Religion* (New York: Alfred A. Knopf, 2010), while Aldon D. Morris provides a close sociological study of black churches and the civil rights movement in *The Origin of the Civil Rights Movement: Black Communities Organizing for Change* (New York: Free Press, 1986). Louis A. DeCaro's *On the Side of My People: A Religious Life of Malcolm X* (New York: New York University Press, 1996) is an important exploration of the religious ideas of the best-known black nationalist of the mid-twentieth century.

In *Conjure in African American Society* (Baton Rouge: Louisiana State University Press, 2007), Jeffrey Anderson follows the black folk religious tradition from its origins to its contemporary expressions, as does Carolyn Morrow Long in *Spiritual Merchants: Religion, Magic, and Commerce* (Knoxville: University of Tennessee Press, 2001). *African Immigrant Religions in America* (New York: New York University Press, 2007), edited by Jacob Olupona and Regina Gemignani, is the most useful study of African immigrants and their religions in recent American history, while Karen McCarthy Brown's *Mama Lola: A Vodou Priestess in Brooklyn* (Berkeley: University of California Press, 2001) is an influential biographical study of an Afro-Caribbean religious leader in contemporary New York City.

For more on black megachurches and the black "gospel of prosperity," see Jonathan L. Walton, *Watch This! The Ethics and Aesthetics of Black Televangelism* (New York: New York University Press, 2009). Studies of the continuing legacy of the black church tradition and its struggles during the post–civil rights era are available in R. Drew Smith, ed., *Long March Ahead: African American Churches and Public Policy in Post–Civil Rights America* (Durham, NC: Duke University Press, 2004), and Marla F. Frederick, *Between Sundays: Black Women and Everyday Struggles of Faith* (Berkeley: University of California Press, 2003). Anthony Pinn's *Terror and Triumph: The Nature of Black Religion* (Minneapolis, MN: Fortress

Press, 2003) is a highly advanced theoretical study of the meaning of African American religious expressions, while those interested in religion and rap music may start with Pinn's edited collection *Noise and Spirit: The Religious and Spiritual Sensibilities of Rap Music* (New York: New York University Press, 2003).

Chronology

1491	Conversion of the Kingdom of Kongo to Christianity.
1619	First importation of black servants to North America.
1664	First law in Maryland stating that baptism will not lead to freedom for slaves.
1701	Formation of Anglican Society for the Propagation of the Gospel in Foreign Parts (SPG).
1706	Francis Le Jau arrives in South Carolina to minister among slaves on behalf of SPG.
1723	Letter from South Carolina slaves to Anglican bishop, arguing for their freedom based on their Christianity.
1727	Ursuline Sisters establish convent in New Orleans, leading to the first black schooling for black Louisiana and later to the creation of Sisters of the Holy Family, a black female religious order.
1739	**September 8–9:** Stono Rebellion in South Carolina.
1740	Great Awakening begins.
1757	Samuel Davies recounts preaching to blacks in Virginia.
1758	First known slave church formed on plantation of William Byrd III in Virginia.
1760s–1770s	Great Awakening comes to the South. Quakers establish the first schools for African Americans.
1775	Evangelist George Whitefield visits Charleston and converts John Marrant.
1784	Methodist antislavery church laws passed.

1786	Formation of Free African Society in Philadelphia, first black fraternal organization and predecessor to African Methodist Episcopal (AME) Church.
1788	Constitution of First African Baptist Church in Savannah, Georgia.
1792 or 1793	Richard Allen leads walkout from St. George's Methodist Episcopal Church in Philadelphia.
1794	Formation of Bethel AME congregation in Philadelphia.
1801	Gabriel Prosser's rebellion in Richmond, Virginia. Publication of first black hymnal by Allen.
1808	End of legal slave importation to the United States.
1816	Constitution of AME Church in Philadelphia.
1820	Daniel Coker sails to Africa as unofficial missionary of the AME Church.
1821	Lott Carey becomes first black Baptist missionary to Africa. Constitution of African Methodist Episcopal Zion Church in New York City.
1822	Denmark Vesey revolt uncovered in South Carolina. Closing of AME congregation in Charleston.
1827	Establishment of black newspaper *Freedom's Journal*.
1829	Publication of Daniel Walker's *Appeal to the Colored Citizens of the World*.
1831	Formation of Liberty County [Georgia] Association for the Religious Instruction of Negroes, with Charles Colcock Jones as a missionary to slaves. **August 21:** Nat Turner revolt in Southampton County, Virginia.
1836	African Methodist female exhorter Jarena Lee publishes her autobiography and spiritual journal.
1843	Black minister Henry Highland Garnet advocates active resistance to slavery, creating controversy within black convention movement.
1844–1845	Baptist and Methodist denominations split over slavery, leading to formation of Southern Baptist Convention and Methodist Episcopal Church, South.
1856	Creation of Wilberforce University, affiliated with AME Church, as first black college in the country.
1861	**April:** Beginning of American Civil War.
1863	**January 1:** Emancipation Proclamation issued.
1865	**January:** Meeting of Gen. William Tecumseh Sherman with black ministers and leaders in Savannah, Georgia. Passage in Congress of the Thirteenth Amendment to the

Constitution. **April:** End of Civil War. Assassination of Abraham Lincoln.

1865–1870   Creation of numerous black schools and colleges affiliated with religious denominations, including Fisk University, Howard University, and Shaw University.

1867   Beginning of Congressional Reconstruction.

1870   Creation of Colored Methodist Episcopal Church as black offshoot of the Southern Methodist Church.

1894   Formation of Church of God in Christ by Charles Price Jones and Charles Harrison Mason.

1895   Formation of National Baptist Convention, largest black denomination in the country.

1896   *Plessy v. Ferguson* decision legalizes segregation as law of the land.

1898   Henry McNeal Turner publishes essay declaring "God is a Negro" and visits South Africa on important mission trip.

1906   Black minister William Seymour leads Azusa Street revivals in Los Angeles, bringing about the birth of Pentecostalism as an international movement.

1915   Beginning of Great Migration of blacks from South to North.

1916   Formation of Elder Lucy Smith's All Nations Pentecostal Church in Atlanta.

1921   Formation of African Orthodox Church, unofficial auxiliary of Marcus Garvey's Universal Negro Improvement Association.

1922   Publication of Carter Woodon's *The Negro Church*, first major history of black Christianity in the United States.

1927   Formation of Moorish Science Temple.

1930   Formation of Lost-Found Nation of Islam in Detroit.

1932   First publication and performance of Thomas Dorsey's "Precious Lord, Take My Hand" marks birth of black gospel music.

1934   Publication of Richard Gregg's *The Power of Nonviolence*.

1938   Publication of Benjamin Mays's *The Negro's God, as Reflected in His Literature*.

1947   Publication of Howard Thurman's *God and the Disinherited*. Mahalia Jackson records "Move On Up a Little Higher," which eventually sells eight million records and kicks off the "Golden Age of Gospel."

1954	*Brown v. Board of Education* decision ends legalized segregation in schools.
1955	**December:** Beginning of Montgomery bus boycott and formation of Montgomery Improvement Association.
1957	Constitution of Southern Christian Leadership Conference (SCLC).
1960	**April:** Formation of the Student Nonviolent Coordinating Committee.
1961	**May:** Freedom Rides through South.
1962	Civil rights campaign in Albany, Georgia.
1963	**April–May:** SCLC campaign in Birmingham, Alabama. **August 28:** March on Washington and Martin Luther King Jr.'s "I Have a Dream" Speech. **September 15:** Bombing of 16th Street Baptist Church in Birmingham.
1964	Passage of Civil Rights Act of 1964. **Summer:** Freedom Summer in Mississippi. **June:** Murder of three civil rights workers in Mississippi.
1965	Passage of Voting Rights Act. **February 21:** Assassination of Black Muslim leader Malcolm X. **Summer:** King's campaign in Chicago and formation of Operation Breadbasket under Jesse Jackson.
1968	**April 4:** Assassination of Martin Luther King.
1969	Publication of James Cone's *Black Theology and Black Power*.
1971	Organization of PUSH (People United to Serve Humanity) by Jesse Jackson.
1984	Jackson makes run for Democratic nomination for president and organizes Rainbow Coalition behind his movement.
1993	Gospel album *Kirk Franklin and the Family* becomes first gospel album to sell over one million copies.
1994	U.S. Supreme Court rules in favor of practitioners of Santería.
1995	Million Man March of Black Muslims in Washington, D.C.
1996	Creation of Potter's House church in Dallas by star black megachurch preacher Thomas Dexter (T. D.) Jakes.
2005	**August:** Hurricane Katrina wipes out scores of black churches in New Orleans.
2008	Election of Barack Obama as president of the United States.

Index

~

About the Author

Paul Harvey is Professor of History and Presidential Teaching Scholar at the University of Colorado, where he has taught since 1996. He is the author of Freedom's Coming: Religious Cultures and the Shaping of the South from the Civil War through the Civil Rights Era (2005), and Moses, Jesus, and the Trickster in the Evangelical South 2011). Together with Edward J. Blum, he edited the Columbia Guide to Religion in American History, and together with Philip Goff is the editor of Themes in Religion and American Culture (2004). Harvey runs the blog Religion in American History, at http://us religion.blogspot.com.